"An authoritative and engaging review of the journey and current position of sustainable development in the EU. Humphreys provides a valuable framework for understanding the concept, its legal and policy context and examines the extent to which the EU meets the legal and political challenges in balancing competing economic, environmental and social interests."

**Professor Toni Hilton**, *Dean Glasgow School for Business and Society, Glasgow Caledonian University*

# Sustainable Development in the European Union

This book undertakes a critical appraisal of the concept of sustainable development in the European Union. In addition to existing issues of sustainability, it examines the development of a European "general principle" of sustainable development. This original, critical approach examines legal, political, and economic implications of the emergence of the principle and places the impact of such in local, national, intranational, and international contexts. While essentially focusing on the development of the principle, the discussion also includes a normative assessment of current policy and practice, and appraises European efforts in the light of international goals.

**Professor Matthew Humphreys,** MBE, is Head of the School of Law, Royal Holloway, University of London. He is also a Professor at the University of Notre Dame, USA.

# Sustainable Development in the European Union
A General Principle

Matthew Humphreys

LONDON AND NEW YORK

First published 2018
by Routledge
2 Park Square, Milton Park, Abingdon, Oxon OX14 4RN

and by Routledge
711 Third Avenue, New York, NY 10017

*Routledge is an imprint of the Taylor & Francis Group, an informa business*

© 2018 Matthew Humphreys

The right of Matthew Humphreys to be identified as author of this work has been asserted by him in accordance with sections 77 and 78 of the Copyright, Designs and Patents Act 1988.

All rights reserved. No part of this book may be reprinted or reproduced or utilised in any form or by any electronic, mechanical, or other means, now known or hereafter invented, including photocopying and recording, or in any information storage or retrieval system, without permission in writing from the publishers.

*Trademark notice*: Product or corporate names may be trademarks or registered trademarks, and are used only for identification and explanation without intent to infringe.

*British Library Cataloguing-in-Publication Data*
A catalogue record for this book is available from the British Library

*Library of Congress Cataloging-in-Publication Data*
Names: Humphreys, Matthew, author.
Title: Sustainable development in the European Union : a general principle / Matthew Humphreys.
Description: Abingdon, Oxon [UK] ; New York : Routledge, 2017. | Includes bibliographical references and index.
Identifiers: LCCN 2017032022| ISBN 9781409447313 (hardback) | ISBN 9781317047926 (adobe reader) | ISBN 9781317047919 (epub) | ISBN 9781317047902 (mobipocket)
Subjects: LCSH: Sustainable development—Law and legislation—European Union countries. | Environmental law—European Union countries. | Subsidiarity—European Union countries. | Proportionality in law—European Union countries.
Classification: LCC KJE6245 .H86 2017 | DDC 343.24/07—dc23
LC record available at https://lccn.loc.gov/2017032022

ISBN: 978-1-4094-4731-3 (hbk)
ISBN: 978-1-315-61147-1 (ebk)

Typeset in Galliard
by Apex CoVantage, LLC

Printed in the United Kingdom
by Henry Ling Limited

# Contents

|   |   |
|---|---|
| *Table of cases* | x |
| *Table of EU secondary legislation* | xii |
| *Table of other authorities* | xvi |
| *Acknowledgements* | xvii |
| *Preface* | xviii |

**1 Introduction**     1
   *The structure of this book* 12

**2 Sustainable development: concept, principles, and practice**     21
   *The concept of sustainable development: its evolution on the international plane* 21
      *Sustainable development: contest and debate of meaning* 25
         *Meaning developed from the Brundtland formulation* 26
         *Meaning developed from the Rio principles* 27
         *'Sustainable development': concept or jargon?* 28
         *Constructionist definitional approach* 29
      *Practical meaning for legal and policy application* 29
      *Sustainable development: legal context and application* 31
      *Key global principles in the sustainable development triad* 32
         *Precautionary principle* 33
         *The polluter pays principle* 34
         *Public participation* 37
   *The international context of sustainable development* 40
   *Conclusion* 41

**3 Sustainable development and general principles of EU law**     42
   *Principled-based sustainable development in EU law* 42
   *General principles in EU law and sustainable development* 47
      *Subsidiarity as a general principle in EU law* 48
      *Proportionality as a general principle in EU law* 50

EU sustainable development in subsidiarity and
proportionality: legal procedural impact 52
The legal effect of EU principle-based sustainable
development 52
Sustainability in subsidiarity and proportionality:
procedural impact 53
Conclusion 57

4 **The precautionary principle and sustainability in EU environmental protection**    59
Precautionary approach to environmental protection 60
EU environmental protection and precaution: law, policy,
and practice 62
Conclusion 71

5 **The polluter pays principle: economic aspects of sustainability in the EU**    72
The polluter pays principle and sustainable development 72
The polluter pays and economic regulation in EU law,
policy, and practice 73
The polluter pays in EU law and policy 73
The polluter pays principle and economic regulation in
practice 76
Transport policy 79
Common agricultural policy 81
Competition and state aid 83
Critical review of polluter pays approaches to policy 85
Conclusion 87

6 **Public participation and access rights in EU law**    88
Public participation principle and sustainable development 88
The Aarhus Convention on public participation and social
justice 90
Right to information – Pillar 1 91
Procedural rights – Pillar 2 91
Access to justice – Pillar 3 91
Aarhus' access rights in EU law, policy, and practice 92
Application of 'access to justice' rights in the EU 96
Access to justice case law 99
Critical review of access rights approach to EU sustainability
policy 103
Conclusion 105

7  **Sustainable development in EU external relations**  107
   *Sustainable development as an international issue for the EU 108*
   *The EU's presence in the international arena: on climate change 110*
   *EU promoting sustainable development 114*
   *Sustainable development and key actors on the international stage 121*
      *The World Trade Organization (WTO) 121*
      *Other key actors' role in sustainable development 126*
         *The United States 126*
         *China 130*
         *Russia 133*
         *India 135*
         *Brazil 139*
   *Conclusion 142*

8  **Conclusion**  145

   *Index*  153

# Table of cases

Case C-28/09 *Commission v Austria* EU:C:2010:854; [2011] ECR I-854
Case C-13/94 *P v S and Cornwall County Council* [1996] ECR I-2143
Case C-144/04 *Mangold v Helm* [2005] ECR I-9981
Case C-84/94 *UK v Council* [1996] ECR I-5755
Canada – Measures Affecting Exports of Unprocessed Herring and Salmon, GATT BISD 35S/98 (22 March 1988)
Case 172/82 *Syndicat National des Fabricants Raffineurs d'Huile de Graissage et al. v. Groupement d' Intérêt Economique 'Inter-Huiles'* (*Inter-Huiles* case) [1983] ECR 507
Case 25/62 *Plaumann & Co. v Commission of the European Economic Community* [1963] ECR
Case C-77/09 *Gowan Comércio Internacional e Serviços v. Ministtero Della Salute* [2010] ECR I-13533
Case C-115/09 *Bund fur Umwelt und Naturschutz Deutschland v Bezirksregierung Arnsberg* [2011] ECR I-3673
Case C-121/00 *Criminal Proceedings against Walter Hahn* [2002] ECR I-9193
Case C-142/05 *Aklagaren v Mickelsson and Roos* [2009] ECR I-4273
Case C-192/01 *Commission v Denmark*, [2003] ECR I-9693
Case C-237/07 *Janecek v Freistaat Bayern* [2008] ECR I-6221
Case C-240/09 *Lesoochranárske zoskupenie VLK v. Ministry of Environment* [2012] ECR I-1255
Case C-254/08 *Futura Immobiliare srl Hotel Futura* [2009] ECR I-6995
Case C-263/08 *Djurgården-Lilla Värtans Miljöskyddsförening v Stockholms kommun genom dess marknämnd* [2009] ECR I-9967
Case C-266/09 *Stichting Natuur en Milieu* [2010] ECR I-13119
Case C-286/02 *Bellio F.lli Srl v Prefettura di Treviso* [2004] ECR I-3465
Case C-302/86 *Commission v Denmark* [1988] ECR I-4607
Case C-321/95P *Greenpeace v Commission* [1998] ECR I-1651
Case C-379/98 *Preussen Elektra, G v Schhleswag AG* [2001] ECR I-2099
Case C-427/07 *The European Commission v. Ireland* [2009] ECR I-6277
Case C-43/10 *Nomarchiaki Aftodioikisi Aitoloakarnanias and Others* [2012] ECR I-560
Case C-463/01 *Commission v Germany* [2004] ECR-I 11705

Case C-50/00P *Unión de Pequeños Agricultores v Council of the European Union* [2002] ECR I-6677
Case C-58/08 *Vodafone Ltd v Secretary of State for Business, Enterprise and Regulatory Reform* [2010] ECR I-4999
Case C-64/05 P *Kingdom of Sweden v Commission of the European Communities and Others* [2007] ECR I-11389
Case T-13/99 *Pfizer Animal Health S.A. v Council* [2002] ECR I-3305
Case T-177/01 *Jégo-Quéré v Commission* [2002] ECR II-2365
Case T-264/04 *WWF-EPP v. Council of the European Union* [2007] ECR II-911
Case T-333/10 *ATC* EU:T:2013: 451

# Table of EU secondary legislation

Commission Directive 2003/46/EC of 4 June 2003 amending Directive 2001/32/EC as regards certain protected zones exposed to particular plant health risks in the Community, 5 June 2003, OJ L138/45
Commission Regulation (EC) No 1122/2009 of 30 November 2009 laying down detailed rules for the implementation of Council Regulation (EC) No 73/2009 as regards cross-compliance, modulation and the integrated administration and control system, under the direct support schemes for farmers provided for that Regulation, as well as for the implementation of Council Regulation (EC) No 1234/2007 as regards cross-compliance under the support scheme provided for the wine sector, OJ L 316/65, 21 December 2009
Council Decision of 17 February 2005 on the conclusion, on behalf of the European Community, of the Convention on access to information, public participation in decision-making and access to justice in environmental matters, 17 May 2005, OJ L 124/1
Council Directive 2003/96/EC of 27 October 2003 restructuring the Community framework for the taxation of energy products and electricity, OJ L 238
Council Directive 2009/28/EC of 23 April 2009 on the promotion of the use of energy from renewable energy sources and amending and subsequently repealing Directives 2001/77/EC and 2003/30/EC, OJ 2009 L 140/16
Council Directive 90/313/EEC of 7 June 1990 on the freedom of access to information on the environment, 23 June 1990, OJ L 158/56
Council Directive 92/43/EEC of 21 May 1992 on the conservation of natural habitats and of wild fauna and flora, 22 July 1992, OJ L 206/7
Council Directive 94/62/EC on Packaging and Packaging Waste
Council Directive 96/62/EC of 27 September 1996 on ambient air quality assessment and management, OJ 1996 L 296/55
Council Regulation (EC) No 73/2009 of 19 January 2009 establishing common rules for direct support schemes for farmers under the common agricultural policy and establishing certain support schemes for farmers; amending Regulations, (EC) No 1290/2005
Decision No 1600/2002/EC of the European Parliament and of the Council of 22 July 2002 laying down the Sixth Community Environment Action Program, 10 September 2002, OJ L 242/1

*EU secondary legislation* xiii

Directive 1999/31/EC on Waste Landfill
Directive 2000/60/EC of the European Parliament and of the Council of 23 October 2000 establishing a framework for Community action in the field of water policy, OJ L 327/1
Directive 2000/60/EC on Water Policy
Directive 2001/42/EC of the European Parliament and of the Council of 27 June 2001 on the assessment of the effects of certain plans and programmes on the environment, 21 July 2001, OJ L 197/30
Directive 2003/35/EC of the European Parliament and of the Council of 26 May 2003 providing for public participation in respect of the drawing up of certain plans and programmes relating to the environment and amending with regard to public participation and access to justice Council Directives 85/337/EEC and 96/61/EC, 25 June 2003, OJ L156/17
Directive 2003/4/EC of the European Parliament and of the Council of 28 January 2003 on public access to environmental information and repealing Council Directive 90/313, 14 February 2003, OJ L 41/26
Directive 2003/87/EC of the European Parliament and of the Council of 13 October 2003 establishing a scheme for greenhouse gas emission allowance trading within the Community and amending Council Directive 96/61/EC, OJ L 275, 25 October 2003
Directive 2004/35/CE of the European Parliament and of the Council of 21 April 2004 on environmental liability with regard to the prevention and remedying of environmental damage, 30 April 2004, OJ L 143/56
Directive 2008/101/EC of the European Parliament and of the Council of 19 November 2008 amending Directive 2003/87/EC so as to include aviation activities in the scheme for greenhouse gas emission allowance trading within the Community
Directive 2008/98/EC of the European Parliament and of the Council of 19 November 2008 on waste and repealing certain Directives, 22 November 2008, OJ L 312/3
Directive 2008/99/EC of the European Parliament and of the Council of 19 November 2008 on the protection of the environment through criminal law, 6 December 2008, OJ L 328/28
Directive 2009/28/EC of the European Parliament and of the Council of 23 April 2009 on the promotion of the use of energy from renewable sources and amending and subsequently repealing Directives, 2001/77/EC and 2003/30/EC OJ EU, L 140/16
Directive 2009/28/EC of the European Parliament and of the Council of 23 April 2009 on the promotion of the use of energy from renewable sources and amending and subsequently repealing Directives 5 June 2009 2001/77/EC and 2003/30/EC, OJ L 140/16
Directive 2009/29/EC of the European Parliament and of the Council of 23 April 2009 amending Directive 2003/87/EC so as to improve and extend the greenhouse gas emission allowance trading scheme of the Community, OJ L 140/63
Directive 2009/30/EC of 23 April 2009 amending Directive, 98/70/EC

Directive 2009/31/EC of the European Parliament and of the Council of 23 April 2009 on the geological storage of C02 and amending Council Directive, 85/337/EEC

Directive 2011/76/EU of the European Parliament and of the Council of 27 September 2011 amending Directive 1999/62/EC on the charging of heavy goods vehicles for the use of certain infrastructures, OJ L 269/1

Directive 2011/92/EU of the European Parliament and of the Council of 13 December 2011 on the assessment of the effects of certain public and private projects on the environment, 28 January 2012 OJ L 26/1

Directive 75/439/EEC on the Disposal of Waste Oils

Directive 94/62/EC OJ L 365/5

Djurgården-Lilla Värtans Miljöskyddsförening v. Stockholms kommun, C-263/08 DLV

Environmental Liability Directive, 2004

European Communities- Measures Concerning Meat and Meat Products, Complaint by the United States (WT/DS26)

*Gabcikovo- Nagymaros Project* (Hungary/Slovakia) 1997, *ICJ Reports* 15 September 1997, GL No. 92 (*Gabcikovo Case*)

*Indian Council for Enviro-Legal Action v. Union of India*, AIR 1996 SC 1446 and *Vellore Citizens' Welfare Forum v. Union of India*, AIR 1996 SC 2715

Measures Affecting Imports of Retreaded Tyres, WT/DS332/AB/R, 17 December 2007

*Pontina Case (2010)*

Regulation (EC) No 1013/2006

Regulation (EC) No 1367/2006 of the European Parliament and of the Council of 6 September 2006 on the application of the provisions of the Aarhus Convention on Access to Information, Public Participation in Decision-making and Access to Justice in Environmental Matters to Community Institutions and Bodies, 25 September 2006, OJ L 264/13

Regulation EC/2493/2000 of the European Parliament and of the Council of 7 November 2000 on measures to promote the full integration of the environmental dimension into the development process of developing countries, OJ L 288/1

Restriction of Hazardous Substances (ROHs) Directive, 2002/95/ EC

*Shrimp Turtle Case* (WT/DS58): Report of the Appellate Body in *WTO DSR* 1998: Vol. VII, 1998

*Southern Bluefin Tuna Cases*, (Australia v. Japan; New Zealand v. Japan) (SBT Cases) Provisional measures Order of 27 August 1999

*State of Tamil Nadu v. Hind Store*, AIR 1981 SC 711

*Tennessee Valley Authority (TVA) v. Hill*, 437 U.S. 153, 174 (1978)

Thailand – Restrictions on Importation of and Internal Taxes on Cigarettes, 7 November 1990, BISD 37S/200

*The MOX Plant Case (Ireland v. United Kingdom), Request for Provisional Measures Order of 3rd Dec. 2001*, (2002) 41 *ILM* 405

United States – Import Prohibition of Certain Shrimp and Shrimp Products, WT/DS58/AB/R, 12 October 1998

United States – Restrictions on the Import of Tuna, DS21/R – 39S/155, 3 September 1991

Waste Electrical and Electronic Equipment (WEEE) Directive, 2012/92/EU, 2002

# Table of other authorities

Air (Prevention and Control of Pollution) Act (1981)
Clean Air Act (CAA)
Clean Water Act (CWA)
Electricity Act (2003)
Forest Conservation Act (1980)
National Environment Appellate Authority Act (1997)
National Environment Tribunal Act (1995)
National Environmental Policy Act
National Green Tribunal Act of 2010
Trade Act of 2002
Water (Prevention and Control of Pollution) Cess Act (1977)
Wildlife (Protection) Act (1972)

# Acknowledgements

The contributions of others made the writing of this book possible – particularly completing it. I would like to recognise the particular contributions made by Alexis Cooke, now of the UK Government Legal Department, and Priscilla Schwartz, at the University of East London. Alexis is unstintingly hard-working, bright and positive to work with: an excellent researcher. Priscilla is a truly generous spirit who helped with the model and the completion. I thank them for each and all of their contributions.

Aiden Irish, currently of EcoAgriculture Partners, and Clare Williams, at SOAS, both helped at key times during the period this book was coming together and I really appreciated their different insights.

I would like to acknowledge the help and assistance from Alison Kirk and Ruth Noble at Taylor & Francis and their faith in this project and perhaps more specifically in me. I know I have not been an easy author and they kept things on track.

Finally, I would like to thank my family for all their support in the last year in particular when so many things happened to us all. Stability at home when everything was so changeable outside enabled the work to continue.

# Preface

Sustainable development is a concept of diverse meanings and significant implications. Its role within the European Union (EU) legal architecture and policy framework is increasingly determinative. Sustainable development has moved over time from minimal implied references to the concept's key ideas to a central place in the Treaties and foundational aims of the Union itself. This book aims to explore the meanings of sustainable development in the EU and how the concept is becoming a defining aspect of EU law. It is not there yet, and there is something about the aspiration of a sustainable development future in the EU which struggles in the delivery. But the sustainable development concept itself in some iterations of meaning expresses aspirational aims requiring a change of mindset and not just an action plan for change. And there are also specific actions and changes undertaken to achieve sustainability too. Both the sustainable development approach and specific legislative and policy actions are considered here.

This book has been finally completed at a time of great flux, with what seems from a historical perspective a remarkable international consensus in 150 states, plus the EU, signing the Paris Accord on the Framework Convention on Climate Change with its commitments that potentially go further than what has been attempted before, and with a reinvigorated EU shaking off the political doldrums of the last few years and perhaps even moving from the quagmire of the combination of the international financial crisis and the semi-associated problems of the creation of a single currency zone. At the same time, US President Trump has stated he will not respect the international commitments of his predecessor regarding climate change and is ditching the US's commitment to the Paris Accord, while the UK enters uncertain times with its inward looking anti-EU vote in the referendum on membership and attempts to negotiate a new relationship with the rest of the EU without a strong and stable government or a clear vision about what it now seeks.

Sustainable development in the EU, and in the UK, remains of remarkable significance and the turbulence of the last few years is unlikely to change the importance of the sustainable development concept, nor of the EU's contribution to understanding what sustainability means. The EU will continue to frame and shape sustainable development, and sustainable development will continue to frame our thinking about the future despite the US's position on international agreements and despite the EU's changing membership. It will be a great shame if contributions from the UK will no longer shape understanding in the EU of sustainability as the UK leaves the EU, but no doubt views in the UK will still make some difference, somehow, to continuing EU Member States.

The development of thinking about sustainable development cannot be anywhere near finished yet, and it is highly unlikely it will be any time soon. Such thinking already has a long history. It is 45 years since Christopher Stone's seminal piece in the *California Law Review*, "Should Trees Have Standing? Toward Legal Rights for Natural Objects", and the UN Conference on the Human Environment at Stockholm. Both key events date from 1972, the year when the UK's European Communities Act passed to enable the UK to join the then community system the following January. And the Brundtland Report, that definitional milestone in sustainable development thinking, itself is 30 years old. So the Brexit vote and the election of President Trump in 2016 may not do that much to impact upon all the work that has been put into sustainable development in the EU, and it is not even certain yet that either will actually impact negatively on sustainability even if it looks like both could. A lot can happen before the UK leaves the EU or even before it decides on adopting its own different approaches to the principles and policies that govern the EU, including sustainable development. And many US regions are signing up for the commitments agreed in the Paris Accord despite the stance of their president.

Of course, 1972 was not really a starting point in the development of the sustainable development idea. Whatever sustainable development as a concept currently is understood as meaning, it has a complex history and many sources. But both the Stockholm Conference and the idea that the environment or natural objects could have legal standing were innovative attempts at the recognition of environmental protection and legal tools to achieve this end. The importance of international cooperation and consensus to achieve sustainable development are also self-evident. Practical initiatives such as these also reflected a shift in thinking. Ideas and debate about the social, economic, and environmental were developed. Environmental ethics suggested a shift from what was seen previously as a social contract towards other frameworks and, to some, even a 'natural contract'. The law was becoming seen not just as a way to defend individual men and women; it is has become seen as something that could defend the world from human action. Anthropocentrism (whereby environmental protection is seen as necessary to enable humanity to live) and deep ecology (whereby environmental protection is seen as a value because of the value of nature and not necessarily because of any human concern) became labels for understanding different perspectives; and in the literature, the debate developed environmental protection ideas while contributing to the critique of modernity. If different perspectives conflicted, a focus on the well-being of living creatures, people, and the environment was developed. This underpins the remarkable idea of sustainable development and the phrasing of what sustainable development means in the language of *Our Common Future* in the Brundtland Report. The social, economic, and environmental balancing that is the sustainable development concept seeks to revalue what has been devalued in our society. Sustainable development is both an aspiration and a technique. It is a journey rather than a destination.

With such a catalogue of literature spanning such a long time period, sustainable development is difficult to define and challenging to implement. But the real risk is not failing at that challenge – the risks of not thinking about a sustainable future greatly outweigh the difficulties associated with understanding the concept. The EU is in a unique place to contribute. Sustainable development can define what the EU is about and what it is for. The EU has made a remarkable and significant contribution to the development of law – both internally and internationally. Its values provide a guide through competing policy fields and project themselves on the international plane in quiet contrast to powerful states or other international blocs. Sustainable development is a principle of the EU legal order and system. Where it lacks force, the opportunity is there for a more robust application of the sustainability concept. Then, if the challenge of balancing economic, social and environmental interests which is the sustainable development ideal can happen in the EU, this can inform how sustainable development operates elsewhere. This book aims to encourage and exhort for more recognition of the sustainable development idea in the EU legal system and in EU policy areas as well as to help with understanding the complex implications of what it means.

# 1 Introduction

Sustainable development attracts diverse meanings and interpretations of its requirements. Much to the frustration of advocates of particular aspects of the concept, how it is understood can vary. These variations are visible in its application in geographical contexts and specific contexts – from political forms of governance to construction industry standards.[1] Over a period of almost thirty years, the meaning and purpose of the term has been gradually defined in a range of international documents,[2] making its first appearance during the 1972 Stockholm Conference, the focus of which was to delineate the 'rights' of the human family to a healthy and productive environment by balancing two opposing positions.[3] The first position was that of developed nations, who were anxious

---

1 See, for example, Stanton, J., *Democratic Sustainability in a New Era of Localism* (London: Routledge-Earthscan, 2014); Kemp, R., Parto, S. and Gibson, R., "Governance for Sustainable Development: Moving From Theory to Practice", *International Journal of Sustainable Development* (2005) 8, nos. 1–2, 12; Fergus, A. and Rowney, J., "Sustainable Development: Lost Meaning and Opportunity", *Journal of Business Ethics* (2005) 60, 17–27; and Spence, R. and Mulligan, H., "Sustainable Development in the Construction Industry", *Habitat International* (1995) 19, no. 3, 279–292.
2 The 1987 Brundtland Report 'Our Common Future' defined sustainable development as "development that meets the needs of the present without compromising the ability of future generations to meet their own needs" (Report of the World Commission on Environmental and Development, Our Common Future (The Brundtland Report), United Nations (1987)). In Principle 27 of the 1992 Rio Declaration, the United Nations Conference on Environment and Development stated its commitment to "the further development of international law in the field of sustainable development". Also in 1992, Agenda 21 elaborated that this involved the "further development of international law on sustainable development, giving special attention to the delicate balance between environmental and developmental concerns". In the 1997 Programme of Action for Further Implementation of Agenda 21, it was deemed "necessary to continue the progressive development and, as and when appropriate, codification of international law related to sustainable development". In its Johannesburg Declaration, the 2002 World Summit on Sustainable Development specifically commits to "assume a collective responsibility to advance and strengthen the interdependent and mutually reinforcing pillars of sustainable development".
3 United Nations, "The History of Sustainable Development in the United Nations", United Nations Conference for Sustainable Development, Rio +20, www.uncsd2012.org/history.html

that the economic development of the third world could have both negative and irreversible consequences for the environment. The second position was that of developing nations, who did not want to have their right to economic development hindered. The notion of sustainable development therefore emerged as a compromise; recognising that the need to protect and defend the environment for future generations was an imperative goal for humankind.[4]

In 1980, the International Union for the Conservation of Natural Resources published the World Conservation Strategy. By asserting that the conservation of nature could not be achieved without the alleviation of poverty through economic development, this strategy provided the precursor to the concept of sustainable development.[5] Later, the World Charter for Nature called for the resources of the world to be "managed to achieve and maintain optimum sustainable productivity".[6]

A Commission, chaired by Gro Harlem Brundtland, was set up to address a growing concern regarding the "accelerating deterioration of the human environment and natural resources and the consequences of that deterioration for economic and social development".[7] After four years of deliberation, the Commission published its report entitled 'Our Common Future' in 1987, according to which:

> The environment does not exist as a sphere separate from human actions, ambitions, and needs, and therefore it should not be considered in isolation from human concerns. The environment is where we all live; and development is what we all do in attempting to improve our lot within that abode. The two are inseparable.[8]

As such, the Commission defined sustainable development as "development that meets the needs of the present without compromising the ability of future generations to meet their own needs,"[9] a formulation at once both simple in its expression and complex in its formation and a mantra capable of many different meanings depending upon the perspective.

While the definition provided in the Brundtland Report remains the principal explanation of the concept of sustainable development, more recent attempts to define it further have resulted in various elements being added to it. For example, in 1992 the Rio Convention provided a more detailed approach to the concept in Agenda 21, cataloguing a number of subsidiary principles connected with the

---

4 Danaher, J., "Protecting the Future or Compromising the Present? Sustainable Development and the Law", *Irish Student Law Review* 14 (2006), 118.
5 "The History of Sustainable Development in the United Nations" (n 3).
6 United Nations General Assembly "42/187 – Report of the World Commissions on Environment and Development", A/RES/42/187, 11 December 1987, 4.
7 Ibid., 1.
8 "The History of Sustainable Development in the United Nations" (n 3).
9 The Brundtland Report (n 2) 27.

achievement of sustainable development, including: the right to development; inter and intra-generational equity; the precautionary principle; the polluter pays principle; and greater transparency, access to information, and participation in environmental decision-making.[10]

At Rio, the governments confirmed the interrelated nature of both environmental protection and economic development as being integral to the achievement of sustainable development. But it was not until 1997 and the Rio+5 that the third element – social development – was added. This rebalancing of the concept of sustainable development to include three fundamental pillars – the economic, the environmental, and the social – was reinforced in the International Law Association's (ILA) 2002 report, considered below.

In their analysis of the principles, Cordonier Segger et al. looked specifically at the extent to which Principles 3, 4, and 5 had been integrated into the above-mentioned triad of sustainable development.[11] They found that nations are capable of integrating different forms of sustainable development, in different ways and to differing extents, at the national, regional, and international level – a conclusion supporting the idea that there is no precise or static definition of the term.[12]

The ever-evolving nature of sustainable development is also reflected in the fact that the concept is exposed to varying interpretations, often depending on the perspective concerned. One of the concept's key strengths is its broad and flexible definition as this has enabled its near-universal acceptance by governments around the world. Yet, for some, this is also one of the concept's primary weaknesses. The vague nature of the definition detracts from the practical impact and meaning of the concept, especially from the perspective of environmental protection.[13]

Some argue that although the broad concept of sustainable development was very successful in managing the political collision between 'development' and 'environment' throughout the 1980s and 1990s, it has proved inadequate for navigating the implementation phase. It has been further argued by advocates of the 'zero growth' approach to environmental economics that the term itself is oxymoronic, since development (and more specifically growth) can never be sustained, as we would eventually exhaust the supply of essential natural assets.[14]

Perhaps, therefore, the means by which States can achieve this relative obligation is by satisfying the absolute obligations imposed by, for example, the component principles of sustainable development, such as integration, environmental

---

10 United Nations, "Rio Declaration on Environment and Development 1992", Principles 3, 10, 13 and 15.
11 Cordonier Segger, M., Khalfan, A., Gehring, M. and Toering, M., "Prospects for Principles of International Sustainable Development Law After WWSD: Common But Differentiated Responsibilities, Precaution and Participation", *RECIEL* (2003) 12, no. 1.
12 Ibid., 67.
13 Danaher (n 4) 123.
14 Danaher (n 4) 124.

protection, the polluter pays and precautionary principles, and inter- and intra-generational equity. If this were the case, parallels could be drawn between the concept of sustainable development and the rule of law. Both seemingly impose a relative obligation on States, the achievement of which can be accomplished by satisfying the absolute obligations imposed by their component elements. The rule of law has been defined as an overarching rule, composed of various elements of law and legal practice to which States must adhere, such as proportionality, legal certainty, access to judicial review, and the protection of human rights.[15]

Similarly, sustainable development is composed of elements which are increasingly integrated into national, European and international law – perhaps more so than sustainable development itself ever will. The precautionary principle,[16] environmental protection,[17] and common but differentiated responsibility[18] all feature in different legal systems. Although there is substantial literature discussing the true definition of the term 'sustainable development', it is worth remembering the limits of such discussions. In practice it seems that less and less importance is accorded to further defining the concept, suggesting to some that the matter, in the eyes of the politicians at least, has been put to rest.[19] Many scholars have done the same and turned their focus on to how the concept, broad and vague though it is, can and is put into practice by those under a legal or moral obligation to do so. However, before examining these approaches further, it is important to understand better the concept's philosophical foundations. To do so makes it easier to conceptualise the future prospects of sustainable development as a key feature of governmental responsibilities.

Commenting on the state of climate change policy, sustainable development more generally and the political environment, Ehrenfeld argues that "we need a new guiding political philosophy for this age of the earth and human history; this is no time for political business as usual".[20] For some, this comment might be considered hopelessly optimistic, hopelessly pessimistic, or perhaps just hopeless. After all, changing political systems is an exceedingly difficult task. However, as change is the human experience, even stultifying, reactionary governance systems, which

---

15 Bingham, T., *The Rule of Law*, 1st edition (London: Allen Lane, 2010).
16 For more on how this principle is integrated into EU case law and legislation, see Chapter 4.
17 Environmental protection is being increasingly recognised as a justification for otherwise legal free movement measures. For more, see Section 3.
18 This is a controversial principle which has been worked into the agreements at the international level, such as in the UNFCCC 'Copenhagen Accord' (2009) and the Rio+20 declaration, 'The Future We Want' (2012).
19 The December 2015 Paris Accord, under the United Nations Framework Convention on Climate Change, avoids definitions while inventing a Sustainable Development Mechanism. There is, further, practically no mention of sustainable development in the Rio+20 declaration 'The Future We Want' other than to recognise its importance and the need to interlink economic, social and environmental concerns so as to "to achieve sustainable development in all its dimensions".
20 Ehrenfeld, D., *Becoming Good Ancestors: How We Balance Nature, Community, and Technology* (Oxford; New York: Oxford University Press, 2009) p. 241.

oppose their own reform, do change in the end. History is littered with such examples, from the remarkable changes in France between Louis XIV's regime and the pre-Napoleonic Directory through to pre- and post-apartheid South Africa.

However, whether this means a new political philosophy can be widely accepted is open to some doubt – there are many more examples of minor reforms than there are of truly transformational changes. Anything is possible, of course. Louis XIV and the dominant philosophy in Bourbon France in 1643 at the time of his accession suggested kings were endowed by God with the authority to rule over their subjects as they saw fit. The revolution that followed a century and a half later overturned everything, not least that philosophy, 400 years after which an entirely different governance theory underpins French society. Viewed in this light, Ehrenfeld's call has precedents even if the obstacles to achievement remain high. Indeed, it may be that a complete revision of political theory is not necessary to achieve sustainable development.

Though often considered a modern appearance in legal frameworks, sustainable development has a long history. The ideas underpinning the concept have many potential origins, including social contract theory. The willing acceptance by citizens of limitations to a generalised free existence in return for security, orderliness, justice, and an improved quality of life is a social governance norm enshrined since the earliest civilisations,[21] and many theories, from Socrates to Thomas Hobbes, have sought to explain this. An implicit component of the social contract is that citizens benefit more from the structured orderliness of society than they would from what Hobbes termed the "state of nature" in all its chaotic horror. Such conceptions of contract theory emphasise the duty of citizens to follow the rule of law in order to reap the benefits of society, most generally those of orderliness and security. But a contract is a two-way agreement and governments have a responsibility to their citizens to fulfil the other side of the bargain. It is this acceptance of governmental responsibility which is an important marker in understanding the aims and aspirations of sustainable development theory.

In the *Second Treatise on Civil Government*, Locke shifted the onus of responsibility from citizen obedience to a government's obligation to provide for its citizens. Failure to meet this responsibility, in Locke's view, could reasonably be considered justification for the rebellion of the governed. Out of this classical liberal view of social contract theory comes the guiding philosophy that is embraced by even the most conservative of European or North American politicians. This view, to some, provided a liberal philosophical legitimisation of many, if not all, revolutions. But there is no settled view, even among social contract theorists, as to when system of governance should be changed to renew the contract, or to rebalance the relationship between the government and the governed. The starting point in this debate remains consideration of the question: what responsibility does a government have for its citizens?

---

21   For example, Hammurabi's Code from Babylon, circa 1772 BC, one of the earliest written justice systems of which we have record.

If the first duty of government is the protection of the physical security of citizens, which is in many ways the basis of the social contract as Socrates illustrated it, our conception of what is needed to secure physical security is influenced by a changing understanding of what is a safe environment. To the protections offered by States to their peoples from the physical threats posed by other States, or from criminality from within the State, we can add health protections, human rights protections, equality protections, and, more latterly, environmental protections. The United Nations Charter on Human Rights is, essentially, a laundry list of the rights now considered basic and foundational to a society that legitimates a government's authority. The list is already much extended to include structural protections, such as the provision of a criminal and civil justice system, and substantive protections, such as rights to free speech, and rights to contribute to the process of government. Thus sustainable development is perhaps more accurately described not as a new philosophy as Ehrenfeld asserts, but as a logical addition to the list of governance responsibilities. However, when applied to the social contract, the concept is made up of different but interrelated components – environmental health, social and societal equity, and the regard for posterity.

The importance of protecting environmental health for human well-being has gained significant traction in recent decades, and scientific discovery has helped to spread this understanding in the western world. Two important lessons have come from understanding environmental systems. First of these lessons is that everything is interconnected and dependent in some way on something else. Lynton Caldwell, a key contributor to the 1969 US National Environmental Policy Act, commented that, "people commonly perceive their 'environment' as a totality of numerous separate interrelationships that have no apparent connections. In fact, these interactive relationships are ultimately, even though remotely, connected".[22] Caldwell's assertion is further supported by the detailed observations of biologists and ecologists such as Wilson.[23] Scientific appreciation of environmental interconnectedness provides the rationale for protecting and sustaining natural systems due to human reliance on those systems. The second lesson suggests, however, that an appreciation of interconnectedness must come before a scientific understanding of those connections.

The quest for scientific understanding is often understood in terms of a journey to a particular end point where conclusions become apparent. For some, however, there will always be mysteries that cannot be understood by science; others will focus on those questions that can be answered and leave the question of interconnected systems and impact hanging. A common tension in the debate about sustainable development, and in understanding what the concept means, relates to the extent to which the concept requires scientific evidence before a particular action is undertaken, or, perhaps more often, before a proposed development is

---

22 Caldwell, L.K., "Is Humanity Destined to Self-Destruct?" *Politics & the Life Sciences* (1999) 18, no. 1, 3–14, 4.
23 Wilson, E.O., *The Creation: An Appeal to Save Life on Earth* (New York; London: W.W. Norton and Company, 2007; 1st reprint edition).

avoided on the basis of the risks posed to our futures. John Locke himself, and his empiricism, teach us that we should consider the evidence for what we think and what we do carefully.

What does this mean in terms of the amount of evidence needed regarding the risk to an ecosystem before any sustainable development is contemplated? Are we in a position where we have the necessary scientific knowledge and tools to identify and understand these risks? Max Planck, famously, was encouraged not to study physics because the popular belief of the age was that there was nothing left to discover in that field. Fortunately he ignored this advice and went on to set out some questions about the field we now call quantum physics. In a famous blunder, William Stewart, the Surgeon General of the US in 1967, after the development of penicillin stated that "the time has come to close the book on infectious diseases. We have basically wiped out infection in the United States".[24] Subsequent discoveries of penicillin-resistant microbes proved Stewart grossly incorrect.

Across the scientific disciplines, similar certainties have been shaken by the realisation of infinite complexity. It seems the more we discover through scientific advance, the more we realise there is to learn. Although it may be impossible to understand everything, there are always more scientific questions, suggesting that there will not always be full evidence of risk because of our understanding of the impact is limited. Sustainable development therefore suggests that society must proceed with caution and with the knowledge that failure to appreciate how little we understand can result in disastrous consequences.

Thus, while Ehrenfeld's assertion that "a new guiding political philosophy" is needed has merit in many respects, it is not entirely accurate. Rather than epitomising a completely new theory of governance, sustainable development actions present the logical evolution of governance theory. The incorporation of both the concept and its component parts into EU governance structures, which is the focus of this book, embodies these amendments to the social contract.

It is against this background that we return to the evolving concept of sustainable development, which, from the perspective of the EU, takes a very similar form to that proposed by the Brundtland Commission. The term is espoused into international principles in the Rio Declaration on Environment and Development, and further developed by the ILA Fifth Environmental Action Programme (EAP) dating from 1993. The ILA not only adopted the Brundtland definition but also stated that sustainable development reflected a policy of "continued economic and social development without detriment to the environment", thus mirroring the three-pillared approach mentioned above. In Article 1 of the 2006 Review of the Sustainable Development Strategy, the EU went further, stating the following:

> Sustainable development means that the needs of the present generation should be met without compromising the ability of future generations to meet their own needs. It is an overarching objective of the European Union

---

24  Bryson, B., *A Short History of Nearly Everything* (Westport, CT: Broadway Books, 2004) p. 315.

set out in the Treaty, governing all the Union's policies and activities. It is about safeguarding the earth's capacity to support life in all its diversity and is based on the principles of democracy, gender equality, solidarity, the rule of law and respect for fundamental rights, including freedom and equal opportunities for all. It aims at the continuous improvement of the quality of life and well-being on Earth for present and future generations. To that end it promotes a dynamic economy with full employment and a high level of education, health protection, social and territorial cohesion and environmental protection in a peaceful and secure world, respecting cultural diversity.[25]

The preamble to the Treaty on European Union (TEU) states that the EU is determined to promote economic and social progress while "taking into account the principle of sustainable development". Moreover, Article 3 TEU refers to the importance of promoting sustainable development through both internal and external action, Article 11 TFEU (Treaty on the Functioning of the European Union) refers specifically to the objective of promoting sustainable development. Despite being a shared competence, the objectives contained in these Articles are broad and allow for the adoption of a wide range of measures by the EU whilst, at the same time, allowing Member States to adopt more stringent national measures.

The Treaties also recognise the importance of some of sustainable development's subsidiary principles stated in the Rio Declaration and by the ILA. These include: the polluter pays and the precautionary principles (Article 191(2) TFEU), intergenerational equity (Article 3(3) TEU), public participation (Article 15 TFEU), the eradication of poverty (Articles 3(5) TEU and 208 TFEU), access to justice (Articles 67(4) and 81(2)(e) TFEU), and good governance (Article 15). The concept itself is not defined within the Treaties, however, when the commitment enunciated in Articles 3 TEU and 11 TFEU are combined with the various subsidiary principles outlined above, it is possible to gain an understanding of what sustainable development at the EU-level might mean and involve.

The EU has also issued various policy documents and official statements, which offer further insight into its understanding of the concept. For example, the sixth and seventh Environmental Action Programmes sought greater integration of environmental concerns into all areas of policy and legislation, both internal and external. In terms of enforcement, experiences to date have demonstrated the important role that the EU plays in the promotion and implementation of both environmental protection and sustainable development within and outside the EU. Beck and Gidden confirm this, referring specifically to the EU as the ideal forum in which "formal sovereignty can be exchanged for real power, national cultures can be nurtured and economic success improved", all for the benefit of environmental, social, and economic development.[26]

---

25 Council of the European Union, "Review of the EU Sustainable Development Strategy", 10117/06, Brussels, 9 June 2006, Article 1.
26 Beck, U. and Giddens, A., "Nationalism Has Now Become the Enemy of Europe's Nations", *The Guardian*, 4 October 2005, www.theguardian.com/politics/2005/oct/04/eu.world

Authors such as Jonker and Welford have also provided an insight into how entities such as the EU can operate to improve the achievement of sustainable development goals. Although their work is tailored to examine businesses seeking better corporate social responsibility, many of their findings are transferable to larger organisations such as the EU and, in any event, provide an interesting commentary on the private sphere's approach to this collectively owned concept. They discuss the importance of private organisations in the achievement of sustainable development and argue that financial gain is no longer the exclusive and ultimate yardstick for organisational and societal success. Rather, with the transformation in the cultural expectations and norms of the business community there has been movement towards greater "quality management", improved environmental performance, and increased social responsibility. It is this evolution, which, they believe, has encouraged the move towards policies consistent with sustainable development.[27]

A key stage in this transformation was the rise in popularity of the 'triple bottom line', a term coined by John Elkington.[28] Elkington was the founder of SustainAbility, a British consultancy firm, whose view was that companies should aim to prepare three different bottom lines. These include: (1) the bottom line of the profit and loss account; (2) the bottom line of a company's personal account – i.e., the extent to which an organisation has been socially responsible in its actions; and (3) the bottom line of the company's planet account – i.e., how environmentally responsible it had been. Only a company that produces a triple bottom line, which measures its financial, social, and environmental performance, is taking account of the full cost involved in doing business.

The formula has enjoyed some success since its inception, especially as the hidden social and environmental costs of business become increasingly transparent. It has been adopted by companies such as Nike and Tesco. It formed the basis of Mission Zero, the ambitious objective of Interface Carpets, a worldwide carpet tile manufacturer. In 1994, Interface Carpet's founder, Ray Anderson, recognised that the carpeting industry as a whole was fundamentally unsustainable and set an ambitious target for the company to meet. Through "Mission Zero", it was his aim to make Interface Carpets fully sustainable by 2020 by reformulating the company's business structure. The objective was to:

1   eliminate waste;
2   make the emissions produced from the consumption of energy benign;
3   reduce the demand for energy while substituting sources with renewable ones;
4   redesign processes and products so that all resources could be recovered and reused, closing the technical and natural loop;

---

27  Welford, R., "Beyond Rhetoric: Identifying Organisational Gaps and Individual Challenges in the Achievement of Sustainable Development", *Estonian Business Review* (2004–2005), 19.
28  Elkington, J., *Cannibals With Forks: Triple Bottom Line of 21st Century Business* (Capstone Trade, 2009).

5   use resource-efficient transportation of both people and products;
6   sensitise stakeholders to the functioning of natural systems and the company's impact on them; and
7   redesign commerce to focus on the delivery of services and value and to encourage external organisations to create like policies and market incentives.

In the space of almost 25 years, the company has made notable progress towards Mission Zero. It has reduced its waste, greenhouse gas emissions, water intake, and non-renewable energy use; increased the use of recycled or bio-based raw materials in the carpet tile manufacturing process, offset the carbon produced by its delivery service and employees travel; and ensured that 99.7% of the products sold in Europe are manufactured in Europe. The company shows us that, on a smaller scale at least, it is possible to integrate sustainable development objectives successfully into all areas of an organisation. And, by setting a sustainable development agenda which pervades the entirety of its processes, Interface Carpets has demonstrated that it is possible to combine sustainable development with financial gain.

Jonker and Welford also argue that, in relation to organisations, there are five gaps in knowledge and doing, of which two are particularly relevant to the focus of this book. The first is the "knowledge gap" which is a "widespread and firmly accepted misunderstanding that knowledge leads automatically to action".[29] Rather, "knowledge in itself is not good enough to create change".[30] The second is the 'organising gap', namely that the basic understanding of organisations as "mechanical and functional entities" operating in a social niche should be abandoned in favour of an understanding that organisations are social communities, accountable to clearly identifiable stakeholders for their social, environmental, and financial results.[31] To help address the 'organising gap', organisations must avoid inertia and instead adapt to embrace change and uncertainty.[32] According to Jonker and Welford, one way of achieving this is by encouraging the greater integration of workers, by enabling participation and involvement in the process of change.[33] They argue that:

> It is not only good business to encourage participation and involvement in the organisation, it is also more consistent with a move towards sustainable development, where people must not only participate in a change process, but must also take on more responsibility for the planet in every aspect of their lives.[34]

Ross, in her analysis looks instead at the UK, a current EU Member State, if not for much longer, and the law of sustainable development. She argues that

---

29  Jonker, J. and Welford, R., "Beyond Rhetoric: Identifying Organisational Gaps and Individual Challenges in the Achievement of Sustainable Development", *Estonian Business Review*, 2004–2005, 22.
30  Ibid., 22.
31  Ibid., 24–25.
32  Ibid.
33  Ibid., 28.
34  Ibid.

implementation in the UK requires institutional change which ensures integration of the concept into all policy and decision-making.[35] This reflects the Organisation for Economic Co-operation and Development (OECD) criteria to deliver sustainable development, namely: a common understanding; clear commitment and leadership; stakeholder involvement and efficient knowledge management; and appropriate integrative mechanisms (including enforcement tools).[36] In view of this, similarly to Jonker and Welford, Ross argues that greater integration should be accompanied by both a cultural change that indoctrinates a clear and consistent understanding of sustainable development, and increased public participation.[37]

Scott discusses how EU measures promoting sustainable development are often justified by a strong normative element, which refers to a *principle* of sustainable development.[38] She argues that the fact that the EU has adopted such a range of strategies which are, directly or indirectly, environmental in nature, "seems to reflect attempts to create an EU-level normative framework".[39]

Jonker and Welford, and Ross, identify a main issue about sustainable development: that it requires a revolution of thought and a rebalancing of the competing economic, environmental, and social interests with the needs of current and future generations. The triad of economic, environmental, and social, having originated from the Brundtland Report,[40] informs much of the sustainability debate including the integration principle.[41] It recognises that, in the twenty-first century, governance cannot be based solely on economic gain. Instead, pervading the various perspectives of what sustainable development represents is the understanding that for development to be sustainable it must be economically viable, socially beneficial and environmentally sound. By achieving an acceptable balance between these three interests, sustainable development can remain relevant, both legally and (perhaps more importantly) politically. However, in view of this need for balance, the challenges to the achievement of sustainable development often arrives either at the policy or implementation level, and this is most frequently the case when the focus has been too heavily concentrated in one area. In this way, the implementation of sustainable development is like, as Ruhl suggests, a Rubik's cube, whereby even though one side of the cube is coming together, the other sides are no further along or even more out of order.[42] Therefore, the key

---

35  Ross, A., *Sustainable Development Law in the UK: From Rhetoric to Reality* (London: Routledge, 2012) pp. 42–43.
36  Ibid., 43–44.
37  Ibid.
38  Scott, J., *Environmental Protection: European Law and Governance* (Oxford: Oxford University Press, 2009) p. 22.
39  Ibid., 22.
40  The Brundtland Report (n 2).
41  For more on the principle of integration in EU law, see Wasmeier, M., "The Integration of Environmental Protection as a General Rule for Interpreting Community Law", *Common Market Law Review* (2001) no. 38, 159–177.
42  Ruhl, J.B., "Law for Sustainable Development: Work Continues on the Rubik's Cube", *Tulsa Law Review* (2008–2009) no. 1, 2, 44.

questions are: to what extent the balancing occurs; how much this balancing is required; and whether such a balancing act should also involve other factors, such as culture, equity, and a greater participatory role for the public.

A further issue is how the concept is most successfully implemented when there are obvious short-term economic gains pervading the EU legislative and policy architecture. It is considered whether the most effective means of achieving sustainable development is by cloaking environmental and social interests in economic incentive. This approach could be particularly viable when aiming to enforce some of the more controversial elements of environmental protection at the international level, and is illustrated in the EU's approach to external trade. It is argued that not only does this make the goal of sustainable development more politically palatable for the twenty-eight Member States, but also enables the EU to incentivise further development both internal and external to the EU.

Another recurring issue is the EU's approach to both the general concept of sustainable development and its subsidiary principles, and the repercussions that such issues have on the purpose and added value of the EU. One such recurring issue is the difference between the rhetoric of the EU institutions in its policy documents and legislation, and the reality of its enforcement. For sustainable development to be fully incorporated and implemented into relevant areas, it is necessary that there is also effective enforcement at both the EU and Member State level.

A line is drawn, however, between the interpretation and enforcement of an overarching principle of sustainable development, and that of the individual subsidiary principles. If we take Barral's suggestion that sustainable development is an obligation of means,[43] perhaps we can see the EU's role and requirement as limited to the achievement of sustainable development through Article 11 TFEU. Alternatively, if we see the EU's role and requirement as entailing obligations of result, the EU can indirectly reinforce the overarching objective of sustainable development by implementing policy and legislation designed to promote its individual subsidiary principles. Leading on from this is the question that, if dividing obligations of means from obligations of result is the preferable approach, what added value does sustainable development have in relation to the EU legal order? One of the things argued at several points throughout the book is that the lack of enforcement of EU measures is detrimental to the attainment of sustainable development at both a regional and international level, and may even damage the Union's credibility and reputation.

## The structure of this book

This introductory chapter discussion has briefly covered some of the main issues around the concept of sustainable development in international and subsequently

---

43 Barral, V., "Sustainable Development in International Law: Nature and Operation of an Evolutive Legal Norm", *European Journal of International Law* (2012) p. 378 and pp. 390–391.

regional law in order to establish, at a basic level, whether there is a specific "European Union" understanding of the term. The introductory issues speak to concerns including how sustainability is understood in the EU context and as a broad lens to illustrate how sustainable development in the EU is rationalised from environmental concerns, the rule of law concept, and from economic, social and political, governance, and participatory rights. Legal issues and mechanism of transposition, implementation, and enforcement within the framework of 'principles' are all noted. Superficially at least, the EU has recognised the importance of sustainable development, in key documents of EU law and policy. Approaches to the EU's interpretation, implementation, and enforcement of sustainable development vary. However, most relate to an understanding that a moral and legal obligation is imposed on the EU to encourage sustainable measures by going further than just acquiring knowledge. Instead, the EU has recognised that any successful sustainable development agenda requires an approach that is beyond the political. The meaning and purpose of the concept of sustainable development from an international perspective is put in context in the next chapter. Sustainable development in international law provokes diverse issues, meanings interpretation, and implementation agendas.

The analysis in Chapter 2 seeks to establish sustainable development as a principle of international law, which is capable of being transposed in EU law through its subsidiary, sub principles. The following questions therefore immediately come to mind: What is sustainable development and its legal purpose? Does sustainable development emerge as a general principle to become an integral part of all relevant EU internal and external initiatives? Is it politically feasible to have a meaningful and operational concept of sustainable development in a twenty-eight-member State Union with membership itself in flux, as the UK leaves and as other States join? Will political leaders ever be willing to allow environmental protection to come before economic policy in a sufficiently consistent way to enable substantial change, both at home and in the wider world? Or, will the general principle that emerges be toothless and simply bolted onto EU initiatives in order to satisfy the self-imposed Treaty obligation merely to promote sustainable development?

In relation to these questions, the main objective is to assess the viability and effectiveness of the EU application of the principle of sustainable development from a legal and institutional outlook regionally and internationally and in relation to other key global actors. The premise seeks to resolve the contestations on the meaning and requirements of sustainable development on the one hand and its application as a principle through EU law, policy, and institutional order including the enforcement modality.

The debate on the meaning of the sustainable development concept is addressed in Chapter 2, with the aim of discerning an appropriate meaning and interpretation to set the framework for analysis of the EU implementation and enforcement methods in subsequent chapters. Chapter 2 presents a critical overview of the varying perspectives on sustainable development bringing out the debate and contested interpretations on its meaning in the legal and policy instruments and

14  *Introduction*

scholarly literature. It shows that sustainable development has popular currency and use in international, regional, and national application through various legal and policy instruments and initiatives; and generally applies to balance social, economic, and environmental objectives in decision-making. It locates sustainable development in the key sub principles that reflect the three main dimensions and objectives of sustainability – its economic, environmental, and social aspects. The key principles specifically examined include the polluter pays principle, the precautionary principle, and the principles of public participation and access to justice. The analysis establishes a framework for understanding the concept, its legal and policy context, and for its practical application through the sub-principles at the international, regional, or domestic level.

What method is apt to apply sustainable development in a meaningful way? First, the analyses show that despite the definitional questions, sustainable development has direct and primary relevance for regulating economic activities for environmental protection, alongside the competing need for ensuring developmental sustainability. It is argued here that sustainable development can be applied through the principles of precaution, the polluter pays, and public participation to address the three dimensions and objectives of sustainability. The legal character of sustainable development beyond legislative and judicial processes includes adjudicatory, administrative, and deliberative processes, and these are also considered in Chapter 2. The scope and purpose of the sustainable development concept's flexibility is considered, allowing for the interpretation of its principles within legal rules to enhance environmental protection at the global or domestic level.

Chapter 3 examines how sustainable development is applied in EU law and various policy areas. Particular consideration is given to the principle-based nature of sustainable development and its application through the principles of subsidiarity and proportionality. These two general principles have been chosen over others – such as non-discrimination – because of their relevance to the concept of sustainable development on the one hand, and their role to regulate governance at the EU level. These EU general principles have been increasingly incorporated into different areas of EU legislation, policy, and case law. This chapter also looks specifically at the interpretation and enforcement of each general principle in the EU.

The potential for the sustainable development concept to become a general principle under EU legal order is considered by looking at whether the concept has been both incorporated and upheld as a basis for legal protection by the Court of Justice. In other words, it examines critically the procedural challenges in EU legislative judicial and institutional mechanisms applying sustainable development. When this framework is applied to sustainable development, it is found that although the EU has made some headway, it has to date largely avoided enforcement. In particular, the Court has failed to uphold the right of future generations to a healthy environment as enshrined in the principle of intergenerational equity, a key element of sustainable development. This chapter therefore demonstrates to the reader the uncertainty as to where the concept of sustainable development sits in EU law and instead raises the potential role that the subsidiary components of principles of sustainable development, or its sub principles, can play when furthering the emergence of general principles in EU law.

The EU legal system transposes the sustainable development concept in two main legal paradigms. Firstly, through specific mention of the need to integrate environmental protection requirements into policy areas by Article 11 TFEU. In this context, sustainable development could fit into either of two camps: It will either remain a guiding principle, referred to in EU policy and legislative documents as an objective of EU law to be considered and – in theory – followed. Alternatively, it will develop in the case law of the CJEU (Court of Justice of the European Union) as a general principle upon which claims for judicial review of EU and Member State measures can be made. The second paradigm reveals that the EU system places sustainable development alongside the fundamental rights and freedoms enshrined in the Charter of Fundamental Rights of the European Union, with which sustainable development has little in common. The inclusion of sustainable development in the Charter suggests its promotion, and its association with fundamental rights of the EU legal order. Here the extent to which the Charter promotes the realisation of sustainable development will depend upon how the Charter will be viewed and used as the relationship between it and the European Convention on Human Rights and Fundamental Freedoms, and the relationship between the Court of Justice and the European Court of Human Rights develop. Although sustainable development is applied in wide-ranging areas of EU law and policy, a lingering gap remains between the rhetoric of the institutions and the reality of enforcement. Sustainable development will not amount to much if it cannot be enforced either under its own name or by means of one of its component principles, and whichever direction the principle takes, the emphasis should be placed on the future role it plays in the judicial scrutiny of EU and Member State measures.

Chapter 4 examines how sustainable development is applied in the EU legal order through the precautionary principle to promote especially the environmental protection dimensions. The precautionary principle is used to illustrate the primary relevance of the environmental protection dimension of sustainability.[44] This chapter demonstrates that the precautionary principle can capably transpose sustainable development through EU law, policy, and practice to promote environmental protection. Principles of precaution and environmental protection provide a transferrable, legal framework in which a general principle of sustainable development could sit.

EU specific methods of transposition are used to illustrate the application of the precautionary principle.[45] Both the interpretation of the principle in legislation

---

44 Note that the polluter pays will be examined in primary relevance to economic aspects of sustainability in Chapter 5; and public participation and access to justice is examined in Chapter 6 in primary relevance to promoting socially sustainable development – both in the EU context. The three principles are not mutually exclusive and therefore may entail overlaps in the objectives that are to be achieved in the respective dimensions from the broader interpretation of sustainable development as an overarching principle.

45 As identified in Chapter 3, the method includes application through policy and legislative documents on the one hand; and on the other hand, its effect in the case law of the CJEU as a general principle upon which claims for judicial review of EU and Member State measures can be made.

and policy and its enforcement by the Court, EU institutions, and the national authorities are examined. Sustainable development and sustainability are rarely referred to by the Court of Justice of the European Union. However, precaution is deeply embedded within the legal framework for environmental protection. It has increasingly favourable application in EU law and wide implementation in various policy areas and in objective interpretations and enforcement by the Court of Justice, the EU institutions, and the national authorities, which bolsters its legal effect; and ensures it as a transferable legal framework for promoting environmental protection dimension of sustainable development. Some of the case law does suggest, in general, ways the re-balancing of economic and environmental protection interests should be attempted. Invariably, the legal effect of the precautionary principle applying the broader sustainable development is not undermined on the basis of enforcement, since enforcement should be done in a way which is sustainable, balancing the competing economic, environmental, and social interests in a way that ensures legal and political credibility.

Chapter 5 examines the application of the polluter pays principle in the EU using mainly the EU method of transposition. It argues that polluter pays principle can capably transpose sustainable development through EU law, policy, and practice primarily to address economic aspects of sustainability. The polluter pays principle requires environmental damage should be a priority, be rectified at the source, and that the polluter should pay (Article 191(2)). The premise is that sustainable development, in EU law and policy, is associated closely with the development of environmental law and policy, which is built on a framework of principles and the polluter pays is key for economic regulation to achieve environmental policy objectives.

The polluter pays is a good illustration of the integration of economic considerations into environmental decision-making to address the regional problem of pollution. The economic aspects of the principle relate to the reliance on market and non-market mechanisms, internalisation, and incentive based economic instruments and measures that balance economic interests for regional pollution regulation and, ultimately, worldwide environmental problems. Economic regulation via the polluter pays, through process and production taxes, effluent charges, or the emissions trading scheme and emissions crediting, can provide an invaluable revenue stream for governments, which could help reduce the total cost of pollution to the environment and control to society. Compliance has increased with aviation and energy standards. The costs of complying with the requirements of pollution standards have lowered and products are redesigned in order to comply with waste packaging and recycling laws. The EU institutions are increasingly interpreting the polluter pays principle as an essential mechanism when developing legislation and policy in a variety of areas, which might result in environmental degradation or social harm. Also, the Court is taking an increasingly environmentally friendly position when balancing economic with environmental and/or social interests.

The analysis of specific policy areas, i.e., transport policy, agriculture policy, and competition policy, shows explicit reference is made to the polluter pays principle, but the emphasis remains limited to the aim of internalising external costs. The internalisation of external costs is an approach, which pervades a large part of transport policy and legislation. This internalisation is done with the aim of supporting and incentivising the creation of sustainable systems, capable of supporting themselves in lieu of State or EU funding. This approach appears in road, marine, and aviation sectors. But the chapter argues there is need for policy makers to consider more fully whether the sanctions for failure to pay 'costs' are sufficient to incentivise change. The policy analysis also uncovers a rather half-hearted integration of environmental protection interests with that of State Aid policy. The explicit integration of State Aid control does permit State subsidies to support efforts by undertakings which go beyond the standards required under the polluter pays principle. This fact distinguishes State Aid from the rest of competition policy.

Chapter 6 considers the social dimension of sustainable development and the right to public participation and access to justice in the decision-making process. It examines the EU system of promoting public participation, namely by placing sustainable development alongside the fundamental rights – economic and social rights – and freedoms enshrined in the Charter that must be balanced with environmental protection. The Aarhus Convention on Access to Information, Public Participation, and Access to Justice in Environmental Matters is analysed by way of a specific example on the protection of rights in relation to sustainable development. Chapter 6 illustrates the various policy and legislative measures enacted by the EU to incorporate the Convention's provisions into EU law, especially the more contentious 'access to justice' element. The relationships between the Charter and the European Convention on Human Rights and Fundamental Freedoms and the relationship between the Court of Justice and the European Court of Human Rights are also discussed. It is argued that in addition to the guarantees of rights in EU treaties and legislation, the promotion of procedural rights could take place through administrative and deliberative processes. One question to determine is whether, if at all, the EU's approach to the Aarhus Convention is representative of its wider approach to the principle of sustainable development in the EU agenda as a whole.

Looking at the EU system on public participation alongside the fundamental rights reveals that there is a successful incorporation of the Rio Declaration principle 10 and the Aarhus Convention provisions into EU law promoting social aspect of sustainability. The focus of the Aarhus Convention is on people, transparency, and accountability. It enables and empowers the public to be informed of and to participate in environmental decision-making and to challenge relevant decisions, which, they believe, are contrary to the interests of environmental protection. There are various policy and legislation, documents, and measures enacted or undertaken by the EU transposing or applying the Aarhus provisions directly of relatively toward social sustainability in environmental decision-making. Certainly, with regard to the first and second pillars, the EU has demonstrated significant willingness to enable greater access to information and participation of the public. However, there are gaps in consistency, specifically in relation to the implementation of the Convention's third pillar which are discussed here.

Chapter 7 reviews sustainable development in EU External Relations. Sustainable development, by its very nature, requires a global approach for it to be fully achieved. For this reason, the concept is, and has always been, one to be considered in an international context. It is generally accepted that external action by the EU in the field of sustainable development is equally as important as internal action. Its credibility has had more bearing as a player in discussions about environmental protection and, to a lesser extent, sustainable development.

The EU considers that promoting sustainable development to the wider world will help both the Union and the Member States to address those issues, which pose a threat, directly or indirectly, to their internal stability. Since both the sources and the impact of unsustainable development do not respect state or regional borders, these threats come in various shapes and guises. One such area of focus is climate change. Chapter 7 first considers whether sustainable development is an international issue for the EU. It then examines the EU's approach to date, to ascertain its effectiveness in encouraging non-Member States to change; or whether it is necessary for the EU to alter course to ensure that the agenda is properly promoted worldwide. Chapter 7 also considers the role that international organisations can play in sustainable development. Many international organisations have contributed to the expansion of sustainable development worldwide by providing a forum within which actors can discuss their sustainability-related challenges and solutions. Moreover, through international law and policy, States are redefining what sustainable development means, identifying the most important priorities, and seeking consensus on how these priorities can and should be addressed. Also, through the arbitration of disputes related to sustainable development, States are gaining valuable guidance from international courts and tribunals on how to resolve problems that require the careful balancing of environmental, economic, and social priorities. The discussion in this chapter focuses on the World Trade Organization (WTO), an organisation which started life as a primarily economic and trade entity and which has subsequently had to adapt to encourage greater environmental protection and sustainable development. The WTO provides a point of comparison to contextualise the EU's approach.

The intention of Chapter 7 is not to enter into a detailed comparison of environmental law and policy, as it is beyond the scope of this book to analyse in depth the material for each State included. Plus, it is not possible to compare directly the EU to any other actor on the international sustainable development stage because nothing is quite like the EU, or, indeed, the WTO. Instead, the aim is to identify the similarities and differences with the EU's approach, and flagging what this might mean for the future of the sustainable development agenda worldwide. It is hoped that such contrast will contextualise the EU's efforts and illustrate the fact that the only realistic way to promote sustainable development. Thus, where the preceding chapters focussed primarily on the EU's internal efforts, Chapter 7 explores the approach taken by the EU to further the sustainable development agenda through external relations.

Furthermore, the chapter aims to discuss what impact this approach might have on the emergence of a general principle of sustainable development. It starts by examining the incentives behind taking a more global approach to sustainable development, looking in particular at what the EU has achieved to date in the efforts to address climate change, a closely associated field. It then looks specifically at the EU's external approach to sustainable development by examining its enlargement, neighbourhood, and foreign trade policies. The goal is to be able to draw conclusions on the extent of the EU's success in promoting sustainable development to third world countries, its credibility in the field of international environmental protection, and its possible future approach to promoting sustainability on an international scale.

The survey of the EU external relations reveal that its international efforts on sustainability generally and specifically on climate change together promote the three dimensions of sustainability and are applicable to implement the precautionary approach, the polluter pays principle, and the public participation and access to justice. The findings also show that in spite of the EU's efforts promoting sustainability in the international arena, the issue of enforcement, as with its internal relations, remains. There is a clear dichotomy between EU's ambitious sustainability agenda and its ability to impose it on others. In this sense, the EU's approach to sustainable development in its external relations appears more as a symbolic Treaty requirement, encouraging the promotion, but not the enforcement, of sustainable development objectives. In other words, rather than seeing the encouragement of sustainable development as a moral obligation to protect the environmental, social and economic well-being of the planet and its inhabitants, the EU sees it as a symbolic, self-imposed Treaty obligation, requiring merely the promotion, and not necessarily the enforcement, of sustainable development.

Although the EU is no exception when it comes to the inconsistent application of political conditionality, it seems that the lack of enforcement could undermine the eventual impact of any genuine carrot-and-stick approach in the future. Such an impact could not only be extremely damaging to the credibility of the EU's reputation in the push towards greater, global sustainable development, but also set a dangerous precedent for other countries looking to revert to old habits. In this sense, more than normative or soft power is required for the EU to make real and lasting changes to how States perceive sustainable development and its subsidiary elements.

Sustainable development is a profound and interesting concept. The EU does many things, and potentially not all of them fit within the parameters of its sustainable development aspirations. That being so, sustainable development is also broader than the EU, its political or legal structures and policies. The United Kingdom's vote on EU membership and subsequent discussions about leaving the EU are unlikely to impact particularly on the contribution the EU makes to understanding the challenges of sustainable development. The EU's voice on this plane is as interesting as its own internal structures and principles. If a study of the EU and sustainable development is ambitious in the fast-changing political climate, it is perhaps inherent the sustainable development concept to consider change. Change is what sustainable development is about.

# 2 Sustainable development
## Concept, principles, and practice

Sustainable development is a concept with popular currency and use in international, regional, and national application through various legal and policy instruments and initiatives. It applies generally to balance social, economic, and environmental objectives in decision-making. This chapter presents an overview of this international concept bringing out the contested debate and interpretations on its meaning in the legal and policy instruments and scholarly literature. It locates sustainable development in its context of key sub principles that reflect the three main dimensions and objectives of sustainability: the economic, the environmental, and the social. The key principles examined are the polluter pays principle (relating to economic aspects), the precautionary principle (relating to environmental aspects), and the principle of public participation (relating to social aspects). The analysis here is intended to establish a framework for understanding the concept, and its legal and policy context, and for its practical application through the sub-principles at the regional or domestic level.[1] It will show that despite the definitional questions, sustainable development has direct and primary relevance for regulating economic activities for environmental protection, alongside the competing need for ensuring developmental sustainability and will put in context the definitional challenges of implementing sustainability at the EU level which are considered subsequently.

### The concept of sustainable development: its evolution on the international plane

The concept of sustainable development is rooted in the quest to introduce change in the exploitative utilisation of natural resources for economic purposes which impact upon the environmental sphere.[2] The 1972 UN Stockholm Conference[3] signalled international attention to environmental protection and

---

1 The analytical framework constructed will serve as a lens through which to discuss the application of sustainable development in EU law, policy, and practice in subsequent chapters.
2 Schwartz, P., "Sustainable Development in International Law", in *Non-State Actors and International Law*, volume 5 (Martinus Nijhoff Publishers, 2005) pp. 127–152 at 128.
3 Stockholm Declaration on the Human Environment adopted June 16, 1972, UN Doc. A/CONF 48/141 Rev. 1 at 3 (1973), 11 ILM 1416 (1972) (Stockholm Declaration).

called on states to safeguard, among other conference outcomes, the natural resources of the earth through careful planning and management, for the benefit of present and future generations.[4] It was agreed states should adopt an integrated approach to development planning to ensure that development is compatible with the need to protect the environment.[5] In 1980, the World Conservation Strategy gave birth to the phrase 'sustainable development', and maintained that "for development to be sustainable, it must take account of social and ecological factors, as well as economic ones".[6] In other words, the conservation of nature could not be achieved without the alleviation of poverty through economic development.[7] Later, the World Charter for Nature called for the resources of the world to be "managed to achieve and maintain optimum sustainable productivity".[8]

The Brundtland Report subsequently presented the phrase 'sustainable development' to the international community with an official definition: "development that meets the needs of the present without compromising the ability of the future generations to meet their own needs".[9] The concept was later adopted in 1992 by an overwhelming consensus of nations through the Rio Declaration and Agenda 21;[10] and recognised subsequently in other international acts.[11] According to Sands, the Rio Declaration anointed the concept formally for legal use within the corpus of international environmental law.[12] It ensured that development henceforth is qualified to possess both economic and ecological sustainability. Then, in 1997 at the Rio+5, the third element – social

---

4 Ibid., Principles 5 and 2.
5 Ibid., Principle 13.
6 *WCS* (1980) https://portals.iucn.org/library/efiles/documents/wcs-004.pdf accessed 01/03/2017
7 "The History of Sustainable Development in the United Nations" (n 3).
8 United Nations General Assembly "42/187 – Report of the World Commissions on Environment and Development", A/RES/42/187, 11 December 1987, 4.
9 Brundtland Report: *World Commissions on Environment and Development (WCED): Our Common Future* (Oxford: Oxford University Press, 1987) p. 43; also United Nations General Assembly "42/187 – Report of the WCED", A/RES/42/187, 11 December 1987, 4.
10 Rio Declaration on Environment and Development, 13 June 1992, adopted by the UNCED at Rio de Janeiro. UN Doc A/CONF. 151/26 (Vol.1) (August 1992) *ILM 874*, 1992 (Rio Declaration); Agenda 21 UNECD Rio de Janerio, Brazil, (3 to 14 June 1992) https://sustainabledevelopment.un.org/content/documents/Agenda21.pdf accessed 9/04/2017
11 *Report of the World Summit on Sustainable Development*, UN Doc A/CONF.199/20 (4 September 2002) (WSSD Report); ILA New Delhi Declaration of Principles of International Law Relating to Sustainable Development' 2002 (ILA/NDD) http://cisdl.org/tribunals/pdf/NewDelhiDeclaration.pdf accessed 01/05/2017; *The Future We Want*, GA Res 288, UN GAOR, 66th sess, 123rd plenmtg, Agenda Item 19, UN Doc A/RES/66/288 (11 September 2012, Rio+20, 2012); *Transforming Our World: The 2030 Agenda for Sustainable Development*, GA Res 1, 70th sess, 4th plenmtg, Agenda Items 15 and 116, UN Doc A/RES/70/1 (21 October 2015) (Agenda 2030).
12 Sands, P., "UNCED and the Development of International Environmental Law", in Handl et al. (Eds.), *YBIEL*, Vol. 3 (London/Dordrecht/Boston: Graham and Trotman/Martinus Nijhoff, 1992) p. 17.

development – was added. The United National Framework Convention on Climate Change, adopted in 1992 and opened for signature at Rio, has led to annual meetings of the signatory parties in conference to assess progress in dealing with climate change. One such conference led to the Kyoto Protocol dealing with commitments until 2020. The 2015 Paris Climate Accord sets out new commitments on the mitigation of greenhouse gases (GHG), and finances for the period as from 2020. As of June 2017, 195 United Nations Framework Convention on Climate Change states have signed the Paris Accord, and 149 have ratified it. The EU itself, as well as its Member States, is also signed up to the Paris Accord. However, President Trump announced early in June 2017 that he would not maintain the United States of America's signature of the Paris Accord and that the US would not then ratify it.[13] A number of the local governments in the US have nevertheless undertaken to respect the commitments set out in the Accord despite the president's statements and the US federal position.[14] The Paris Accord includes a Sustainable Development Mechanism "to contribute to the mitigation of greenhouse gases and support sustainable development".[15] The structure and processes of this mechanism are not yet developed, and there will be extensive debate about its governance and purpose. It is hoped it will do better than what it replaces, the Kyoto Protocol's Clean Development Mechanism, and it is an innovative initiative specifically creating a mechanism that formally links the combat of greenhouse gases with initiatives in 'support' of sustainable development, but this mechanism can also add to the complexity of sustainable development's many meanings.

Although the Rio instrument does not define the sustainable development concept, the Rio Declaration sets forth twenty-seven general and specific principles that establish objectives, targets, and standards for a meaningful elaboration or application.[16] Of these principles, those representing aspects of sustainable development most relevant to protection of the environment – as opposed to socio-economic development – include environmental protection, integration, intergenerational equity, sustainable utilisation, the polluter pays and the precautionary principle, environmental impact assessment (EIA), and public participation. Environmental protection is a primary objective of sustainable development in the Rio Declaration and "should constitute an integral part of the development process, and cannot be considered in isolation from it".[17]

The intergenerational principle and principle of integration derive from Principles 3 and 4. These sanction the conduct of development activities, while also

---

13 "Trump Will Withdraw US From Paris Climate Agreement", *New York Times*, 1 June 2017.
14 See, for example, "Miami-Dade Backs Paris Climate Agreement That Trump Rejected", *Miami Herald*, 20 June 2017.
15 Paragraph 6 of the Paris Accord.
16 For a detailed compendium of all the Rio principles see Viñuales, J.E. (Ed.) *Rio Declaration on Environment and Development: A Commentary* (Oxford, UK: Oxford University Press, 2015).
17 See Rio Declaration (n 10) Principles: 4.

seeking to condition such activities to require the factoring in of environmental concerns. Both principles highlight the need to maintain a balance between pursuit of 'development' to satisfy the 'needs' of the current generation while also recognising that future generations interests should be protected. The intergenerational principle could invoke a strict interpretation, requiring that natural capital is preserved intact for future generations. This is a 'strong' sustainability. Strong sustainability can be contrasted with an alternative interpretation of what the principle requires, or 'weak' sustainability, which sees substitution between different forms of natural and manmade capital.[18] The International Law Association (ILA) describes the integration principle as the very 'backbone' of the concept of sustainable development.[19]

The principle of sustainable utilisation requires states and peoples to pay due care to the environment and to make prudent use of the natural wealth and resources within their jurisdictions, and to eliminate "unsustainable patterns of production and consumption".[20] Principle 15 of 'precaution' directs that if a risk is not certain, this will not be used as an excuse to prevent measures that could mitigate harm. Principle 16 prescribes the polluter pays principle requiring national authorities to ensure that environmental and social costs of activities are met by the polluter either through the internalisation of such costs, or by use of economic instruments like environmental taxes, charges, and permits to ensure the costs are carried by the polluter even where the market itself does not ensure it.

Rio Declaration principle 17 requires that "as a national instrument, EIA shall be undertaken for proposed activities that are likely to have significant adverse impact on the environment, and are subject to a decision of a competent national authority". Rio Principle 10 provides that participation "of all concerned citizens" is made a precondition for any effective determination of environmental issues at the national level. To affect this, public authorities must make environmental information available to the public.[21]

These principles convey the practical value of sustainable development, fulfil its purpose by instilling social and environmental considerations into development activities, and impute responsibility on developers for the ultimate objective of sustainability. This is why former Director-General of the WTO Gro Harlem Brundtland calls it the "Declaration on legal principles for sustainable development", and Sands considers it as providing basis for defining the concept and its application.[22]

---

18 Schwartz, P., *Sustainable Development and Mining in Sierra Leone* (Kent: Pneuma Spring, 2006).
19 ILA, *Report of the 70th Conference* (New Delhi/London: ILA, 2002) pp. 390, 391.
20 Rio Declaration (n 10) Principle 8.
21 Rio Declaration, (n 10); Participants must include women, youth, other local communities and indigenous people (Principles 20, 21 and 22) respectively.
22 Brundtland, G.H., "Our Common Future and Ten Years After Rio: How Far Have We Come and Where Should We Be Going?", in Dodds, F. (Ed.), *Earth Summit 2002: A New*

The ILA New Delhi Declaration (NDD) certifies the Rio sustainable development concept but compresses the principles into seven core aspects:[23]

- the duty of states to ensure sustainable use of natural resources;
- the principle of equity and the eradication of poverty;
- the principle of common but differentiated responsibilities;
- the principle of precautionary approach to human health; natural resources and ecosystems;
- the principle of public participation and access to information and justice;
- the principle of good governance;
- the principle of integration and the interrelationship in particular relating to human rights, and social and economic and environmental objectives.

The objective is to integrate economic drivers and outcomes, social protection, and the political process of decision making underpinning any development. This aims at the sustainable use of natural resources, environmental protection, a fair standard of living, a fair distribution of benefits, and participation of the interests of future generations.[24] The ILA/NDD (New Delhi Declaration) considers that, "the application . . . [of these] principles of international law relevant to the activities of all actors involved, would be instrumental in pursuing the objective of sustainable development in every way".[25] This prediction has been validated by Cordonier Segger et al. who showed that nations are capable of integrating different forms of sustainable development, in different ways and to differing extents, at the national, regional, and international level in the application of the integration of the principles to the sustainability triad.[26]

### Sustainable development: contest and debate of meaning

The omission of a formal definition of sustainable development in the Rio Declaration has engendered several definition paradigms. To enhance clarity and analytical ease, the various views on the definition and meaning of sustainable development are dissected into four categories. These include a category of scholarship that relies on the Brundtland formulation as a general definitional reference point. Another category applies the elements and principles of sustainable development in the Rio Declaration, or other international instruments, either as guide to discerning the true content of the concept, or as means of achieving it. The

---

*Deal* (London: Earthscan, 2000) p. 255; Sands, P., *Principles of International Environmental Law* (Cambridge: Cambridge University Press, 2003) p. 53.
23 ILA New Delhi Declaration (n 11).
24 Ibid., para. 13.
25 Ibid., para. 15.
26 Cordonier Segger, M., Khalfan, A., Gehring, M. and Toering, M., "Prospects for Principles of International Sustainable Development Law After WWSD: Common But Differentiated Responsibilities, Precaution and Participation", *RECIEL* (2003) 12, no. 1.

third category derives the meaning of sustainable development by focusing on the words of the phrase themselves. The final category constructs a meaning from a blend of the previous three sources – the Brundtland formulation, the Rio principles, and the sustainable development phrase itself – and employs a descriptive definitional method that identifies 'sustainable development' as a process, or as a concept with an instrumental role in affecting change in development patterns.

*Meaning developed from the Brundtland formulation*

The approach taken by those relying on the Brundtland formulation for meaning is to infer in the concept either a utilitarian perspective, an anthropocentric view, and a development-orientated view of our environmental resources. The ILA is among the proponents supporting the utilitarian view, stating that the concept entails "a rational system of resource management that can operate in so far as the resources on which it depends are not exhausted and the environment is not irreparably damaged".[27] Handl also agrees that sustainable development imposes restraints on developmental activities in so far as these would undermine the environmental basis for further development.[28]

Supporting the anthropocentric view, Boer believes that political, economic, and social contexts, including the particular economic activity to which it is applied, will shape the meaning of the concept, opening up to a variety of application to meet human needs.[29] Pearce et al. impute within the concept a development-orientated view of environmental resources to achieve an increase in 'development indicators'; 'capital accumulation' or 'welfare maximisation', all for improving human condition.[30] Collins captures the contest and debate between utilitarian groups, the arguments about the requirements of a high level of environmental protection with less consumption of valuable resources and the arguments about anthropocentric outcomes with industry encouraging the exploitation of natural resources to facilitate development.[31] Other scholars have imputed in the concept a conditioning of development activities to recognise environmental protection. According to Shiva, sustainability "implies maintaining the integrity of nature's processes, cycles, and rhythms"; therefore,

---

27 ILA, *Report of the Sixty-Sixth Conference*, Crawford, J. and Williams, M. (Eds.) (Buenos Aires, Argentina/London: ILA, 1994) p. 128.
28 Handl, G., "Sustainable Development: General Rules Versus Specific Obligations", in Lang, W. (Ed.), *Sustainable Development and International Law* (London/Dordrecht/Boston: Graham and Trotman/Martinus Nijhoff, 1995) p. 36.
29 Boer, B., "Implementation of International Sustainability Imperatives at the National Level", in Ginther, Denters, and De Waart (Eds.), *Sustainable Development and Good Governance* (Dordrecht/Boston/London: Martinus Nijhoff Publishers, 1995) p. 104.
30 Pearce, D., Markandya, A., and Barbier, E. *Blueprint for Green Economy* (London: Earthscan, 2000) p. 33; see also Redclift, M., *Sustainable Development: Exploring the Contradictions* (London: Routledge, 1984) pp. 32–33.
31 Collins, L., "Revisiting the Doctrine of Intergenerational Equity in Global Environmental Governance", *Dalhousie Law Journal* (2007) 30, no. 79, 131–132.

production processes and markets, she claims, should be reshaped in line with nature's logic of returns, not the logic of profits, capital accumulation, and returns on investment.[32] She warns against the danger in upholding interpretations which suggest "sustaining not nature, but development itself," with disregard for the "limits of nature".[33] Along this line, Jacob claims that the meaning of the degradation of environmental wealth is crucial to understanding sustainability and must underline sustainable development.[34]

*Meaning developed from the Rio principles*

The International Court of Justice (ICJ) is among those supporting the application of the Rio Declaration principles or international instruments (e.g., ILA/NDD principles) to find meaning in the sustainable development concept.

The Court defined the concept in terms of its sources in the *Gabcikovo Nagymaros* case,[35] holding that sustainable development can be inferred from "new norms and standards" that are "set forth in a great number of instruments"; and must be given proper weight when states contemplate 'new activities' or when continuing with activities began in the past.[36] In other words, the courts identify sustainability as a regulatory tool for activities and hold that what the concept denotes at any given time will depend on its context in an instrument.

Dupuy supports this perspective on seeking meaning "from various principles essential to its realization".[37] Barral similarly holds that there are a vast array of legal standards and principles closely connected to the realisation of sustainable development. She argues that sustainable development evolves "according to circumstances, and in particular according to the time, the area, or the subjects concerned" and that it is important to have a non-exhaustive list of essential elements which, when combined, enable progress towards sustainable development.[38] Barral distinguishes between obligations of means and obligations of result, placing sustainable development in the former of the categories and its component, subsidiary principles in the latter. Accordingly, although states are

---

32 Shiva, V., "Resources", in Sachs, W. (Ed.), *The Development Dictionary* (London: Zed Books, 1992) p. 217.
33 Ibid.
34 Jacobs, M., *The Green Economy: Environment, Sustainable Development and the Politics of the Future* (London: Pluto Press, 1991) p. 84.
35 *Gabcikovo-Nagymaros Project* (Hungary v Slovakia) Case (1997), *ICJ Reports* 15 September 1997, GL No. 92.
36 Ibid para. 140.
37 Dupuy, P.M., "*Ou en est le droit international de l'environnement a la fin du siecle?*" RGDIP (1997) 101, no. 873, 886, cited in Barral (n 15) 378. On the same line, see also Danaher, J., "Protecting the Future or Compromising the Present? Sustainable Development and the Law", *Irish Student Law Review* 14, no. 131, 117.
38 Barral, V., "Sustainable Development in International Law: Nature and Operation of an Evolutive Legal Norm", *European Journal of International Law* (2012) 381–382 and 390–391.

28  *Sustainable development*

under an obligation to strive to achieve sustainable development, "they are not bound to achieve it".[39] By contrast, subsidiary principles require concrete actions to achieve concrete results. Vinuales, however, argues that "even the more elaborated version of the concept, as consisting of three pillars . . . tells us little about what should be our strategic priorities in tackling environmental degradation or poverty".[40]

### *'Sustainable development': concept or jargon?*

Critique of both the developed Brundtland and Rio meanings has come from those who have sought a narrow reading from the two-word phrase 'sustainable development'. In this perspective, the term has been assessed as 'vague' or 'theoretically obscure',[41] as lacking content, 'logically redundant' or 'basically flawed'.[42] Beckerman argues that 'sustainable development' mixes up together the technical characteristics of a particular development path, programme, or project, with a moral injunction to pursue it. Ruhl argues that the word 'sustainable' has become shorthand for the claim that the proposed action or policy will advance economic, environmental, and equity interests in perpetuity. The intended effect of such a broad definition is that everyone supports the proposal or policy, but does not know what it is, a situation which, in his view, may seem like window dressing or even as a deceptive way of masking problems.[43]

Despite this obscurity, the International Institute for Sustainable Development identifies a strength in the ambiguity of the words, and consider their flexibility as responsible for nearly universal adoption of the concept.[44] "This strength, however, is also a liability because various interpretations have led to confusion and compromised implementation".[45] But Jacobs identifies a practical definitional values that entails three 'core ideas': a discussion of the operational objectives required to achieve sustainable development; the management of principles needed to generate more sustainable policies; and the articulation of policies

---

39  Ibid.
40  Vinuales, J.E., "The Rise and Fall of Sustainable Development", *Review of European Community & International Environmental Law* (2013) 22, no. 1, 4.
41  See Malanczuk, P., "Sustainable Development: Some Critical Thoughts in the Light of The Rio Conference", in Ginther, Denters and De Waart (Eds.), *Sustainable Development and Good Governance* (Dordrecht/Boston/London: Martinus Nijhoff Publishers, 1995) p. 26; Lowe, V., "Sustainable Development and Unsustainable Arguments", in Boyle and Freestone (Eds.), *International Law and Sustainable Development* (Oxford: Oxford University Press, 1999) pp. 30–31.
42  Beckerman, W., "Sustainable Development: Is It a Useful Concept?", in *Environmental Values 3* (Cambridge, UK: The White Horse Press, 1994) p. 205.
43  Ruhl, J.B., "Law for Sustainable Development: Work Continues on the Rubik's Cube", *Tulsa Law Review* (2008–2009) 44, no. 1, 1.
44  International Institute for Sustainable Development, "Sustainable Development: From Brundtland to Rio 2012: Background Paper prepared for consideration by the High Level Panel on Global Sustainability at its first meeting, 19 September 2010", September 2010, 9.
45  Ibid.

and practices required to achieve sustainability. Each represent as components of making sustainable development 'meaningful' and operational in practice.[46]

### Constructionist definitional approach

Constructionist definitional approaches to sustainable development blend the other three forms of interpretation just considered and employ a descriptive definitional method, which identifies sustainable development as a process, or as a concept with an instrumental role in affecting change in development patterns.[47] Gaines and Linder are proponents of this understanding of the sustainable development concept. They view the concept as implying a permanent process requiring emphasis on process issues for it to be achieved and maintained. In this interpretation, the concept requires a continuous process of change and adaptation.[48] Linder sees in this process resource exploitation, investments, technology, and institutional change interrelate in harmony to enhance current and future needs and aspirations.[49]

The instrumental role of sustainable development is advanced by judicial bodies and tribunals. Judge Weeramantry emphasised the capacity of the concept to direct robust processes, and for solving fundamental problems in international environmental and development law, while seeking to reconcile and harmonise the needs while steering a course between them.[50] This instrumental role could save 'normative anarchy', its significance resting on resolution of tensions and 'environmentally related disputes'.[51] The WTO Appellate Body also used the concept as an aid to define the extent to which environmental objectives can be pursued within national and international trade policies.[52]

### Practical meaning for legal and policy application

Perspectives on the definition and meaning of sustainable development continue to abound and this work holds little space for all of their inclusion. In practice,

---

46 Jacobs, M., "Sustainable Development as a Contested Concept", in Dobson, A. (Ed.), *Fairness and Futurity*, (Oxford: Oxford University Press, 1999), p. 27.
47 Schwartz, P., "Sustainable Development in International Law", in *Non-State Actors and International Law* (Leiden: Martinus Nijhoff Publishers, 2005) 5, no. 2, 127–152 at 133.
48 Gaines, S.E., "International Trade, Environmental Protection and Development as a Sustainable Development Triangle", *Receil* (2002) 11, no. 3, 264; Lindner, W.H., "Sustainable Development: Its Social Political and Economic Implications", in *Environmental Liability* (Graham and Trotman: London/Dordrecht/Boston, 1991(IBA Series)) p. 6.
49 Ibid., 6.
50 See Separate Opinion of Judge Weeramantry in the *Gabcikovo-Nagymaros Project* (Hungary v Slovakia) Case (1997), *ICJ Reports* 15 September 1997, GL No. 92 pp. 86–87.
51 Ibid., 95.
52 The *Shrimp Turtle Case* (WT/DS58): Report of the Appellate Body in *WTO DSR* 1998: Vol. VII, 1998, Cambridge p. 275ff. See also Sands, P., "International Courts and the Application of the Concept of 'Sustainable Development'", in *Max Planck Yearbook of United Nations Law, Vol.3.* (1999) p. 398.

less importance is accorded to further defining the concept, which suggests that to some, or to some politicians at least, that the matter and the questions about what sustainable development means has been put to rest.[53] The variation in interpretations seems to be warranted by confusion over the scope of the concept and instead the focus is on the practical meanings that can have legal and policy application.

Underpinning the various definitional approaches is a balancing of socio-economic development, on the one hand, and environmental protection, on the other. Clearly, all the Rio and ILA principles identified above reflect some form of international consensus on general and specific objectives of sustainable development. But without a yardstick that delimits the scope, the concept becomes less practical in this form. To enhance practicability for use in policy and legal guidance particularly, the meaning of sustainable development should always be discerned from the context in which it is employed to determine primarily its purpose or the goals it is meant to achieve. This exercise involves a determination of whether the concept is an articulation of international – regional or national – development policy, strategy, programmes, or agenda, or whether it is to inform or direct development activities, for example, through ventures, projects, or investment.

In the context of a wider development agenda, for instance, the environment becomes an indication factor for economic growth and development, a category that best defines the concept of international law in the field of sustainable development.[54] This branch of law is identified in principle 27 of the Rio Declaration, it refers to processes, principles, and objectives, as well as to a large body of international agreements on environmental, economic, civil, and political rights. In relation to sustainable development, this field may have relevance only in interpretation and development of varying fields of international law as opposed to an objective to regulate specific economic activities that may entail environmental and social implications.

In terms of developmental activities or projects, however, sustainable development represents primarily as a principle in international environmental law that should inform and guide activities toward a sustainable course for environmental protection. The application of its elements in this case will depend on the kind of venture sought to be undertaken (i.e., agriculture, fishing, or manufacturing); by whom (i.e., public or private capital, aid or subsidy); the nature and extent of use that must be made of natural resources (i.e., land, air, water, and biodiversity); and the responsibilities of those embarking on such activities. On this premise, therefore, while not purporting to define the concept, it is submitted that sustainable development has direct primary relevance for environmental protection, in

---

53 There is practically no mention of it in the Rio+20 declaration "The Future We Want" other than to recognise its importance and the need to interlink economic, social, and environmental concerns so as to "to achieve sustainable development in all its dimensions".
54 Schwartz, P., 2005 (n 47) 135.

the way resources are managed – or exploited – and in the conduct of economic activities to enhance either domestic, regional, or international development objectives. The legal mandates, policies, or processes that direct such economic activities could achieve or undermine sustainability.

*Sustainable development: legal context and application*

Sustainable development has already acquired legal standing, function, and currency pursuant to its invocation by international judicial bodies.[55] However, it must also have an appreciable legal context by which it can be understood, interpreted, transposed, and implemented at the international, regional, or national levels. Legality could either be defined by the nature of the term, its status, or by its transposition and effect.

It is not clear whether international law imposes an obligation on states to achieve or implement sustainable development. Boyle and Freestone perceive that since substantial discretion is left with states on how to interpret and give effect to sustainable development, and given the absence of any justiciable standards for review, a general international obligation cannot be assumed.[56] Supporting this view, Handl claims that it does not provide the basis from which 'specific obligations' can be deduced or 'individualised rights' tested.[57] It is, rather, regarded as "an area in which law-making and other law-related activities take place".[58] However, there is still a sense in which sustainable development can infer a legal obligation. For instance, international law requires development decisions to be the outcome of a process which promotes sustainable development, and to establish appropriate processes for requiring this.[59] In this sense, the objectives and principles of the concept are set as a prescription on achieving sustainable development and should be employed in policy formulations and decision-making. In fact, some principles may emerge as a legal rule rather than a norm or become relevant when courts apply or interpret them.[60]

Sustainable development has also acquired legality by status in terms of the extent to which the objectives of the concept are reflected in existing areas of international, regional, and national law. There is ample reference to the concept in binding and non-binding international instruments, policy documents of international bodies, or in the application by judicial bodies, for the concept

---

55 *Gabcikovo-Nagymaros Case* (n 35) pp. 86–87, The *Shrimp Turtle Case* (n 52) 275ff.; Sands, P., "International Courts" (n 35) 395 and 404.
56 Boyle, A. and Freestone, D., *International Law and Sustainable Development*, Boyle and Freestone (Eds.) (Oxford: Oxford University Press, 2001) pp. 16–18.
57 Handl, G. (n 28) p. 36.
58 Lang, W., "How to Manage Sustainable Development", in Ginther, Denters and De Waart (Eds.), *Sustainable Development and Good Governance* (Dordrecht/Boston/London: Martinus Nijhoff Publishers, 1995) p. 93.
59 Boyle, A. and Freestone, D. (n 56) pp. 17 and 18.
60 Schwartz, P., 2005 (n 47) 137.

to qualify as having legal status in international law. Though the obligations created may not be of universal application, the legality acquired through treaty obligations, or judicial pronouncements, for instance, is challenged less because they are linked to binding sources of law. According to Schrijver and Weiss, the concept has already successfully established its credentials as a legal concept in law through three dimensions of legality: as "possessing widely recognised legal core"; as a main policy objective of states and non-state actors; and as "central to a bewildering variety of practice rooted in law".[61]

A further method by which sustainable development has derived a legal character is through transposition or application. The legal effect here suggests it is informative or for guidance; the concept is employed in judicial reasoning, administrative decision-making, treaty negotiations, or policy formations. In this sense, the legal effect is akin to a directing principle, providing guidance on choices and methods concerning measures to limit environmental risks and damage with the aim of guaranteeing citizens' rights to enjoy a healthy environment.[62] Higgins's call for "international law's normative system to be harnessed to the achievement of common values, and which should be able to contribute to solving today's problems",[63] supports this model of transposition and the application of sustainable development.

This meaning or interpretation of sustainable development is distinctive in that it limits the legality of the concept to 'treaty obligations', and judicial pronouncements will not reveal its true legal character. The approach allows the principle to retain its peculiar character of adaptability whenever its elements are to be clarified, interpreted, modified, or distinguished in the context in which they may be employed. Therefore, while international environmental law is essentially a 'legislative process',[64] we distinguish the legal character of sustainable development as an aspect of that law in legislative and judicial processes that may confer obligations relevant for pursuing sustainability. Further we include administrative, adjudicatory, and deliberative processes within it.

### Key global principles in the sustainable development triad

All the principles of sustainable development in the Rio Declaration identified above are relevant in specific and general context for implementing the objectives of the concept. But the analysis here focuses on three key principles: the precautionary principle, the polluter pays principle, and the public participation

---

61 Schrijver, N. and Weiss, F., *International Law and Sustainable Development*, Boyle and Freestone (Eds.) (Oxford: Oxford University Press, 2001) pp. xiii–iv.
62 De Sadeleer, N., *Environmental Principles: From Political Slogans to Legal Rules* (Oxford: Oxford University Press, 2002) pp. 5–6.
63 Higgins, R., *Problems and Process: International Law and How We Use It* (Oxford: Clarendon Press, 1994) pp. 2–3.
64 Boyle, A., "Codification of International Environmental Law and the International Law Commission: Injurious Consequences Revisited", in *International Law and Sustainable Development*, 1999 (n 41) p. 63.

principle. These three are the focus because of their popularity, their wide transposition in international, regional, and domestics systems, and because they exemplify the three dimensions of sustainability – environmental protection, economic, and social development – in the analysis that follows.

*Precautionary principle*

The principle is incorporated in Principle 15 of the Rio Declaration, as an approach that will secure protection of the environment and efficient use of natural resources in carrying out socio-economic activities. The precaution approach is triggered, in the Declaration, only for environmental protection: the relevant environment must be under threats 'of serious or irreversible damage'. In such case, irrespective of whether or not there is scientific proof of, or the likelihood of damage occurring, measures should be employed in order to prevent or contain the damage. To trigger its application it is sufficient that a risk be suspected, conjectured, or feared, so that it does not require a perfect understanding of risk or complete knowledge of the threat. It differs from 'prevention', which is generally a separate environmental principle. Prevention applies when the risk is known, and preventive measures are needed.[65]

The precautionary principle is deemed central in international law relating to sustainable development because it expresses a duty on states to take preventive measures to protect human health, natural resources, and the environment.[66] The approach is reflected in most international environmental treaties, natural resource management regimes, in application by courts and tribunals, and is increasingly being adopted by national legal systems.[67]

The precautionary principle can be applied through different types of measures in the regulation of diverse economic activities, with different ways of affecting

---

65 Cordonier Segger *et al.* "Prospects for Principles of International Sustainable Development Law After WSSD: Common But Differentiated Responsibilities, Precaution and Participation", *Receil* (2003) 12, no. 1, 55–61.
66 ILA NDD Principle 4:4:1 (supra chapter 2, p. 50, n 51) ILA New Delhi Declaration of Principles of International Law Relating to Sustainable Development (NDD), 2002, www.ila-hq.org and UN Doc.A/57/329.
67 Some examples of instruments endorsing the precautionary principle or approach include: Helsinki Convention on the Protection of the Baltic Sea Area (1992) *3 YBIEL* (Article 3(2)); The OSPAR Convention, 1992, *32 ILM, 1069* (1993) (Article 2(2)(a)); Maastricht Treaty on European Union, (1992) *31 ILM 247*; ITLOS – *Southern Bluefin Tuna Cases*, (Australia v. Japan; New Zealand v. Japan) (SBT Cases No. 3 and 4) Provisional measures Order of 27 August 1999, www.itlos.org/cases/list-of-cases/case-no-3-4/
*Gabcikovo Case* (n 35); the WTO *Hormones case*; European Communities-Measures Concerning Meat and Meat Products, Complaint by the United States (WT/DS26) and Canada (WT/DS48), *Report of the Appellate Body; WTO DSR 1998, Vol. 1*, Cambridge pp. 135ff. For regional and national endorsement of the principle see Hey, E., "The Precautionary Concept in Environmental Policy and Law: Institutionalising Caution", *Georgetown Environmental Law Review* (1992) IV, pp. 303–318. Note also that the principle is reflected as a general principle for environmental policy for most organisations.

the environment.⁶⁸ Its application criteria allow for some flexibility within which decision makers can determine every potential impact of the particular development activity, and enables them to assess the method of prevention or adaption that is most cost-effective and can be adopted.⁶⁹ Capability will determine the cost-effectiveness of the measure to be applied, but in all cases, it must have an effect of prevention of harm or protection of the environment.

The application of the precautionary principle relates to the manner and the extent of the measures to be taken. These are to be employed in accordance with state's 'capabilities' and are to be 'cost-effective'.⁷⁰ The obligations created hereunder are of a relative nature since they depend upon economic and financial capabilities. The ILA NDD also identifies precautionary measures as including: accountability for harm caused, planning based on clear criteria and well-defined goals and EIA.⁷¹

However, the principle has drawn criticisms in respect of its operation especially its inherent reliance on some form of scientific and/or economic assessment for its operation, necessitating the need to conduct a cost-benefit-analysis (CBA), which itself is deemed to be ruled by uncertainties.⁷² This uncertainty increases the possibility for ecological interests to be systematically compromised and for non-targeted risks to arise.⁷³ While these concerns raise lots of questions, it is difficult to dispute that the operation of the principle is always going to require a balancing process in decision-making. And since the emphasis on precaution is primarily in favour of environmental protection, it is hard to see how ecological concerns could be compromised. Its objective bias in favour of environmental protection in sustainable development is grounded at the point of decision-making, anticipating environmental harm before it occurs. Precaution evidences in several characters and measures, by which its goal is achieved, and with flexibility that allows developers, decision-makers, policy planners, and judges to be able to interpret, infer from obligations, or implement policies that promote environmental objectives. The principle can foster effective and credible environmental law and policy.

### *The polluter pays principle*

Rio Declaration Principle 16 is orientated at economic regulation primarily for pollution control. The polluter pays principle (PPP) calls on:

> National authorities [to] endeavour to promote the internalization of environmental costs and the use of economic instruments, taking into account

---

68 Nollkaemper, A., "What You Risk Reveals What You Value and Other Dilemmas Encountered in the Legal Assault on Risk", in Freestone, D., and Hey, E. (Eds.), *The Precautionary Principle and International Law: The Challenge of Implementation* (The Hague/London: Kluwer Law International, 1996) p. 80.
69 Note that EIA, ERA, Environmental Auditing, and Monitoring all have direct connections with the implementation of the principle, as mechanisms to determine the propensities of risks.
70 Rio Declaration (n 10) Principle 15.
71 ILA New Delhi Declaration (n 11) (Principle 4:2 (a)–(c)).
72 De Sadeleer (n 62) pp. 169–170.
73 Ibid., 171.

the approach that the polluter should, in principle, bear the cost of pollution, with due regard to the public interest and without distorting international trade and investment.

The principle was first applied by the OECD in the 1970s, as an instrument for allocating the costs of pollution prevention and control in order "to encourage the rational use of scarce environmental resources and to avoid distortions in international trade and investment".[74] The Rio formulation sets out a global policy for pollution control that aims to make polluters bear the cost of pollution and ensure sustainable activities.[75] Principle 16 requires a determination by authorities of who is a polluter, the obligation arising from pollution having occurred, the costs of polluting, and the ascription of such cost, both of pollution resulting directly from the activity or pollution arising subsequently and indirectly.

Debate and discussion about the polluter's personality, the types of polluting activity, and the scope of polluter responsibility continue to evolve in academic literature, in treaties, and in state practice. Global practice tends to identify polluter personality with states, corporations, industries, and individuals who engage in a polluting activity. That being so, the regulatory focus in practice is largely on corporations.[76] Understanding of polluting activity has also evolved beyond industrial emissions to include uses of natural resource that contribute to environmental deterioration;[77] the financial and emission reduction burden on developed states under the common but differentiated responsibility principle;[78] and producer responsibility for products environmental impacts.[79] These dimensions of polluter obligation reflect the complex regulatory dynamics that Principle 16 evokes in promoting economically efficient and environmentally sustainable development.

Principle 16 specifies environmental costs as the cost burden the polluter pays principle seeks to allocate, and suggests methods by which the polluter could address these costs. The methods are a mechanism to ensure the internalisation of costs, and a package of economic instruments. The way in which 'environmental' costs are framed enables the inclusion of other costs that may be connected with pollution regulation and management to address the many pollution challenges

---

74 OECD Recommendation of the Council Concerning International Economic Aspects of Environmental Policies, C(72)128, (1972) 128.
75 For a detailed exposition of the PPP, see Schwartz, P., "The Polluter- Pays Principle", in Viñuales, J.E. (Ed.), *Rio Declaration on Environment and Development: A Commentary* (Oxford, UK: Oxford University Press, 2015) p. 429.
76 Council Recommendation of 3 March 1975 regarding cost allocation and action by public authorities on environmental matters (75/436/EURATOM, ECSC, EEC) para. 2 – "Polluter" is defined as "natural or legal persons governed by public or private law who are responsible for pollution".
77 This may be for economic or social purposes. See Agenda 21 (n 10) ch 8, 8:28.
78 United Nations Framework Convention on Climate Change UNFCCC/INFORMAL/84 GE.05–62220 (E) 200705 (United Nations 1992) Arts., 3(1); 4(2)(a)&(b); (UNFCCC 1992).
79 See Directive 2012/92/EU on waste electrical and electronic equipment.

deriving from modern economic activities and technology and the variety of methods needed to tackle them.[80] The polluter's costs burden could therefore include *inter alia*: the cost of achieving prescribed environmental quality or remedying accidental pollution or environmental damage; the cost of the clean up or reinstatement of the environment; and the cost of exceptional measures needed to protect human health and social costs. Measures which distort international trade and investment are prohibited. To ensure this caveat is applied, the polluter's costs burden could also translate to financial costs. Such costs may include: the remaining external cost of investment on technology; the cost incurred of banned polluting activity; indemnity costs; operational costs, loss of profit, costs associated with trade-offs, off-sets, and subsidies; and the cost of promoting best practices and best available technology.[81]

The principle has a condition requiring states to have due regard to the public interest the polluter pays. Polluters not paying for their pollution represent a market failure, or a distortion of international trade and investment. The polluter pays principle's requirement of cost internalisation, its economic instruments, and market mechanisms, have direct bearing on trade and investment, and the obligation on states to avoid distortions in trade and investment. Trade taxes such as the carbon tax and emissions trading, subsidies, and other incentives for investment in technologies are important tools in the international pollution regulation strategy. For example, by application of the WTO General Agreement on Tariffs and Trade (GATT) system, environmental costs measures, which introduce differential treatment by taxing carbon-intensive activities or products, or which provide subsidies to carbon-efficient activities or technologies, could be viewed as trade distortive, and the polluter pays principle is an economic tool to contrast with the regulatory combat of pollution.[82]

Also, by prohibiting distortions, Principle 16 should secure a competitive environment between varying polluter-businesses who may seek to use economic instruments through international trade and investment aims on the one hand while recognising the variations in the levels of countries' development, trade, and investment capabilities on the other. The polluter pays principle consideration of the public interest is warranted especially in use of economic instruments to address pollution costs, given the disparity in the wealth of nations, where their use may raise revenues for the government, which it could use to cut the total costs of programmes.[83]

A key challenge facing the prohibition of distortion of trade and investment involves the balancing of 'environmental costs' with investment costs, and with

---

80 See Case C-254/08 *Futura Immobiliare srl Hotel Futura* [2009] ECR I-6995 paras 47–48.
81 These costs are identified in treaties, statutes and academic literature; Schwartz, P., "Polluter Pays Principle", in Fitzmaurice, Ong and Merkouris (Eds.), *Research Handbook on International Environmental Law* (Edward Elgar, 2010) pp. 243–261 at 248–250.
82 Export duties, tariffs, or taxes are acceptable forms of protection generally permitted under WTO rules: Article III:I and III:2 and VIII.
83 Schwartz, P. 2010 (n 75).

the public interest. This is so especially where the investment costs may heavily influence decision-making and leave a disproportionate share of the burden on the public. Trade and investment rights are guaranteed by the Rio formulation with the implementation of the polluter pays principle.

The polluter pays principle has a firm legal basis as a principle of law deriving from a variety of legal sources including in international and regional treaties, domestic legislation, and as a regional custom, particularly in Europe. Some treaties require that the polluter pays principle be used as an approach that forms the basis for fulfilling their mandate, or urge members to be 'guided' by the principle, 'take it into account', or 'apply' it in their respective contexts.[84] Other instruments require regulated entities to pay the costs of meeting national environmental standards demonstrating responsibility for polluting activities or their potential effects.[85] It has also been applied in international liability regimes, which impute responsibility to persons dealing with dangerous substances.[86] The polluter pays principle is also prominently applied in EU law and policy relating to waste landfills, packaging of wastes, climate change emissions reduction, renewable energy, and civil aviation; and by the Court of Justice in providing specific guidance on the scope of polluter responsibility in certain activities in the EU Directives.[87]

Thus, this international pollution policy and regulatory tool has such wide application in law and practice to become a legitimate legal principle. Its consistent application in the OECD and the EU, in binding treaties, and EU secondary legislation cements its legal status. Similarly the wide practice of carbon trading and investments in renewable energy to address emissions reduction commitments certifies the polluter pays principle as a regional custom certainly in the EU, and potentially in many countries.

*Public participation*

The social emphasis in the principle of participation is settled. Public participation as a central concept derives from three parallel paths: it is an integral and essential component of the environmental impact assessment (EIA) procedure; and it obtains from other spheres of general environmental decision-making,

---

84 See London Protocol to the Convention on the Prevention of Marine Pollution by Dumping of Waste and other Matters, 1996: art 3(2); Rotterdam Convention on the Protection of the Rhine, 1998: art 4.
85 UNFCCC Kyoto Protocol, 2303 UNTS 148, Annex I.
86 Some examples include: Convention on the Establishment of an International Fund for Compensation for Oil Pollution Damage, 1971 (replaced by Protocol of 1992), (The Fund Convention); International Convention on Liability and Compensation for Damage in Connection with the Carriage of Hazardous and Noxious Substances by Sea, 1996 (HNS Convention).
87 See further Chapter 5 herein for the applicable instruments in EU law and policy context, and Schwartz, P., 2010 (n 81) p. 436 for illustration of applicable instruments.

such as environmental planning, conservation, and resource allocation issues. This dimension represents in general international environmental law and policy, and the broader developmental perspective of sustainability that interprets 'Good Governance' or 'environmental Human Rights' aspects.[88] The third aspect of participation addresses Rio Declaration Principle 10, as a distinct element of sustainable development in a narrow and specific context of regulating 'activities' especially to ensure socially sustainable development in the local context.

The principle has recognition in the global – regional and national – arena, under different international instruments for resources management, and environmental protection efforts and policy prescriptions of institutions and organisations aiming to:

- create participatory rights for their public to have either access to environmental information;
- participate in environmental decision-making; or
- gain access to a form of redress for environmental wrongs, commonly described as 'access to justice'.[89]

While some of the international instruments clearly require all three elements of information, participation and justice,[90] others represent only one.[91] Another set of instruments, usually requiring public participation in EIA procedures, generally adopt two forms of the elements.[92]

Principle 10, on the other hand, provides guidance on the general application of the principle with evident practical dimensions. Firstly participation 'of all concerned citizens' is made a precondition for any effective determination of environmental issues. Second, its proper forum is at the national level, where the relevant public authorities must make available to the public two categories

---

88  See ILA, *Report of the 70th Conference* (New Delhi/London: ILA, 2002) pp. 834–835.
89  Pring, G. and Noé, S., "The Emerging International Law of Public Participation Affecting Global Mining, Energy and Resource Development", in Zilman, D., Lucas, A. and Pring, G. (Eds.), *Human Rights in Natural Resources Development*, (Oxford: Oxford University Press, 2002) p. 44.
90  Some examples include: UN/ECE: Convention on Access to Information, Public Participation in Decision-Making and Access to Justice in Environmental Matters (Aarhus) UN Doc. ECE/ CEP/ 43 (1998) at www.unece.org/env/pp/treatytext.htm; ILA Declaration (n 11) Principles 5:2 and 5:3.
91  See: UNFCCC (1992) 31 *ILM* 848 Art. 6(a)(ii); The OSPAR Convention, 1992, *32 ILM, 1069* (1993) Art. 9(1) (Information); UN Convention on Non-Navigational Uses of International Watercourses, 1997, *32 ILM 700* (the Watercourse Convention) Art. 32 (access to justice).
92  UNEP Guidelines on Goals and Principles for Environmental Impact Assessment (1987) (UNEP Guidelines) UN DOC. UNEP/Z/SER A/9 (1987) Principles 7–9; the 1991 Protocol on Environment Protection to the Antarctica Treaty (Madrid Protocol) *30 ILM* 1461 (1991 annex 1 Art. 3(3)); UNECE Convention on Environmental Impact Assessment in the Trans-boundary Context 1991(Espoo); *30 ILM* (1991) 802; EEC Directive on Access to Environmental Information, Council Directive 90/313/1990, OJ C 158/56.

of environmental information: on the state of the national environment; and concerning environmentally adverse activities conducted in particular local communities. In respect of the latter, a further responsibility is imposed on states to 'facilitate' such participation.[93]

The Aarhus Convention is the first legally binding participation-specific international instrument, containing the broadest and most detailed requirements to date, for public participation in decision-making; and by far the most impressive elaboration of Principle 10 of the Rio Declaration, with global effect, despite its regional application.[94] The application of this instrument is analysed in depth in Chapter 6. Its broad framework defines participatory rights in terms of its information, participation, and justice elements, as a means through which the public can exercise their right to life and well-being in a healthy environment and also perform their duty to protect it for future generations. It extends the category of persons with the obligation to provide these elements to include natural or legal persons performing public administrative functions under national law or those who have responsibility in specified institutions of any regional economic integration organisation.[95] It also extends the category of participants – the 'public' – beyond the citizens of the state to include human beings, corporations, companies, organisations, associations, or groups formed by these and which are recognised under national law and practice.[96] Aarhus helps to shed light on what participation under the Rio declaration must entail, in other to achieve the objectives of sustainable development.

Academic debate has interpreted or affirmed the participatory principles variedly as requiring education of the public about the relationship between environment and development; as posing the strongest argument for human rights to the environment; or as catering for "legal standing of intermediary groups on the basis of right to development".[97] But as an element that must inform environmental policies, environmental laws, and development decision-making at the national level, 'public participation' cannot be assumed under one encompassing definition, but must be structured within the earlier discussed ideals to deal with the situations that present themselves.

---

93 See Rio Declaration (n 10) Participants must include women, youth, other local communities and indigenous people (Principles 20, 21, and 22) respectively.
94 Pring and Noe, "The Emerging International Law of Public Participation Affecting Global Mining, Energy and Resource Development", in Zilman, Lucas and Pring (Eds.), *Human Rights in Natural Resources Development* (Oxford: Oxford University Press, 2002) p. 43; Kofi Annan (UN Secretary General); UNECE, Environment and Human Settlements Division: "Introducing the Aarhus Convention" at www.unece.org/env/pp
95 Aarhus Convention Article 2(a), (b), (c) and (d).
96 Ibid., Art. 2 (4).
97 Malanczuk, P. (n 41) p. 12; Picolotti, R., "Agenda 21 and Human Rights", in Picolotti, R., and Taillant, G. (Eds.), *Linking Human Rights and Environment* (Tucson, Arizona: University of Arizona Press, 2003) p. 56; ILA, *Report of the 70th Conference* (New Delhi/London: ILA, 2002) p. 390.

## The international context of sustainable development

The international political context of sustainable development is crucial to the concept's meaning and operation. The concept received an outstanding pass in demonstrating the willingness of states to address global environmental and developmental concerns. The political underpinning of sustainable development was the desire of states "to reconcile the visions of the affluent countries to that of the populations concerned with their own development".[98]

The divergence in interest between rich and poor states impressed within an environmental protection narrative the content of 'development' and placed human beings at "the centre of concern for sustainable development" in Principles 1 and 2 of the Rio Declaration. This is widely held to undermine environmental goals.[99] 'Developing states', through the common but differentiated responsibility (CBDR) principle, have diluted environmental responsibility and this reflects a political dichotomy. Alongside the dichotomy of sustainable development including the protection of international trade and investment, which today largely involves the multinational corporations of developed states,[100] there are significant problems in applying any standard.[101] But even more important for international relations and application of the concept is "the persistent divergence between the poor and rich" in interpreting the concept.[102]

However, Principle 27 of Rio Declaration calls for the fulfilment of all its principles based on international cooperation among states, in good faith and in the spirit of partnership. This principle is not regarded as "a further normative postulate, but an authentic operational directive for future implementation of the Rio Declaration as a whole".[103] The main method by which such cooperation could be demonstrated is by the "further progressive development of international law in the field of sustainable development". The application of the concept should also promote cooperation between states and people and industry in public-private

---

98  Dupuy, P.M., "The Philosophy of Rio Declaration", in Viñuales, J.E. (Ed.), *Rio Declaration on Environment and Development: A Commentary* (Oxford, UK: Oxford University Press, 2015) p. 6.
99  These critiques include: Pallmearts, M., "International Environmental Law From Stockholm to Rio: Back to the Future?" *Reciel* (1992) 1, no. 3, 256; Porras, I., "The Rio Declaration: A New Basis for International Co-Operation", *Reciel* (1992) 1, no. 3, 246.
100 Rio Declaration (n 10) Principles 7, 12, and 16.; see: Cullet, P., "Common But Differentiated Responsibility", in Viñuales, J.E. (Ed.), *Rio Declaration on Environment and Development: A Commentary* (Oxford, UK: Oxford University Press, UK) pp. 229–244; Young, M., "Environment and Trade", in Viñuales J.E. (Ed.), *Rio Declaration on Environment and Development: A Commentary* (Oxford, UK: Oxford University Press, 2015) pp. 325–348; and Schwartz, P., 2015 (n 75).
101 See Viñuales, J.E., *Foreign Investment and the Environment* (Cambridge: Cambridge University Press, 2002) pp. 261–262.
102 Dupuy, P.M. (n 98) p. 65.
103 Sand, P.H., "Cooperation in the Spirit of Global Partnership", in Viñuales, J.E. (Ed.), *Rio Declaration on Environment and Development: A Commentary* (Oxford, UK: Oxford University Press, 2015) p. 618.

partnerships and especially to ensure corporate accountability.[104] A new wave of flexible pilot schemes of 'voluntary agreements' and 'eco-contracts' between industry and state organs in Europe are reportedly achieving the reconciliation of environmental protection in economic progress.[105]

## Conclusion

This chapter presents an overview of the international concept of sustainable development and some key principles. It seeks to show the construction of a logical analytical framework for understanding the concept and for deriving practical meaning therefrom that ensures its application in regional and domestic legal, policy, and political contexts. The concept is capable of varying perspectives, meaning, and interpretations discussed at length in existing literature. Despite the definitional questions, the chapter shows that sustainable development has direct and primary relevance for regulating economic activities for environmental protection, alongside competing need for ensuring developmental sustainability. It also finds that sustainable development can be applied through key sub-principles to address the three dimensions and objectives of sustainability: the polluter pays principle and economic aspects; precautionary principle and environmental aspects; and public participation and social aspects. Sustainable development has a legal character beyond those legislative and judicial processes which may confer obligations relevant for pursuing sustainability. It includes adjudicatory, administrative, and deliberative processes. It has a flexibility that allows for the interpretation of its principles within legal rules to enhance environmental protection at the global or domestic level. The analytical framework constructed will serve in the subsequent chapters as a lens through which to examine the application of sustainable development in EU law, policy, and practice through the principles of polluter pays, precaution, and public participation.

---

104 Johannesburg Declaration: (n 11) para. 49; WSSD/POI: (n 11) para. 18. For analysis on corporate accountability at WSSD, see: Cordonier Segger, M., "Sustainability & Corporate Accountability Regimes: Implementing the Johannesburg Summit Agenda" *Receil* (2003) 12, no. 3.
105 Rest, A., "Implementation of Rio Targets-Preliminary Efforts in State Practice" *EPL* (1995) 25, no. 6, 139.

# 3 Sustainable development and general principles of EU law

As established in the previous chapter, sustainable development is as an international principle with primary relevance for regulating economic activities for environmental protection, alongside the competing need for ensuring developmental sustainability. It entails a flexibility that allows application in regional and domestic legal and policy contexts, to enhance environmental protection. This chapter examines how sustainable development is applied in EU law and also in various policy areas. Particular consideration is given to the principled-based nature of sustainable development and its application through the principles of subsidiarity and proportionality. These two general principles have been chosen over others – such as non-discrimination – because of the relevance of proportionality and subsidiarity to the concept of sustainable development on the one hand, and because of the role of both proportionality and subsidiarity in regulating governance at the EU level. We critically discuss the procedural challenges in EU legislative, judicial, and institutional mechanisms applying sustainable development. It is argued that although sustainable development is applied in wide-ranging areas of EU law and policy, a lingering gap remains between the rhetoric of the institutions and the reality of enforcement.

## Principled-based sustainable development in EU law

The majority of EU environmental policy documents are framed in the language of sustainable development.[1] There are also many pieces of legislation and policy documents which refer explicitly to the objective of sustainability which must be attained when dealing with matters such as environmental strategy,[2] soil

---

1 See, for example, Commission Communication, A Sustainable Europe for a Better World: A European Union Strategy for Sustainable Development: Communication from the Commission of the European Communities to the Gothenburg European Council of 15 May 2001, COM(2001) 264 final; Commission Communication of 9 February 2005, the 2005 Review of the EU Sustainable Development Strategy: Initial Stocktaking and Future Orientations, COM(2005) 37 final; and Commission Communication 24 July 2009, Mainstreaming sustainable development into EU policies: 2009 Review of the European Union Strategy for Sustainable Development, COM(2009) 400 final.
2 The 7th EAP also makes several references to the objective of sustainable development, covering various elements of environmental, social, and economic growth, see Decision of

*General principles of EU law* 43

protection,³ rural development,⁴ common agricultural policy,⁵ maritime policy,⁶ fisheries policy,⁷ transport policy,⁸ and energy security.⁹ There are also many other documents which refer specifically to the "principle of sustainable development", including Commission communications on air transport,¹⁰ energy resources¹¹ and sustainable European tourism.¹² Directives assessing issues such as environmental liability,¹³ flood risks,¹⁴ pollution prevention,¹⁵ air quality,¹⁶ marine policy,¹⁷ and pesticides¹⁸ also make specific reference to the sustainable development concept.

---

the European Parliament and of the Council on a General Union Environment Action Programme to 2020 "Living well, within the limits of our planet", Decision 1386/2013/EU.
3 Strategy for Soil Protection COM(2006) 231 final (no 45).
4 Council Decision 2006/144/EC on Community strategic guidelines for rural development (programming period 2007 to 2013), OJ L 55/20 of 25 February 2006.
5 See Commission Communication of 18 November 2010, The CAP towards 2020: Meeting the food, natural resources and territorial challenges of the future, COM(2010) 672 final and Commission Guidelines for state aid in the agriculture and forestry sector, (2006) OJ C 319/01.
6 See Commission Communication of 10 October 2007 on An Integrated Maritime Policy for the European Union, COM(2007) 575 final.
7 Commission Communication of 13 July 2007 on Reform of the Common Fisheries Policy, COM(2011) 417 final and (EU) No 1380/2013 of 11 December 2013 on the Common Fisheries Policy, OJ L 354/22 of 28 December 2013.
8 European Commission White Paper – Roadmap to a Single European Transport Area – Towards a competitive and resource efficient transport system, COM(2011) 144 final of 28 March 2011.
9 Commission Communication of 13 November 2008 on an EU Energy Security and Solidarity Action Plan, the Commission Communication an Energy Policy for Europe, COM(2008) 781 final.
10 Commission Communication of 1 December 1999 on Air transport and the environment – Towards meeting the challenges of sustainable development, COM(1999) 640 final.
11 Commission Communication of 25 January 2006 on External Action: Thematic Programme For Environment and Sustainable Management of Natural Resources including Energy, COM(2006) 20 final.
12 Commission Communication of 19 October 2007 for a sustainable and competitive European tourism, COM(2007) 621 final.
13 Directive 2004/35/EC (n 44).
14 Directive 2007/60/EC of 23 October 2007 on the assessment and management of flood risks, OJ L 288/27.
15 Directive 2008/1/EC of 15 January 2008 concerning integrated pollution prevention and control, OJ L 24/8.
16 Directive 2008/50/EC of 21 May 2008 on ambient air quality and cleaner air for Europe, OJ L 152/1.
17 Directive 2008/56/EC of 17 July 2008 establishing a framework for community action in the field of marine environmental policy (Marine Strategy Framework Directive), OJ L 164/19.
18 Directive 2009/128/EC of 21 October 2009 establishing a framework of Community action to achieve the sustainable use of pesticides, OJ L 309/71. See also, Directive 2004/35/EC (n 44); Directive 2006/21/EC of 15 March 2006 on the management of waste from extractive industries and amending Directive 2004/35/CE, OJ L 102/15; Directive 2008/98/EC (n 46); and Regulation (EU) No 1304/2013 of 17 December 2013 on the European Social Fund and repealing Regulation (EC) No 1081/2006, OJ L 347/470.

## 44  *General principles of EU law*

In addition, the principle of sustainable development is accorded a place in the EU Charter of Fundamental Rights and Freedoms. Article 37 of the Charter states:

> A high level of environmental protection and the improvement of the quality of the environment must be integrated into the policies of the Union and ensured in accordance with the principle of sustainable development.[19]

There is substantial evidence to suggest that sustainable development has legal application as a general principle in the framework of EU law, with the principle integrated not only into primary law – through Article 11 TFEU and Article 37 of the Charter – but also with the principle finding expression in soft law covering a range of EU policy areas. No other requirement or principle has such a provision for integration across the legal order,[20] suggesting a particularity to sustainable development in EU law as well as its status as a principle of law.

The principle of sustainable development is further transposed in EU legal framework through the concept of intergenerational equity, identified in the Rio Declaration as a sub-principle of the broader principle of international sustainable development.[21] In the formulation of policy and legislation, the EU institutions have sought to consider the interests of future generations.[22] The incorporation

---

19  There will be further discussion below as to what practical effect the inclusion of the principle in the Charter has.

20  Certain cross-arching concepts, principles, or rules are self-evident and so they do not need to be expressed in this way, and perhaps many of the propositions associated with democracy and the rule of law as set out in the opening articles of the TEU do not require an integration provision like Article 11 TFEU on the basis of their fundamental status. However, the unusual status of the specific requirement that environmental protection requirements be integrated into policy stands.

21  See note 1.

22  In "Environmental Rights for the Future? Intergenerational Equity in the EU" (n 96) Collins argues that there is even evidence of the EU institutions working within the Weiss framework of duties: With regard to the duty to conserve resources, the EU's Biodiversity Strategy calls for an end to the loss of biodiversity within the EU by 2010 enacting the Birds Directive and the Habitats Directive. Also, the EU has passed a number of directives aimed at the reduction of waste (such as Directive 94/62/EC and Directive 2000/53/EC). In terms of the duty to ensure equitable use, the EU has taken an active role in facilitating sustainable development both within the less developed regions within its own borders, and in the developing world. This includes financing projects to assist developing countries in sustainably accessing their natural resources. Regarding the duty to avoid adverse impacts on the environment, the EU has enacted a comprehensive regime of anti-pollution measures, and broadened the scope of the ETS to help combat climate change. The EU has addressed the duty to avoid adverse impacts by codifying and operationalising the procedural environmental rights outlines in the Aarhus Convention. Lastly, the institutions address the duty to prevent disasters, minimise damage and provide emergency assistance by implementing various pieces of legislation to address the prevention and mitigation of climate change, marine spills, chemical accidents, nuclear safety, forest fires, and floods. Certainly within this framework of protecting the environment for future generations, sustainable development seems to be widely recognised and codified as an important objective of EU law.

of intergenerational equity in EU policy "implicitly or explicitly", is deemed to suggest "some ambiguous notion of responsibility to future generations".[23]

The 'intergenerational equity' principle was first identified in the works of Professor Edith Brown Weiss.[24] According to her doctrine, current generations are both beneficiaries of a Planetary Trust passed down from our ancestors and trustees of the planet for the benefit of future generations. This trusteeship gives rise to three principles[25] and, within those three, five duties of use.[26] Some scholars maintain that the concept is deemed to have spread into the broader generalities and language of sustainable development owing to questions over its practicability.[27]

Yet 'intergenerational equity' is identified by Redgwell to "constitute a 'guiding principle' in the application of substantive norms, including existing treaty obligations under international law"; while Sand and Peel describe it among the "legal elements of the concept of 'sustainable development', as reflected in international legal agreements".[28] Thus, the idea of protecting "third generation rights"[29] is accepted as justifiable, especially given the profound vulnerability of future generations to harm resulting from present environmental degradation.[30]

From the point of view of procedural impact, the principle of sustainable development is not yet openly used as grounds for judicial review in a case involving intergenerational equity. However, it is possible that, within the framework of the EU Charter, and more specifically Article 37, the principle could be relied upon to justify the protection of the interests of the future.

The Charter certainly recognises the rights of future generations. The Preamble states explicitly the responsibilities and duties incumbent upon the current generation to ensure the enjoyment of rights of future generations.[31] Moreover, the requirement of accordance with the principle of sustainable development in Article 37 entails, by definition, some protection of the interests of future generations.

---

23 Collins, L., "Environmental Rights for the Future? Intergenerational Equity in the EU", *RECEIL* (2007) 16, no. 3, 325.
24 Weiss, E.B., "The Planetary Trust: Conservation and Intergenerational Equity", *Ecology Law Quarterly* (1984) 11, 495–582.
25 The principle of conservation of options, the principle of conservation of quality, and the principle of conservation of access.
26 The duty to conserve resources; the duty to ensure equitable use; the duty to avoid adverse impacts; the duty to prevent disasters, minimise damage, and provide emergency assistance; and the duty to compensate for environmental harm.
27 Warren, L., "Legislating for Tomorrow's Problems Today – Dealing With Intergenerational Equity", *Environmental Law Review* (2005), 167–169.
28 Redgwell, C., *Intergenerational Trusts and Environmental Protection* (Manchester: Manchester University Press, 1999); Sands, P. and Peel, J., *Principles of International Environmental Law*, 3rd edition, (Cambridge: Cambridge University Press, 2012) p. 207.
29 Douglas-Scott, S., "The European Union and Human Rights After the Treaty of Lisbon", *Human Rights Law Review* (2011) 11, no. 4, 651.
30 Collins, L., "Are We There Yet? The Right to Environment in International and European Law", *McGill International Journal of Sustainable Development and Policy* (2007), 149.
31 Charter of Fundamental Rights of the European Union, OJ C 364/01 of the 18 December 2000; see penultimate paragraph of the preamble.

But, in 2007, the enforceability of Article 37 – and more specifically the principle of sustainable development – was greatly undermined by the introduction of Article 52(5) to the Charter. In this Article, the drafters attempted to distinguish rights and principles, providing that:

> The provisions of this Charter which contain principles [such as Article 37] may be implemented by legislative and executive acts taken by institutions, bodies, offices and agencies of the Union, and by acts of Member States when they are implementing Union law, in the exercise of their respective powers. They shall be judicially cognisable only in the interpretation of such acts and in the ruling on their legality.[32]

The extent of this exclusion, and how it can operate, is not clear. In the view of Douglas-Scott, this paragraph means that principles in the Charter such as sustainable development are "incapable of creating any directly enforceable rights",[33] which suggests either actions brought under the Charter will fail, or more broadly that the general principle of sustainable development in all contexts is unable to give rise to enforceable rights. However, if the CJEU wished to base a judgment on sustainable development, it could rely on Article 11 TFEU instead of the Charter, where no exclusion applies.

If sustainable development is more broadly incapable of creating enforceable rights and the Article 52(5) exclusion is simply evidence of the limitation rather than the cause, Article 52(5) is still in direct conflict with the widespread use of other principles included in the Charter. For example, the principle of equality – enshrined in Article 23 of the Charter – has been relied upon in many cases before the CJEU regarding the legality of national measures, and its scope of application continues to expand even now.[34]

In either case, the exclusion and the questions around the utility of the sustainable development concept need to be considered in the light of the location of the principle of sustainable development alongside other rights and fundamental freedoms included in the Charter. This position suggests equivalence between the rights. The Charter attempts to encompass a range of rights, spanning from the human rights already well established in the European Convention of Human Rights to social and economic rights and freedoms. The Charter itself does not resolve the question of where a principle of sustainable development fits within this range of rights.

There is a sense in which one might perceive the incorporation of the principle into Article 37 of the Charter and the location in Article 52(5) as undermining

---

32　Ibid., Art. 52(5).
33　Douglas-Scott (n 29) 652.
34　First used as a means of ensuring equality (or non-discrimination) between males and females in the workplace, it has since been developed to encompass cases relating to race, sexual orientation and age. For example, see C-13/94 *P v S and Cornwall County Council* [1996] ECR I-2143 and C-144/04 *Mangold v Helm* [2005] ECR I-9981.

its justiciability to render the principle less workable. It may also suggest that the EU is uncertain as to where sustainable development should fit in the EU legal order, in terms of the potential enforceability. Surely to keep sustainable development as a guiding principle without justifiability for generational equity does not really allow it to have the full influence required ensuring a "high level of environmental protection" as required by Article 11 TFEU. It is not enough for EU institutions to have considered the principle in their decision-making; the principle must also be enforced, otherwise the interests of future generations will not be protected. Without some form of procedural impact, the EU institutions and the measures they enact are able to avoid judicial scrutiny and not only does this undermine the importance attributed by the EU institutions themselves to the principle of sustainable development, but it is also contrary to the rule of law itself.

It is useful perhaps to reflect on the historical and political context of how the intergenerational equity principle came to be enshrined as an element of sustainable development in the Rio Declaration, as relevant for understanding the unenforceable non-justiciable approach adopted by the EU system. The intention behind the formulation of the intergenerational equity as Principle 3 was to stress the 'right to development' of present generations rather than future ones.[35] But the "emphasis has progressively moved away from development as a mere present concern and towards a conception more sensitive to the temporal dimension"; and is increasingly regarded as "a statement of intergenerational equity than of the 'right to development'".[36] It is arguably the 'right to development' content of the principle that the Charter attempts to protect to encompass a range of rights, including economic, social, and environmental rights under the human rights frame. In line with this reasoning protection of rights could come from other component principles of sustainable development – such as the precautionary, polluter pays and public participation principles to address the three dimensions of sustainability from a *right's* frame, as well as principled-based.

## General principles in EU law and sustainable development

Clearly, the EU institutions have recognised sustainable development as a primary objective of the EU, and both the TEU and TFEU include specific references to sustainable development as a guiding theme for the EU. The treaties indicate that a principle of sustainable development may emerge in EU law.[37] But

---

35 Molinari, C., "From a Right to Development to Intergenerational Equity", in Viñuales, J.E. (Ed.) *Rio Declaration on Environment and Development: A Commentary* (Oxford: Oxford University Press, 2015) p. 141.
36 Ibid., 144.
37 See the preamble to the Consolidated Version of Treaty on European Union, OJ C 326/13, 26 October 2012, and Article 11 of the Consolidated Version of Treaty on the Functioning of the European Union, OJ 326/47, 26 October 2012.

it is important to examine the form of the principle-based sustainable development under the subsidiarity and proportionality principles, which are fundamental in regulating EU governance the exercise of powers by the EU. To locate sustainable development within EU legal order of subsidiarity and proportionality should help illustrate the nature of the principle, its impact, and its future role for environmental protection alongside developmental objectives in the EU legal order – at the institutional and national level.

### *Subsidiarity as a general principle in EU law*

The primary role of subsidiarity is to regulate governance at the EU level and, in particular, to promote good governance, a key element of sustainable development. Moreover, the principle respects the diversity of the current twenty-eight Member States, a feature which is particularly relevant to sustainable development due to the latter's transboundary nature. Such transboundary issues are best dealt with consistently and subsidiarity provides structure, which allows for decisions on such issues which are best taken at the EU level to be made at the EU level, thus ensuring minimum harmonisation across all twenty-eight Member States where relevant and appropriate.

Currently, the principle and its rules of application can be found in Article 5 TEU and in Protocol 2 respectively. According to these documents, the principle of subsidiarity acts to regulate the exercise of powers by the EU. It requires that, in an area of joint competence, the Union can only take action when it is clear that the objectives of the proposed action cannot be sufficiently achieved by the Member States. In doing so, the principle ensures that the existing diversity between the States is not repressed by excessive and unjustified EU-wide harmonisation.[38] When the concept of subsidiarity was formally introduced as a general principle of Union law in the Maastricht Treaty on European Union in 1992, the principle was not a new one. In fact, it had already been implemented by several of the federalised Member States, such as Germany.[39]

In the EU context, the application of the principle is governed by the sufficient attainment test, which is used to ensure that the EU takes action only if the Member States cannot achieve the aim of the measure themselves. A second, better attainment test is also used to ensure that Union action is preferred to Member State action, provided it will bring demonstrable advantages. On the face of it, therefore, subsidiarity seems to be a standard by which Member States

---

38 Bjerregaard, R., "Policy Review: Subsidiarity and Environment", *European Environment* (2000) 10, 107.
39 As succinctly put by the House of Lords "[t]he principle developed in political thought in the 19th century and found expression in political liberalism and Catholic social theory. The political liberals used the principle to limit state intervention in individual lives. Socialist Catholics used it to invite state intervention where necessary and efficient and prevent interference where it was neither necessary nor efficient"; House of Lords Select Committee on European Union, "Fourteenth Report – Chapter 2: Exploring Subsidiarity", 2005, para. 46.

can challenge retrospectively either the validity of legislation adopted without reference to it, or its appropriateness when alternative national or regional legislation could have achieved the same aim.[40]

Furthermore, the principle of subsidiarity plays a crucial role in the field of environmental policy, since competences in this area are shared between the EU and its Member States.[41] In terms of application of the general principle, there is substantial evidence that the EU institutions recognise its important role as a principle in its decision-making, referring to it in general strategy documents[42] and in various specific policy documents, relating to matters such as: water policy;[43] civil and criminal liability for environmental damage;[44] soil protection;[45] waste;[46] and renewable energy.[47] It appears also that the EU institutions can easily satisfy the principle when taking initiative for environmental measures. Certainly, in some circumstances, the EU is better placed to act than the Member States. In matters of a transboundary nature, which encompass key environmental issues like climate change, damage to the ozone layer, biodiversity, and pollution (both water and air),[48] the institutions have recognised that EU-level action is more appropriate.[49]

---

40 Horspool, M. and Humphreys, M., *European Union Law*, 9th edition (Oxford: Oxford University Press, 2016) p. 132.
41 See Article 4(2)(e) TFEU and Case C-114/01 *AvestaPolarit Chrome* [2003] ECR I-8725, para. 56.
42 Such as in Article 1 of the 7th EAP – Decision of the European Parliament and of the Council on a General Union Environment Action Programme to 2020 "Living well, within the limits of our planet", Decision 1386/2014/EU.
43 Paragraph 18 of Directive 2000/60/EC of the European Parliament and of the Council of 23 October 2000 establishing a framework for Community action in the field of water policy, OJ L 327/1, 21 December 2000.
44 Paragraph 3 of Directive 2004/35/CE of the European Parliament and of the Council of 21 April 2004 on environmental liability with regard to the prevention and remedying of environmental damage, OJ L 143/56, 30 April 2004 and paragraph 14 of Directive 2008/99/EC of the European Parliament and of the Council of 19 November 2008 on the protection of the environment through criminal law, OJ L 328/28, 6 December 2008.
45 Page 6 of the Communication from the Commission to the Council, the European Parliament, the European Economic and Social Committee and the Committee of the Regions Thematic Strategy for Soil Protection, COM(2006) 231 final.
46 Paragraph 49 of Directive 2008/98/EC of the European Parliament and of the Council of 19 November 2008 on waste and repealing certain Directives, OJ L 312/3, 22 November 2008.
47 Paragraph 96 of Directive 2009/28/EC of the European Parliament and of the Council of 23 April 2009 on the promotion of the use of energy from renewable sources and amending and subsequently repealing Directives 2001/77/EC and 2003/30/EC, OJ L 140/16, 5 June 2009.
48 de Sadeleer, N., "Principle of Subsidiarity and the EU Environmental Policy", *Journal for European Environmental Planning Law* (2012) 9, no. 1, 64–65.
49 The 2009 revised impact assessment guidelines includes an explicit set of provisions on subsidiarity in transnational matters and the role the EU has to play in their management. See European Commission, Impact Assessment Guidelines, 2009, SEC(2009) 92, 23; Humphreys and Horspool (n 60) 133.

Furthermore, due to the differences that can often occur between the Member States in their varying approaches to environmental policies, EU action through harmonising measures – even if set at the level of the lowest common denominator – ensures that a certain standard of environmental protection applies in all EU Member States.[50] Without this potential for harmonisation, the efforts of even the most environmentally minded Member States would be quickly undermined by the inaction of others.[51] As an illustration, the harmonising Directive on engine emissions[52] has continued to set high standards for motor vehicle engines for more than forty years. Instead of entrenching the efforts of the lowest common denominator, the Directive requires Member States to meet the same quality standard as those countries, which had successfully pushed the boundaries of what could be achieved in lowering engine emissions. Despite the extraordinary growth of the market for vehicles and the corresponding impact on pollution – particularly in large urban areas – this should not detract from the significance of the milestone achieved by setting such an engine emission standard.

The forgoing illustration of EU subsidiarity shows that it is possible for the application of sustainable development within the frame, especially for achievement of environmental policy objectives. In fact, it sits well with nature of transposing the sustainability to include legislative, judicial, deliberative, and institutional processes. Granted there seen to be an issue over the effectiveness of CJEU judicial role of subsidiarity in ensuring the balancing that is necessary for promoting sustainability, giving the wide discretion affording to union institutions, in face of the unwillingness of the court to second guess the Union institutions to justify action at the Union level. In spite of this shortcoming, subsidiarity could promote sustainable development as it allows flexibility for the principle to be inferred from the context and to guide institutional decision-making including on environmental policy.

## *Proportionality as a general principle in EU law*

The general principle of proportionality seeks to regulate the exercise of powers by the EU.[53] This is essential if the EU is to legitimise its action in relation to contentious issues and, as such, is often considered alongside subsidiarity. At a conceptual level, proportionality mirrors certain characteristics of the international principle of sustainable development in terms of its broadness and flexibility and balancing role. For example, proportionality is deliberately flexible to afford the Court of Justice wide grounds for judicial review. It also involves a balancing of

---

50 de Sadeleer Principle of Subsidiarity (n 48) 64–5.
51 Ibid.
52 Council of the European Union, Council Directive on the approximation of the laws of the Member States on measures to be taken against air pollution by emissions from motor vehicles, Directive 70/220/EEC (consolidated), 20 March 1970, 1970L00220.
53 The ECJ confirmed that proportionality was a general principle of law in Case 11/70 *Internationale Handelsgesellschaft* [1970] ECR 1125, 1128–9.

different interests (for example environmental and economic), an essential task when legitimising EU action in a certain area.

Enshrined in Article 5 TEU and in the second Protocol, proportionality requires that the involvement of the institutions in decision-making be limited to what is necessary to achieve the objectives of the Treaties.[54] Moreover, the principle has three key functions in EU law:

(i) as a ground for the judicial review of measures;
(ii) as a ground of review of national measures affecting one of the four fundamental freedoms;
(iii) to govern the exercise by the EU of its legal competence.[55]

As with subsidiarity, when first codified in EU law, the proportionality principle had already been present at the national level for some time. However, unlike subsidiarity, the principle is notorious for its flexibility of application, which is achieved by the Court by the use of three tests. These are suitability (that the measure is appropriate to achieve the given aim); necessity (that the measure is necessary to achieve the given aim); and proportionality *stricto sensu* (that the measure is disproportionate if it imposes an excessive burden on the individual).[56]

One feature of the principle of proportionality, therefore, is the varying levels of judicial scrutiny it entails and, as a consequence, the *ad hoc* nature of its application from case to case.[57] This can be both a positive and a negative. From a positive perspective, it demonstrates the flexibility of the application of the principle, arguably a desirable characteristic of a general principle, which covers a broad range of policy areas. From a negative perspective, such *ad hoc* interpretation can be detrimental to the legal certainty surrounding the application of the principle and, as such, contrary to the rule of law the CJEU seeks to uphold.

When concerned with measures designed specifically to address environmental degradation, the proportionality principle is applied in two ways. First, it is acknowledged as a core element in the EU-level policy measures and legislation, which guides the exercise of EU powers in the particular field concerned and, as in the case of the subsidiarity principle, legitimises them.[58] Second, the general principle is often used by the CJEU as a test to determine whether certain

---

54 See Case C-331/88 *Fedesa* [1990] ECR I-4023.
55 Tridimas, T., *The General Principles of EU Law*, (Oxford: Oxford University Press, 2nd edition, 2007) p. 89.
56 Harbo, T., "The Function of the Proportionality Principle in EU Law", *European Law Journal* (March 2010) 16, no. 2, 165.
57 Ueda, J., "Is the Principle of Proportionality the European Approach? A Review and Analysis of Trade and Environment Cases Before the European Court of Justice", *European Business Law Review* (2003), 563.
58 For example: paragraph 3 of Directive 2004/35/CE (n 44); para. 49 of Directive 2008/98/EC (n 46); para. 14 of Directive 2008/99/EC (n 44); paragraph 96 of Directive 2009/28/EC (n 47).

environmental measures (implemented by either the EU or its Member States) are proportionate in terms of their potential impact on other fundamental legal principles, such as free movement.[59] In such cases, the Court usually applies the general principle by means of a disproportionality test.[60] This enables the effective balance of environmental concerns with other social or economic concerns, and thereby reinforces the legitimacy and appropriateness of the measure taken.

The tests for proportionality namely – suitability, necessity, and cost-burden-proportionality – coupled with the flexibility in application makes it apt to transpose the principle of sustainable development from a contextual standpoint. What sustainable development applies to address, as has been mentioned need to be inferred from the context of its use and in reference to the objective sought – to regulate activities for environmental protection and balancing developmental needs, on the one hand, and effectively regulate EU governance within its legal framework.

## EU sustainable development in subsidiarity and proportionality: legal procedural impact

### *The legal effect of EU principle-based sustainable development*

The EU Treaties indicate that a principle of sustainable development may emerge in EU law.[61] General principles have long played an important role in the development of EU law. However, the form that any such principle will take including sustainable development depends greatly on how the EU institutions attempt to incorporate it into their decision-making and interpret it in the Court. Broadly speaking, a general principle should transcend all areas of law and, depending on its nature, fulfil at least one of several roles. They can perform different acts in the development of case law, such as fill gaps in written law;[62] aid the Court in the interpretation of written law;[63] provide the grounds for the judicial review of an EU measure; and, if the prior aim is achieved, engage liability for damages.[64]

In addition to their use in Court, general principles can also assist in rationalising and legitimising decision-making at the EU level, and they are, as a consequence, often referred to in the preambles of most legislation and policy documents. In referring to these general principles, EU institutions can maintain

---

59 For more on the application of the environment-economic balance in CJEU case law, see Chapter 3.
60 Ueda (n 57) 589.
61 See the preamble to the Consolidated Version of Treaty on European Union, OJ C 326/13, 26 October 2012, and Article 11 of the Consolidated Version of Treaty on the Functioning of the European Union, OJ 326/47, 26 October 2012.
62 Tridimas (n 55) 9.
63 Ibid., 17.
64 Tridimas (n 55) 19 and 22.

a consistent approach and, thereby, enable greater legal certainty in EU law as a whole.[65]

Due to these varying purposes, each general principle has a different influence on the development and interpretation of EU law. For example, some principles are more guiding in nature and are used more as a point of reference in the development of case law, legislation, or policy. Others are characterised by more robust, procedural effect, both forming the basis of political and legislative legitimacy in decision-making and providing the grounds for the judicial review of measures. Where sustainable development sits on the spectrum of general principles will determine how its future interpretation and enforcement is framed by the courts. If at the guiding end of the spectrum, a general principle of sustainable development would help policy to develop in a manner which is superficial only, an approach which may prove more politically palatable in the diverse member States of the Union. Alternatively, if the concept sits at the other end of the spectrum, any general principle which emerges would be characterised by a more aggressive integration and enforcement of sustainable development in all relevant areas of EU law and policy.

This variety in the interpretation and implementation of general principles is something to be borne in mind when comparison is made between their respective legal frameworks and whether these frameworks can truly be transplanted onto the concept of sustainable development. This does not mean to say that sustainable development is not or cannot be a general principle in its own right. Indeed, the discussion below will show how the concept guides the development of EU policy and decision-making and, potentially, allows for judicial review of certain measures. Rather, the fact that the framework of one principle may not fit comfortably onto another merely illustrates the differing nature of general principles and reinforces the uncertainty of whether a single concept of what constitutes a general principle can really be defined.

### *Sustainability in subsidiarity and proportionality: procedural impact*

As mentioned above, the principles of subsidiarity and proportionality are referred to in most legislative documents and openly recognised by the EU institutions as core considerations for action, and sustainable development may validly be transposed through this regime at institutional and national levels.

With respect to subsidiarity, cases are often brought against the EU institutions, which challenge their competence to act in certain areas. However, the CJEU rarely rules explicitly on the application of the subsidiarity principle. It tends to focus instead at the legal basis of the act or (prior to the Lisbon Treaty reforms to the EU) the division of competences according to the Treaties. Procedurally the CJEU has demonstrated its capacity to handle arguments based on

---

65 Harbo (n 56), 160 and 162.

subsidiary, but in practice the principle appears to have significant shortcomings when striking down legislation or decisions made in breach – environmental or otherwise.[66] Similarly, subsidiarity is often not used to challenge the legality of measures that may be in breach of the principle and, as such, lacks procedural impact.

The procedural complications derive from the fact that first, the Union institutions have a wide discretion in the application of the principle. The European Parliament itself has admitted that the Court's jurisdiction over the application of the principle has grown "in inverse proportion to the extent to which the Member States are effectively involved in a decision on substance and scale of the measure under consideration".[67] Secondly, Protocol 2 provides that the CJEU has jurisdiction on grounds of the infringement of the principle of subsidiarity. However, the threshold at which the Court analyses the respect of subsidiarity by the institutions is set low.[68] The Court, it seems, will not second-guess the European Institutions where considered reasons have been given to justify action at the Union level.[69]

For example, in C-84/94 *UK v. Council* [1996] and C-233/94 *Germany v. European Parliament* [1997] the Court found that a measure's compliance with the principle was sufficiently covered by the Commission's requirement to state reasons.[70] In the latter case, the Court held that this requirement is met even if the principle is not explicitly referred to, provided it is clear from the recitals as a whole that the principle has been complied with.[71] Moreover, it is difficult to imagine how the CJEU can rule on what remains essentially a political choice as to the most appropriate forum for making a decision or the most appropriate source for a piece of legislation.[72] Indeed, this was the point raised by the Council in the mobile phone roaming charges case C-58/08 *Vodafone v Secretary of State for Business* [2010].[73]

In view of these issues, it is perhaps easier to see subsidiarity in the 'guiding' sense, requiring institutions to consider – and prove that they have considered – the principle, rather than using it as a standard against which the legality of the

---

66 Humphreys and Horspool (n 40) 132.
67 European Parliament, The Principle of Subsidiarity, Summary Paper, 2012, 3.
68 Humphreys and Horspool (n 40) 132.
69 House of Lords Select Committee on European Union, "Fourteenth Report – Chapter 5: The Role of the European Court of Justice", 2005, 221.
70 See Cases C-84/94 *UK v Council* [1996] ECR I-5755, 47 and C-233/94 *Germany v European Parliament* [1997] ECR I-2405, 26–8; The Principle of Subsidiarity, Summary Paper (n 74) 3.
71 C-233/94 *Germany v European Parliament* [1997] ECR I-2405, 28; The Principle of Subsidiarity, Summary Paper (n 74) 3.
72 See Joined Cases C-154/04 and C-155/04 *Alliance for Natural Health* [2005] ECR I-6451
73 See both AG opinion and judgment in Case C-58/08 *Vodafone Ltd v Secretary of State for Business, Enterprise and Regulatory Reform* [2010] ECR I-4999, 42–48.

legislation be evaluated.⁷⁴ Moreover if, like in the *Vodafone* case, the Court is deferential to the legislator, stating that on the basis of the legislation alone the need for Union action is clear, then the principle will remain weak and lacking in the procedural impact necessary to escape this category.⁷⁵

Indeed, it is arguably unwieldy for the Court to adjudicate on the principle, due to the political nature of the division of competences the principle aims to guarantee. Nonetheless, failure to implement the principle of subsidiarity in such a way robs it of its power to substantiate claims for judicial review and, as such, leaves it at the 'weak' end of the spectrum.

The principle of proportionality, on the other hand, is often used as a means of challenging the legality of certain measures under EU law. The flexible application of the principle illustrates the potential extent of its procedural impact and highlights the important role it has to play in legitimising decision-making at EU-level. As such, the proportionality principle's legal framework including the proportionality test is especially important for sustainable development and is a good point for mapping it application in EU legal framework. To what extent, then, has the Court deemed sustainable development as sufficient either to justify a measure otherwise in violation of EU law, or to strike down legitimate legislation due to its inconsistency with the requirements of sustainable development, or other negative impact?

Certainly environmental protection, a subsidiary principle of sustainability, has been accepted by the Court as a justification for limiting the freedom to move goods.⁷⁶ Arguably, in view of the difference between relative versus absolute obligations this interpretation could indicate an attempt to ensure that EU Member States strive towards the general principle of sustainable development. This argument would go further if a stand-alone right to environmental protection were to emerge.⁷⁷

However, even if there were to be such a stand-alone right, there is little indication in the cases to date that the Court is willing to interpret environmental

---

74 Humphreys and Horspool (n 40) 132.
75 Humphreys and Horspool (n 40) 133.
76 See, for example, Case C-28/09 *Commission v Austria* EU:C:2010:854.
77 The objectives of environmental protection and the promotion of human rights are "increasingly seen as intertwined, complementary goals, and part of the fundamental pillars of sustainable development" (See OHCHR [Office of the United Nations High Commissioner for Human Rights] and UNEP [United Nations Environment Programme], "Human Rights and the Environment, Rio+20: Joint Report OHCHR and UNEP" (2012) p. 21.) However, discussion of such a right has yielded few conclusive results. Rather, there has been a growing acceptance that environmental degradation may violate already protected human rights enshrined in the European Convention of Human Rights (ECHR), such as the rights to life, security of the person, and family life. This has thus lead to a 'greening' of some human rights law, the obvious limitation being that remedy for the impact of environmental degradation can only be claimed under a violation of a right protected by the ECHR. See Collins, L. (n 98) 321. See also the Council of Europe, *Manual on Human Rights and the Environment*, 2nd edition (2012).

protection in a way that reinforces a general principle of sustainable development. In such judgments, the Court makes little or no reference to Article 11 TFEU or to prior judgments on general principles.[78] Despite this, in C-43/10 *Nomarchiaki Aftodioikisi Aitoloakarnanias* [2012], the Court did refer to the general "objective" of sustainable development.[79]

When asked to interpret whether Directive 92/43 on the conservation of natural habitats and of wild fauna and flora[80] permits "the conversion of a natural fluvial ecosystem into a largely man-made fluvial and lacustrine ecosystem", the Court had to balance overriding public interests with preservation on the grounds of sustainable development.[81] Although this was a reference for a preliminary ruling and, as such, required only an interpretation of EU legislation by the Court, it could suggest that the Court is willing to consider sustainable development and the impact it can have on national measures, which affect the protection of the environment.

Similarly, in C-302/86 *Danish Bottles* [1988], the Court used the proportionality principle to mitigate the exception to the free movement of goods regime allowed for in the interests of the environment and, in doing so, kickstarted the emergence of the mandatory requirement of environmental protection.[82] According to the Court, a deposit and return scheme, which only permitted the use of certain types of containers, was acceptable under the scope of the free movement of goods because of the environmental protection aim it pursued.[83]

Yet, the Court also ruled that a restrictive scheme which permitted the return of only certain types of containers, despite being designed for the same environmental aim, was disproportionate.[84] However, in C-142/05 *Mickelsson and Roos* [2009], a ruling some years after *Danish Bottles*, the Court took a different approach, finding that even when a less restrictive means of protection exists, Member States may still adopt an alternative path, provided it is required by their specific national circumstances.[85] These contrasting opinions again demonstrate the principle's wide-ranging and flexibility of application.

Thus interpretation or transposition of sustainable development in EU legal and policy framework including through its subsidiarity and proportionality

---

78 Similar results can be found where the court has ruled upon the application of the precautionary principle. For more on the application of the precautionary principle in EU case law, see Chapter 4.
79 Case C-43/10 *Nomarchiaki Aftodioikisi Aitoloakarnanias and Others* [2012].
80 Council Directive 92/43/EEC of 21 May 1992 on the conservation of natural habitats and of wild fauna and flora, 22 July 1992, OJ L 206/7.
81 *Nomarchiaki Aftodioikisi Aitoloakarnanias* (n 118) 134–139.
82 Case C-302/86 *Commission v Denmark* [1988] ECR I-4607.
83 Ibid., 13.
84 *Commission v Denmark* (n 82) 21.
85 Case C-142/05 *Aklagaren v Mickelsson and Roos* [2009] ECR I-4273, 36.

regime for environmental protection, and developmental objectives could be discerned from two basic premises:

1. whether the principle is considered and referred to in legal and policy documents as an objective which must be satisfied to the best of the EU's abilities when pursuing an agenda;
2. whether it can be used as grounds for the judicial review of Union or national measures.

Where sustainable development is established in the first context of consideration, then arguably the principle can be aligned with other principles of a guiding nature, such as subsidiarity. It could inform decision-making on the application, for instance, of its sub-principles (e.g., precaution, polluter pays, or participation) in regulation of EU governance potentially to achieve environmental protection or economic or social objectives which already enjoy wide treaty application in the EU.

The context of transposition or implementation could also demonstrate the characteristics in both premises: In such scenario sustainable development would apply in form more similar to robust general principles such as proportionality. This case may be more effective if it can be used as a ground upon which actions for judicial review can be brought, whereby claimants can argue that, on balance, a measure otherwise in violation of or in conformity with EU law is set aside or justified, because it either supports the general principle of sustainable development or undermines it.

Clearly, the international principle of sustainable development does have wide application in the EU. However, in order for the EU to achieve its integration into economic, social, and environmental interests Europe-wide, and thereby enhance its role as a leader in global change, it must not only recognise the importance of the concept in relation to their decision-making, but also facilitate ways by which the principle can be upheld before the Court. In other words, it could demonstrate a robust commitment towards pursuing the objective of sustainable development through its various policy areas it is desirable that the two requirements be satisfied and an endeavour to eliminate the lingering gap remaining between the rhetoric of the institutions and the reality of enforcement.

## Conclusion

The analysis reveals that the international concept and principle of sustainable development is capable of application at a regional level, and specifically in the EU. It shows that sustainable development has application in wide-ranging areas of EU law and policy, including through the principles of subsidiarity and proportionality.

The EU legal system transposes the sustainable development concept in two main legal paradigms. Firstly, through specific mention of the need to integrate environmental protection requirements into policy areas by Article 11 TFEU. In this context, sustainable development could fit into either of two camps: It will either remain a guiding principle, referred to in EU policy and legislative documents as an objective of EU law to be considered and – in theory – followed. Alternatively, it will develop in the case law of the CJEU as a general principle upon which claims for judicial review of EU and Member State measures can be made.

The second paradigm reveals that the EU system places sustainable development alongside the fundamental rights and freedoms enshrined in the Charter, with which sustainable development has little in common. The inclusion of sustainable development in the Charter suggests its promotion, and its association with fundamental rights of the EU legal order. Here the extent to which the Charter promotes the realisation of sustainable development will depend upon how the Charter will be viewed and used as the relationship between it and the European Convention on Human Rights and Fundamental Freedoms, and the relationship between the Court of Justice and the European Court of Human Rights develop. The instance of the intergenerational equity in the transposition of EU's sustainable development raises issues particularly regarding the lack of mechanism for judicial scrutiny.

It finds that although sustainable development has wide application in EU legal order, a lingering gap remains between the rhetoric of the institutions and the reality of enforcement. Sustainable development will not amount to much if it cannot be enforced either under its own name or by means of one of its component principles. Whichever direction the principle takes in the years to come, this analysis demonstrates the emphasis which should be placed on the principle of sustainable development and the future role it has to play in the legal and judicial scrutiny of EU and Member State measures.

# 4 The precautionary principle and sustainability in EU environmental protection

The international principle of sustainable development has been shown to have application in wide-ranging areas of EU law and policy, including through the principles of subsidiarity and proportionality. Its legal context for application was revealed to entail under the broad principle of sustainability or by means of its component principles. This chapter examines how sustainable development is applied in the EU legal order through the precautionary principle to promote, in particular, the environmental protection dimensions of sustainable development. The precautionary principle is used to illustrate its primary relevance for environmental protection in the context of the other two dimensions.[1]

The analysis here will apply EU specific methods of transposition that have been identified in Chapter 2. These include the application through policy and legislative documents as an objective of EU law to be considered and followed; and its effect in the case law of the CJEU as a general principle upon which claims for judicial review of EU and Member State measures can be made. It presents both the interpretation of the principle in legislation and policy and its enforcement by the Court, by other EU institutions and by national authorities to argue that the legal effect of the principle is not undermined on the basis of enforcement. It suggests that enforcement itself should be done in a way, which is, in itself, sustainable, balancing the three competing interests – economic, environmental, and social – in a way that ensures legal and political credibility. It demonstrates that the precautionary principle can capably transpose sustainable development through EU law, policy, and practice to promote environmental protection. The principles of precaution and environmental protection provide a transferrable, legal framework in which a general principle of sustainable development could sit.

---

1 The polluter pays principle will be examined in primary relevance to economic aspects of sustainability in Chapter 5; and public participation and access to justice is examined in Chapter 6 in primary relevance to promoting socially sustainable development – both in the EU context. The three principles are not mutually exclusive and therefore may entail overlaps in the objectives that are to be achieved in the respective dimensions from the broader interpretation of sustainable development as an overarching principle.

## Precautionary approach to environmental protection

The objective of environmental protection is an integral part of the development process to achieve sustainable development.[2] A distinction should be maintained between environmental protection generally as a principle of international environmental law,[3] and environmental protection as an element of sustainable development.[4] Environmental protection as an indication of sustainable development, will thus include a commitment to reduce pollution, to avoid environmental degradation, promote efficient use of resources, maintain environmental capacities, and sustain consideration for economic and social component as the right to utilise the 'resource environment' in a certain manner.[5] In other words, environmental protection forms the basis upon which exploitative economic activities can be said to be sustainable.

The precautionary principle provides a regulatory oversight in the balancing that must take place between environmental protection, economic development, and social justice. The international formulation of the principle in the Rio Declaration recommends that:

> In order to protect the environment, the precautionary approach shall be widely applied by States according to their capabilities. Where there are threats of serious or irreversible damage, lack of full scientific certainty shall not be used as a reason for postponing cost-effective measures to prevent environmental degradation[6]

Atapattu deems the precautionary principle to have evolved from the discipline of international environmental law in three stages. The first was characterised by the repairing of environmental damage. The second involved an anticipatory approach to environmental protection, which was limited by its reliance on *existing* scientific knowledge. The third stage derived from a recognition that some environmental problems (such as global warming) could not be predicted with scientific certainty and, therefore, a precautionary approach would need to be

---

2 Rio Declaration on Environment and Development, 13 June 1992, adopted by the UNCED at Rio de Janeiro. UN Doc A/CONF. 151/26 (Vol. 1) (1992); *ILM* 874, 1992 (Rio Declaration) Principle 4.
3 This envisages a wider scope of regulation under international environmental law, and could include issues like protecting the environment from wars, hazardous substances, transboundary pollution, protection of global atmospheric components, and control mechanisms (liability regimes) for environmental protection at the international level.
4 The latter is a more narrowly defined dimension of protection that interprets in context of particular development activities, as undertaken in specific environments, and in relation to the environmental resources or persons that would be employed, or impacted by such activities; see Schwartz, P., *Sustainable Development and Mining in Sierra Leone* (Kent, UK: Pnuema Spring, 2006) p. 74.
5 Schwartz, P., 2006 (n 4).
6 Rio Declaration (n 2) Principle 15.

applied to force countries to take preventive measures even when scientific evidence was inconclusive.[7]

In its international frame, the principle has been prominent in regulating sustainable use of the planet's natural resources,[8] balancing social issues such as human health, and showcasing the importance of science based decision-making for sustainable development.[9] The link between the precautionary principle and environmental protection has ushered within it 'protection', framed as 'environmental rights', generally referenced in context of human rights.[10] There is a broad range of judicial perspective and literature on the principle entailing discussions over its legality, in terms of conferring a positive obligation to take protective measures; on the guiding nature of the principle requiring consideration of other policy areas; and on the instance of the burden of proving that the activity is not potentially harmful.[11]

Precaution is adjudged to reflect the necessity of making environment-related decisions, in the face of scientific uncertainty, about potential future harm of a particular activity;[12] or to "activities which may cause serious long-term or irreversible harm".[13] So that the effects of any form of development activities on the environment (and people) must be contemplated in order to avoid, reduce, or minimise the impact on the environment. The operation of the principle is likely

---

7 Atapattu, S.A., *Emerging Principles of International Environmental Law* (Ardsley: Transnational Publishers, 2006) p. 203.
8 Freestone, D., "International Fisheries Law Since Rio: The Continued Rise of the Precautionary Principle", in Boyle and Freestone (Eds.), *International Law and Sustainable Development* (Oxford: Oxford University Press, 2001) p. 135.
9 Plan of Implementation (POI) Report of the World Summit on Sustainable Development, UN Doc A/CONF.199/20 (4 September 2002) (WSSD Report) para. 23.
10 For analysis on environmental rights, Redgewell, C., "Life, the Universe and Everything: A Critic of Anthropocentric Rights", in Boyle and Anderson (Eds.), *Human Rights Approaches to Environmental Protection* (Oxford: Claredon Press, 1998); Handl, G., "Human Rights and Protection of the Environment", in Eide, A., Krause, C. and Rosas, A. (Eds.), *Economic, Social and Cultural Rights* (Leiden: Brill, 2001).
11 See *Southern Bluefin Tuna Cases (Australia v. Japan; New Zealand v. Japan)* (SBT Cases) Provisional measures Order of 27 August 1999; *The MOX Plant Case (Ireland v. United Kingdom), Request for Provisional Measures Order of 3 December 2001* (2002) 41 *ILM* 405; *Gabcikovo- Nagymaros Project* (Hungary/Slovakia) 1997, *ICJ Reports* 15 September 1997, GL No. 92 *(Gabcikovo Case)*; WTO *(Hormones case)* European Communities Measures Concerning Meat and Meat Products, Complaint by the United States (WT/DS26) and Canada (WT/DS48); Trouwborst, A., *Evolution and Status of the Precautionary Principle on International Law* (New York: Kluwer Law International, 2002); O'Riordan, T., Cameron, J. and Andrew, J. (Eds.), *Reinterpreting the Precautionary Principle* (London: Cameron, May 2001); Freestone, D. and Hey, E., *The Precautionary Principle and International Law: The Challenge of Implementation* (Boston: Kluwer Law International, 1995).
12 Judge Wolfrum (Separate Opinion), *The MOX Plant Case (Ireland v. United Kingdom), Request for Provisional Measures Order of 3 December 2001* (2002) 41 *ILM* 405.
13 International Law Association, New Delhi Declaration of Principles of International Law Relating to Sustainable Development' 2002 (ILA/NDD) Principle 4.3 (d) at http://cisdl.org/tribunals/pdf/NewDelhiDeclaration. pdf accessed 01/05/2017

to allow for proper consideration to be given to environmental and related concerns, and will invariably enhance environmental awareness if not absolute protection. The yardstick for precaution is not one of certainty of damage (or not), but potentiality.[14] The principle could be applied as an 'approach' rather than the 'principle' ensuring a certain degree of flexibility in its application.[15]

As with the international plane, sustainable development in EU law and policy is associated closely with the development of environmental law and policy. Article 191 TFEU sets out the framework for environmental policy and bases that upon principles. The objectives of environmental policy are to preserve, protect, and improve the quality of the environment; protecting human health; rationalising the utilisation of natural resources; promoting measures at international level to deal with regional or world-wide environmental problems, and in particular combating climate change. Article 191(2) TFEU identifies a role in environmental protection for the precautionary principle.

## EU environmental protection and precaution: law, policy, and practice

The precautionary principle is important to the aim of sustainable development due to the very uncertain and unpredictable nature of environmental damage.[16] By encouraging the understanding that, even without scientific evidence, certain actions cannot necessarily be tolerated by the environment, the precautionary principle ensures that measures are taken which, although not substantiated today, may prove immensely effective in slowing the degradation of our environment in the future.

In line with the international direction of the principle for environmental protection, the EU legal framework embeds the precautionary principle as an aspect of environmental protection activity broadly transposed as "policy in the sphere of the environment".[17] It was omitted in the Treaty of Rome but subsequently included into the Maastricht Treaty to read as:

> Community policy on the environment shall aim at a high level of protection taking into account the diversity of situations in the various regions of the Community. It shall be based on the precautionary principle and on the principles that preventive action should be taken, that environmental damage should as a priority be rectified at source and that the polluter should pay.[18]

---

14 Schwartz, P., 2006 (n 4) p. 93.
15 See Sep. Op. of Judge Laing *The MOX Plant Case* (n 11).
16 Dernbach, J.C., "Sustainable Development as a Framework for National Governance", CASE W. RES. L. REV. 49(1) (1998) cited in Atapattu, *Emerging Principles* (n 7) 278–279.
17 The Single European Act of 1986.
18 Article 174(2) para. 1, *Maastricht Treaty on European Union* (1992) *31 ILM 24*: see also TFEU Article 191(2). Note that the polluter pays principle is discussed at length in Chapter 5 and only precaution is examined herein.

The precautionary principle was the last to be added to the list of environmental principles in the Treaties.[19] Wolf and Stanley claim that the precautionary principle enables or requires States to take action where a risk to human health or the environment exists, but where there is evidential uncertainty as to the existence or extent of the risk.[20]

The EU expression is different in language to the formulation of the Rio Declaration; it does not specifically mention the nature of threats – 'serious or reversible harm', the question of 'scientific uncertainty', or qualify the precautionary measure by reference to 'capabilities' and 'cost-effectiveness'. But, it aims at a 'high level' of environmental protection in consideration of 'diversity of situations'. However the TFEU, Article 191(3) directs the Union to consider inter alia "available scientific and technical data", and "potential benefits and costs of action or lack of action" in preparing its policy on the environment.[21]

However, the Court of Justice has recognised the precautionary principle as a general principle of EU law,[22] more recently restating the jurisprudence on the application of the principle in *Gowan*:

> A correct application of the precautionary principle presupposes first, identification of the potentially negative consequences for health of the proposed used of the substance at issue, and, secondly, a comprehensive assessment of the risk to health based on the most reliable scientific data available and the most recent results of international research.[23]

Despite the potentially wide scope of application of the principle, when it was first included in the Treaty, it was not accompanied by a formal definition. This lack of definition was raised in subsequent case law and, in response, the European Commission produced a communication setting out the guidelines on using the principle.[24] These have been supplemented by principles and guidance developed

---

19 de Sadeleer, N., *Environmental Principles: From Political Slogans to Legal Rules* (Oxford: Oxford University Press, 2005) p. 24.
20 Wolf, S. and Stanley, N., *Environmental Law*, 5th edition (London: Routledge, 2010) pp. 16–17.
21 Other criteria include consideration of environmental conditions in the various regions of the Union, the economic and social development of the Union as a whole, and the balanced development of its regions.
22 Case T-13/99 *Pfizer Animal Health S.A. v Council* [2002] ECR I-3305, paras 114–115. In Case T-333/10 *ATC*, the Court of Justice reinforced its position that the precautionary principle is a general principle of EU law and stated precedence should be given to precautionary requirements over economic interests. EU:T:2013: 451 at paragraph 79.
23 Case C- 77/09 *Gowan Comércio Internacional e Serviços L v.Ministtero Della Salute* [2010] ECR I-13533 para. 75 – in that case, the European Commission had placed severe restrictions on pesticide uses of fenarimol, even though it had on previous risk assessment concluded that the substance caused limited harm. The Court upheld the measure challenged.
24 European Commission, Communication from the Commission on the Precautionary Principle, Brussels 2 February 2000, COM(2000) 1; Bell, S. and McGillivray, D., *Environmental Law* (Oxford: Oxford University Press, 2008) p. 67.

by the Court of Justice, including on the circumstances in which the precautionary principle may apply, especially regarding the threshold and seriousness of risk, the adequacy of scientific data, consensus on scientific research the objectivity in the risk assessment, and balancing of economic and social interests with environmental protection.

According to the Court of Justice, action on grounds of precaution may not justify where the risk is either "purely hypothetical" or based on "mere suppositions not yet scientifically verified".[25] The risk must be "adequately backed up by the scientific data available at the time".[26] An objective appreciation of the level of potential risk will be a sufficient trigger and claimants need not wait "until the reality and seriousness of those risks become fully apparent".[27] In other words the principle could only be applied in situations where the risk could not be demonstrated completely.[28]

In the landmark case T-13/99 *Pfizer*, the Court circumscribes two tests that must be fulfilled for the application of the principle: First, the Community institutions must choose an acceptable level of protection relative to the scientific evidence, but also other social, political, or other factors.[29] The second test relates to the risk assessment that Community institutions must ascertain – e.g., hazard and the risk posed to human health – prior to making a decision on the measures necessary for achieving its chosen level of protection.[30]

In the first test, the consideration by community institutions of social, political, and other factors relative to the scientific evidence to determine the risk threshold imports discretion in the balancing exercise that may warrant the possibility for judicial review in application of the principle.[31] In case of such review, the Court will only seek to ascertain whether the Community institutions decision was "manifest error or a misuse of powers" or have "clearly exceeded the bounds of their discretion".[32] The Court also states that where institutions are "required to make complex assessments" judicial review must be limited.[33] In addition to the stipulation of the threshold of risk and the requirement of scientific evidence in the first test, the second test introduces the element of proportionality of

---

25 Case 236/01, *Monsanto* [2003] ECR I-08105, para. 106; Case E-3/00, *EFTA Surveillance Authority v Norway* EFTA Court Reports 2000–20001, p. 73, paras. 36–38.
26 Case T-13/99 Pfizer (n 22).
27 Joined Cases T-74/00 etc., *Artegodan* [2002] ECR II-4945, para. 185, *Pfizer* and *ATC* (n 22) above, para. 139. See previously Case C-180/96 *United Kingdom v Commission* [1998] ECR I-2265, para. 99, (the BSE judgment) Case T-199/96 *Bergaderm and Goupil v Commission* [1998] ECR II-2805, para. 66.
28 Bell, S. and McGillivray, D., *Environmental Law* (Oxford: Oxford University Press, 2008) p. 68.
29 *Pfizer* (n 22) above, paras. 151–153.
30 Ibid., 154–156.
31 Ibid., 166–169. Note that Judicial review is, however, limited to procedural and administrative guarantees.
32 Ibid.
33 Ibid.

risk – i.e., the measure chosen must be proportionate to the risk.[34] The two-part test analysed above has also been applied to the acts of Member States, who may exercise their own discretion provided the level of protection is not based on a purely hypothetical risk.[35]

Indeed, case law has provided the primary basis upon which the precautionary principle has developed. Judgments of the Court of Justice have defined the principle's meaning, scope, and limitations, all the while demonstrating increasing evidence of the re-balancing of environmental, economic, and social interests. According to Faure and Skogh, industrial optimism, i.e., the belief that benefits normally exceed the harm of industry, was particularly strong during the twentieth century.[36] Furthermore, economic growth and the development of social security systems were intended to compensate for the potential damage caused. Now, although the belief remains that the benefits of industrial operation outweigh the costs, this industrial optimism has lost its dominant position in our society, to be replaced by other interests and beliefs.[37]

This view is supported by the decision in *Artegodan and Others v Commission* by finding that standard of integration of 'high level protection' necessary for operation of the precautionary principle, and applicable to other policies, demands that the protection of human health take precedence over economic interests.[38] The General Court held that the principle was designed to ensure that any regulatory choice must "comply with the principle that the protection of public health, safety and the environment is to take precedence over economic interests".[39] Thus, by means of the precautionary principle, the objectives of environmental protection and social welfare have taken an increasingly important role in the deliberation of costs and benefits.

In C-28/09 *Commission v. Austria*,[40] the Court of Justice described the objectives of health and environmental protection as being "closely linked".[41] But it also held that, despite being precluded by Union law on the free movement of goods, a national measure prohibiting lorries from carrying certain goods on the

---

34 *Artegodan* (n 27) para. 185, citing Case C-180/96 *United Kingdom v Commission* (n 27) above, para. 99; Case C-157/96 *National Farmers' Union and Others* [1998] ECR I-2211, para. 66.
35 See, for example, Case C-463/01 *Commission v Germany* [2004] ECR-I 11705, para. 74; Case C-192/01 *Commission v Denmark*, [2003] ECR I-9693; Case C-121/00 *Criminal Proceedings Against Walter Hahn* [2002] ECR I-09193; Case C-286/02 *Bellio F.lli Srl v Prefettura di Treviso* [2004] ECR I-3465.
36 Faure, M. and Skogh, G., *The Economic Analysis of Environmental Policy and Law: An Introduction* (Cheltenham: Edward Elgar, 2003) pp. 23–24.
37 Ibid.
38 Artegodan (n 27, this chapter) paras. 183–184. The Court thus places a limitation on the discretionary powers of community institutions identified in case T-13/99 *Pfizer* (n 22, this chapter).
39 Ibid., 186.
40 Case C-28/09 *Commission v Austria* EU:C:2010:854.
41 Ibid., 122.

grounds of the protection of air quality could be justified by an objective of public interest such as public health or environmental protection.

Interestingly, this preference for environmental or social interests over economic ones is increasingly prevalent in internal market measures, all of which have primarily economic aims. In the realisation of the internal market, the EU has come to recognise the competing policy objectives and social imperatives that will, on occasion, hamper the realisation of a full internal market, the CJEU itself seemingly conceding that the internal market project should not be a purely economic exercise.[42]

In the trade context, which usually has an inherent economic bias, the precautionary principle has been applied under Article 34 TFEU which prohibits quantitative restrictions on imports and all measures affecting free movement of goods. The Treaty provides for general exceptions, including the protection of human, animal, or plant life or health, provided it does not constitute unjustifiable discrimination.[43] The Court of Justice defined this prohibition in terms of "all trading rules enacted by member states which are capable of hindering, directly or indirectly, actually or potentially, intra-community trade" between Member States.[44] The breath of coverage of "all trading rules" and the potentiality of impact thereto imports within it also considerations of protection of human, animal, or plant life or health.

In effect, a Member State's decision to withdraw a product from the market in the name of precaution may constitute a technical barrier to the free movement of goods.[45] Yet, there is now an increasing recognition that the existence of a risk to public health may permit a Member State to impose such a restriction to the free movement of goods. In order to assess whether such a health hazard exists, the Court must refer to the results of international scientific research and, in doing so, define the scope and limitations of the precautionary principle.

The Court has ruled that Member States can uphold trade barriers for the purposes of health protection. This includes cases where there has been insufficient evidence or lack of scientific consensus;[46] and where scientific research was being undertaken but "appeared not to be sufficiently advanced to be able to determine with certainty the critical quantities and the precise effects" of the goods affected.[47]

---

42  See Case C-341/05 *Laval un Partneri Ltd v Svenska Byggnadsarbetareförbundet and Others (Laval)* [2007] ECR I-11767.
43  Article 36 TFEU.
44  Case 8–74 *Procureur du Roi v Benoit and Gustave Dassonville* [1974] ECR 837, para. 5.
45  de Sadeleer, *Environmental Principles* (n 19) 361.
46  Case 53/80 *Officier van Justitie v Koninklijke Kaasfabriek Eyssen* [1981] ECR I-409, Case 174/82 *Sandoz* [1983] ECR I-2445, C-247/84 *Motte* [1985] ECR I-1329, C-304/84 *Ministère public v Muller* ECR I-1511; See also de Sadeleer, *Environmental Principles* (n 19) 361.
47  See Cases C-227/82 *Van Bennekom* [1983] ECR I-3883 and C-473/98 *Toolex* [2000] ECR I-5681.

In case C-58/10 *Monsanto*, the Court was required to consider the conditions according to which the French authorities could adopt an emergency measure affecting a GMO product, in accordance with Article 23 of Directive 2001/18/EC on the deliberate release into the environment of GMOs.[48] It established a standard for determining what may likely constitute a risk to human health, animal health, or the environment. The Court held that the risk "must be established on the basis of new evidence based on reliable scientific data" and that "the protective measures in question cannot validly be based on a purely hypothetical approach to the risk, founded on mere assumptions which have not yet been scientifically verified".[49]

However, this broad interpretation of scientific findings is not without limits. For example, in 74/82 *Commission v. Ireland*, the Court found that, even in cases of scientific uncertainty, the precautionary principle cannot be used to justify measures that disproportionately restrict the free movement of goods.[50]

This prioritisation of social welfare over economic concerns could be seen as even more evident if we were to follow Sunstein's distinction between strong and weak interpretations of the precautionary principle.[51] On the one hand, a weak interpretation would mean that the potential for a precautionary measure must be modified by balancing the costs and benefits of taking action.[52] And, on the other hand, a strong interpretation would prohibit any action, resulting in significant or irreversible environmental harm, regardless of the cost of doing so.[53]

Despite arguing that the latter interpretation, if consistent, would demonstrate the Court's more favourable approach towards environmental or social interests, Sunstein acknowledges that the EU has demonstrated evidence of both versions of the principle, seemingly vacillating between the two ends of the spectrum.[54] The case *Pfizer* provides a pertinent example. The General Court upheld a ban in *Pfizer* even though "no risk assessment had been conducted, when there was limited or no evidence of such bacterial resistance arising, when there was no present need for the use of such antibiotics in human medicine," and even when the EU's Scientific Committee for Animal Nutrition (SCAN) had recommended against the ban.[55] This application of the precautionary principle is in line with Sunstein's strong version.

---

48  C-58/10 *Monsanto and Others* [2011] ECR I-7763; OJ L 106/1, 17 April 2011.
49  Ibid., 76–77.
50  Case 74/82 *Commission v Ireland* [1984] ECR I-317; de Sadeleer, *Environmental Principles* (n 19) 362.
51  Sunstein, C.R., *Laws of Fear: Beyond the Precautionary Principle* (Cambridge: Cambridge University Press, 2005) p. 21.
52  Bell and McGillivray (n 28) 70.
53  Ibid.
54  Sunstein (n 51) 21.
55  *Pfizer* (n 22); Sunstein (n 51) 21–22.

Similarly in T-70/99 *Alpharma Inc v Council* the Court found that there is no need to conduct a formal assessment, even when the risk was highly speculative and SCAN had recommended against a ban.[56]

> It is sufficient that the risk exists, that serious concerns have been expressed in scientific literature and in the reports of various conferences and bodies and that, if such transmission actually occurred, it could have serious consequences for human health.[57]

At the other end of the spectrum, Sunstein argues that the Court of Justice has been more cautious about the precautionary principle, applying a more 'weak' approach. In C-236/01 *Monsanto Agricoltura Italia* the Court of Justice ruled that in order for Italy's ban on genetically modified maize to be upheld, at least some evidence must show that consumption threatens human health, the mere possibility of danger is not enough.[58]

In addition to the above developments, there is increasing evidence that the use of the precautionary principle extends further than cases of human health to matters of environmental protection. However, it seems that the results of such cases differ in terms of the balance between economic and environmental interests.[59] For instance, an anomaly in the application of the precautionary principle has been identified by Chenye,[60] regarding the definition of 'waste' in the interpretation of the Framework Waste Directive with respect-recycled materials, because the term 'discard' is itself not defined.[61] So that in *Van de Walle*,[62] involving a leak of petroleum onto land, the Court held that the term 'discard' could not be given a restrictive interpretation because of the environmental protection objective and especially the need to implement the precautionary principle underpinning the Directive.[63] In effect it finds the term 'discard' included

---

56 Case T-70/99 *Alpharma Inc v Council*; Sunstein [2002] (n 51) 21–22.
57 Ibid.
58 C-236/01 *Monsanto Agricultura Italia* [2003] ECR I-8725; Marchant, G.E., and Mossman, K.L., *Arbitrary and Capricious: The Precautionary Principle in the European Union Courts* (Washington DC: American Enterprise Institute, 2004) pp. 54–63, cited in Sunstein (n 51) 22.
59 Fleurke, F.M., "Analysis: What Use for Article 95(5) EC?", *Journal of Environmental Law*, (2008) 20, no. 2, 267, 4.
60 See Cheyne, I., "The Definition of Waste in EC Law", *Journal of Environmental Law* (2002) 14, 61–73;
61 Council Directive 91/156/EEC of 18 March 1991 amending Directive 75/442/EEC on waste [1991] OJ L 78. Waste is defined in the Directive as anything which falls in a list contained in Annex I: The list includes production or consumption residues, off-specification or out-of-date products, and contaminated materials.
62 Case C-1/03, *Criminal Proceedings Against Paul Van de Walle, et al.*, 7 September 2004, nyr.
63 Para. 45, relying on Joined Cases C-418/97 and C-419/97 *ARCO Chemie Nederland and Others* [2000] ECR I-4475, paras. 36–40.

accidental leakage and thereby the leaked hydrocarbons and the contaminated soil were both regarded as waste.

A similar issue of interpretation to give effect to the precautionary principle in order to protect the environment via the Habitats Directive is examined in the case of *Waddenzee*.⁶⁴ By Article 6(3) of that Directive, public authorities must not authorise plans or projects likely to have significant effect on the environment until they ascertain that it would "not adversely affect the integrity of the site concerned". Applying the precautionary principle, the Court employed a very strong interpretation of the requirement to infer obligation on the authorities to "make sure" or be "convinced" that no adverse effects will occur; or to refuse authorisation where "doubt remains as to the absence of adverse effects".⁶⁵ Authorisation must only be given where "no reasonable scientific doubt remains as to the absence of such effects".⁶⁶

When it comes to harmonisation of the internal market and environmental protection through application of the precautionary principle, it seems that the European institutions are unwilling to tip the balance in favour of environmental interests. This is, *inter alia*, to the fact that the right that Member States would otherwise enjoy to choose individual levels of protection may be extinguished by exhaustive EU harmonisation in relevant area.⁶⁷ Article 114(5) TFEU sets out the provisions for Member States wanting to introduce more stringent domestic standards than those set out in a harmonisation measure. In such cases, the Member State concerned must fulfil an even more onerous set of requirements than those wishing to maintain standards under Article 114(4).

They must demonstrate that there is new scientific evidence relating to the protection of the environment or to the working environment which was not previously available and thus not considered by the Commission when the harmonisation measure was introduced. Concerned Member States must also show that the issue at hand and the reason for the required stricter standards is "specific to that Member State".⁶⁸ Moreover, unlike under Article 114(4) TFEU, the exceptions listed in Article 36 TFEU cannot be used to justify a national derogation made under Article 114(5) TFEU.⁶⁹ These requirements have been interpreted strictly by the Court as it is assumed that the EU institutions were

---

64 Case C-127/02, *Landelijke Vereniging tot Behoud van de Waddenzee* v *Staatssecretaris van Landbouw, Natuurbeheer en Visserij*, 7 September 2004, nyr.
65 Ibid., paras. 55–57.
66 Ibid., para. 59.
67 On the difficulty in establishing exhaustiveness of Community harmonisation and how other flexibilities apply in practice into community legislation, see Scott, J., "International Trade and Environmental Governance: Relating Rules (And Standards) in the EU and the WTO", *European Journal of International Law* (2004) 15, no. 15, 307–354.
68 Humphreys, M., "Consistency in European Environmental Protection: Towards a General Principle?" *Columbia Journal of European Law* (2013) 19, 313, 13; Art. 114(5) TFEU.
69 Humphreys (n 68) 13; Case C-512/99 *Germany v Commission* [2003] ECR I-845, 40–41 and Case C-3/00 *Denmark v Commission* [2003] ECR I-2643, 57–58, cited in Barnard (n 5) 620.

aware of legislation and specific issues at the time of drafting the measure, but chose not to act differently.[70] This, in turn, implies a high threshold, whereby it is not possible for a Member State to seek a higher level of protection, or to rely on the precautionary principle, unless this is justified by new science.[71]

Nevertheless, the outlook is more promising in case law relating to matters outside the scope of Article 114(4) and (5) TFEU. For example: the conservation of biodiversity (*Bluhme*), waste management (*Commission v Denmark*), water protection (*Standley*), and prevention of climate change (*Preussen Elektra*), have all been recognised by the Court as pursuing an objective of general interest under which the precautionary principle is sufficient to restrict basic economic rights.[72]

Furthermore, in C-219/07 *Nationale Raad van Dierenkwekers en Liefhebbers VZW*, the Court held that:

> Where it proves impossible to determine with certainty the existence or extent of the risk envisaged because of the insufficiency, inconclusiveness or imprecision of the results of the studies conducted, but the likelihood of real harm to human or animal health or to the environment persists should the risk materialize, the precautionary principle justifies the adoption of restrictive measures.[73]

According to *de Sadeleer*, the result of such an interpretation of the precautionary principle goes much further than initially thought. By interpreting risk in such a way, the Court acknowledges that the principle can "lower the scientific hurdles that [EU] or national regulators face while trying to protect environmental values to the detriment of certain economic rights".[74] This demonstrates a significant step forward in the balancing of the triad in favour of social and environmental interests.

Although sustainable development and sustainability are rarely referred to by the Court of Justice, the sub-principle of precaution is deeply embedded within the legal framework for environmental protection. The Court of Justice seems already prepared to tip the balance between economic interests and

---

70 See also the strict interpretation of Art. 114(5) in Commission Decision 2003/653/EC and the judgments in Joined Cases T-366/03 and T-235/04 *Land Oberösterreich v Commission* [2005] ECR II-4005 and Case C-430/05P *Land Oberösterreich v Commission* [2007] ECR I-7141.
71 Fleurke (n 59) 4.
72 See Cases C-67/97 *Bluhme* [1998] ECR I-8033, C-302/86 *Commission v Denmark* [1988] ECR I-4607, C-293/97 *The Queen v Minister of Agriculture, Fisheries and Food, ex parte Standley and Others* [1999] ECR I-2603, C-379/98 *PreussenElektra* [2001] ECR I-2099; de Sadeleer (n 216) 4–5.
73 Case C-219/07 *Nationale Raad van Dierenkwekers en Liefhebbers VZW* [2008] ECR I-4475, 38, cited in N. de Sadeleer, "The Precautionary Principle in EC Health and Environmental Law", *European Law Journal* (2006), 139–172.
74 Ibid., 4–5.

environmental protection in a way that favours the latter. Without doubt, the increasingly favourable application of EU law, the wide implementation in various policy areas and the interpretation by the Court of Justice could represent a transferable legal framework for promoting environmental protection dimension of sustainable development through the precautionary principle.

There is need to caution that transferability of the framework for application in the EU context of interpretation and case law analysis may be unwieldy and could therefore prove difficult to impose to broader and undefined concept of sustainable development as oppose to it appreciation as a principle. Some of the case law does suggest, in general, ways the re-balancing of economic and environmental protection interests should be attempted.

Both in the free movement of goods and in harmonisation, it has demonstrated, albeit inconsistently, a willingness to allow environmental protection and social welfare concerns to displace those of the establishment of the internal market.[75] While the principle may have been restated and expounded in typical European community legal context, it still trails along the central objective established in the international sustainable development.

## Conclusion

Sustainable development has application in the EU legal order through the precautionary principle and especially promotes the environmental protection dimensions of sustainable development. This chapter has shown that precautionary principle can capably transpose sustainable development through EU law, policy, and practice to promote environmental protection. Both the principles of precaution and protection provide an appreciable legal framework in which a general principle of sustainable development could sit.

The analysis reveals that although sustainable development and sustainability are rarely referred to by the Court of Justice, sub-principle of precaution is deeply embedded within the legal framework for environmental protection. The increasingly favourable application of EU law, the wide implementation in various policy areas and the objective interpretations by the Court of Justice ensures a transferable legal framework for promoting the environmental protection dimension of sustainable development through the precautionary principle.

Interpretation of the precautionary principle in legislation and policy and its enforcement by the Court, the EU institutions, and the national authorities bolsters the legal effect of the principle including on the basis of enforcement. Enforcement as a process itself can be sustainable, by balancing the three competing interests – environmental, economic, and social – in a way that ensures legal and political credibility. Some of the case law does suggest, in general, ways the re-balancing of economic and environmental protection interests should be attempted.

---

75 See Humphreys (n 68) 313, for further discussion.

# 5 The polluter pays principle
## Economic aspects of sustainability in the EU

Chapter 4 considered how sustainable development could be applied through the precautionary principle to promote environmental protection in the EU legal order. It noted the specific methods of transposition in the EU: through policy and legislative documents as an objective of EU law; through administrative actions; and through the effect of the case decisions in the Court. These methods of transposition are considered again in this chapter in examining the application of the polluter pays principle. The polluter pays principle can capably transpose sustainable development through EU law, policy, and practice primarily to address economic aspects of sustainability. The economic aspects relate to the reliance on market and non-market mechanisms, internalisation- and incentive-based economic instruments and measures that balance economic interests for regional pollution regulation and ultimately worldwide environmental problems. The premise is that sustainable development, in EU law and policy, is associated closely with the development of environmental law and policy, which is built on a framework of principles and the polluter pays is key for economic regulation to achieve environmental policy objectives. The rationale of the polluter pays principle is that environmental damage should, as a priority, be rectified at the source and that the polluter should pay (Article 191(2)).

### The polluter pays principle and sustainable development

The polluter pays principle, like the precautionary principle, is one of the well-established legal concepts in EU environmental law, intrinsically linked to the objective and realisation of sustainable development. The OECD was the first to identify the principle as a useful instrument for allocating the costs of pollution prevention and control. The OECD applied it to distinguish the role of the principle in environmental matters from its origin as an economic rule of 'external' cost allocation.[1]

---

1 Recommendation of the Council Concerning International Economic Aspects of Environmental Policies, C(72)128, (OECD 1972). It aims: "to encourage the rational use of scarce environmental resources and to avoid distortions in international trade and investment".

The principle was adopted in the Rio Declaration as a global strategy for pollution control that would minimise the regulatory burden on states. It called on national authorities to take steps – through cost 'internalisation' and through the use of 'economic instruments' – to make persons who engage in polluting activities bear the environmental costs, i.e., the full costs, including prevention and control measures.[2] By seeking to integrate environmental protection and economic activities to internalise the costs of pollution, the polluter pays principle enshrines the principle of integration.

The polluting conduct or activity that incurs a cost could include varying polluter obligations such different levels of responsibility for industrial emissions; uses of natural resources for economic or social purposes that cause environmental deterioration; and producer responsibility to improve the waste profile of their products.[3] The identification of 'environmental' as the costs burden widens the concept of costs to include many pollution challenges that derive from modern economic activities and technology and the variety of methods needed to tackle them.[4]

The polluter pays principle has a firm legal basis as a principle of law deriving from a variety of legal sources including international and regional treaties, domestic legislation, and as a regional custom, particularly in Europe.[5] It takes varying legal forms in international treaties as a principle of guidance, as an approach to consider or apply, and as a way to impute responsibility in some dangerous cases.[6]

## The polluter pays and economic regulation in EU law, policy, and practice

### The polluter pays in EU law and policy

The principle was noted in the First Environmental Action Programme (1973–1976), according to which the polluter would be responsible for the costs occasioned by the prevention and control of nuisances. The procedures for applying

---

2  Rio Declaration on Environment and Development, 13 June 1992, adopted by the UNCED at Rio de Janeiro. UN Doc A/CONF. 151/26 (Vol. 1) (August 1992) ILM 874, 1992; For the formulation of the principle see supra Chapter 1, p. 14.
3  Categorised as: 'polluter pays principle, 'polluter responsibility principle', 'beneficiary pays principle', 'user pay principle', 'producer responsibility', 'extended polluter responsibility'; See Schwartz, P., "Polluter Pays Principle", in Fitzmaurice, M. D., Ong, D. and Merkouris, P. (Eds.), *Research Handbook on International Environmental Law* (Cheltenham: Edward Elgar, 2010) pp. 243–261 at 247–248.
4  For the environmental and other costs that may be connected with economic regulation of pollution for sustainability see Chapter 2 (note 78). See Schwartz, P., "The Polluter-Pays Principle", in Viñuales, J.E. (Ed.), *Rio Declaration on Environment and Development: A Commentary* (Oxford, UK: Oxford University Press, 2015) p. 433.
5  Ibid., 435–436.
6  See Chapter 1 supra (n 81–84) p. 16.

the principle were specified in Recommendation 75/436/Euratom, ECSC, EEC of 3 March 1975, which broadly replicated the rules elaborated by the OECD.[7] The polluter pays principle has appeared in the founding Treaties of the European Union (then Community) since the 1986 Single European Act.[8]

The concept of polluter has evolved first in respect of personality category to include states, corporations, industries, and individuals.[9] The second development is in relation to the nature and effects of conduct or activity, extending these to include natural resource use for economic or social purposes and attaching liability to direct or indirect environmental consequences.[10]

The principle encourages the use of economic and fiscal instruments to influence the behaviour of producers and to promote technologies and processes, which are consistent with resource conservation.[11] Making any polluter pay damages links the legal enforceability of a penalty with the economic imperative of efficiency. In other words, no one should get something for nothing and everything has a value. As such, the principle in itself and, in particular, its enforcement, can bring about the achievement of sustainable development.[12]

The polluter pays principle, therefore, has a source and context within the EU legal order, and to some extent the Treaties give the principle meaning and force. It is prominently transposed and applied in law and policy relating to climate change emissions reduction, civil aviation,[13] and renewable energy incentive schemes.[14] The EU has also applied the principle in policy areas of environmental cost allocation generally concerning, disposal of waste oils, waste landfills, and water policy, and, quite recently, to nuclear liabilities respectively.[15]

---

7   de Sadeleer, N., *Environmental Principles: From Political Slogans to Legal Rules* (Oxford: Oxford University Press, 2005) p. 28.
8   See Single European Act (1986) Art. 130(r)(2) and Art.174(2); Council Recommendation of 3 March 1975 regarding cost allocation and action by public authorities on environmental matters 75/436/EURATOM, EEC.
9   EC Recommendation (1975) ibid para. 2 – "'Polluter' is defined as 'natural or legal persons governed by public or private law who are responsible for pollution'".
10  See Schwartz, P., (2010) (n 3) p. 247.
11  Horspool, M. and Humphreys, M., *European Union Law*, 7th edition (Oxford: Oxford University Press, 2012) p. 494.
12  Humphreys, M., *Sustainability in European Transport Policy* (London: Routledge, 2010) Chapter 3.
13  Directive 2008/101/EC of the European Parliament and of the Council of 19 November 2008 amending Directive 2003/87/EC so as to include aviation activities in the scheme for greenhouse gas emission allowance trading within the community.
14  Council Directive 2009/28/EC of 23 April 2009 on the promotion of the use of energy from renewable energy sources and amending and subsequently repealing Directives 2001/77/EC and 2003/30/EC, OJ 2009 L 140/16.
15  See, for instance, *Council Recommendation Regarding Cost Allocation and Action by Public Authorities on Environmental Matters,* 1975: 1; Directive 75/439/EEC on the Disposal of Waste Oils, 1975: Arts 13 and 14; Directive 1999/31/EC on Waste Landfill: Article 10; Directive 2000/60/EC on Water Policy Article 9.

'Producer responsibility' applies to place responsibility for the environmental impact associated with a product onto the producers of that product. This is done through directives on packaging waste, waste electronic and electrical equipment, and end-of-life vehicles.[16] Under the Waste Packaging Directive, for example, those involved in the production, use, import, and distribution of packaging and packaged products should, in accordance with the polluter pays principle, accept responsibility for such waste.[17] The interrelationship between producers of products and users of products has been severally expressed as 'apportionment of liability'[18] and 'appropriation of burden' and 'burden sharing'.[19] Also, 'extended polluter responsibility' (EPR) has been used to describe "a policy in which the producer's financial and or physical responsibility for a product is extended to the post-consumer state of the product's life cycle".[20] EPR assumes that polluters will improve the waste profile of their products, by increasing the possibility of reuse and recycling.

In the context of EU liability regimes which transpose the polluter pays principle functions to establish a framework for environmental liability that works to prevent and remedy environmental damage. Alternatively it serves as a complement to state responsibility in international law.[21]

In the judicial context, the Court of Justice has applied the polluter pays principle, providing specific guidance on the scope of polluter responsibility in activities under the regime of certain EU Directives.[22] The principle has been held by the Court to be applicable in financing indemnities for undertakings relating to collecting and/or disposing of waste oils,[23] where the Court clarified that Member States may "choose the form and the methods to be applied in order to attain that result", including by means of a tax or of a charge or in any other manner.[24] The Member States have a broad discretion, when laying down national rules developing or giving concrete expression to the polluter pays principle.[25]

Its consistent application in the EU, in Treaties, and in secondary legislation cements its legal status. Both the OECD and EU are considered to have transformed a mere economic rule into a true legal principle that has transcended its

---

16 Schwartz, P., 2010 (n 3) p. 248.
17 Council Directive 94/62/EC on Packaging and Packaging Waste.
18 Environmental Liability Directive, 2004/35/CE: Article 22.
19 Restriction of Hazardous Substances (ROHs) Directive 2011/65/EU, 2011; Waste Electrical and Electronic Equipment (WEEE) Directive 2012/92/EU, 2012).
20 Schwartz, P., 2010 (n 3) p. 248
21 Article 1 Environmental Liability Directive 2004/35/EC.
22 See *Pontina Case* (2010) – ECJ interpreting Directive 1999/31 Article. 10; and Case C-254/08 *Futura Immobiliare srl* [2009] ECR I-6995 – interpreting Directive 75/442 and Directive 2006/12.
23 Case 172/82 *Syndicat National des Fabricants Raffineurs d'Huile de Graissage et al. v. Groupement d' Intérêt Economique 'Inter-Huiles'* (1983) ECR 555.
24 *Futura Case* (n 22) paras 47–48.
25 Ibid., paras 52 and 55.

mandate from one of recommendations, to binding treaties and EU secondary legislation, with the status of regional custom in most OECD and EU States.[26]

Despite this wide representation of the principle, EU law does not define the meaning of the polluter pays principle. This, for some, results in several gaps, which need to be filled before the principle can really be deemed as 'operational'.[27] There is little in law or policy to support the view that somehow the principle creates obligations or duties. It helps shape policy rather than itself providing any sort of remedy.[28]

That is not to say that the polluter pays principle is to all intents and purposes meaningless, or completely within the discretion of those setting out environmental policy.[29] A principle of law is almost by definition difficult to pin down, and it is in this flexibility that a principle is preferred to a legal absolute.[30] At first reading of Article 191(2), while it is clear that polluters should pay, there is some expectation that generally they do not. This tells us two things: firstly, a principle of law is not an enforceable standard, or not as enforceable as a statement declaring that polluters will or must pay for their pollution. Secondly, there is nevertheless some sort of commitment to adjust legal norms to make polluters pay more than they currently do. A principle, therefore, plays a role in the legal order, even in the absence of setting an enforceable, commonly applicable standard.[31]

### *The polluter pays principle and economic regulation in practice*

The broad concept of polluter paying[32] can accommodate 'environmental costs' and other costs that may be connected with pollution regulation, including inter alia the cost of achieving prescribed environmental quality and protecting human health and the environment; and the social costs, including investment on technology, subsidies, and bans on activities.[33]

The regulatory economic approaches make the polluter pay identified costs including internalisation, use of economic instruments, and emissions standards.

---

26 de Sadeleer, N., *Environmental Principles – From Political Slogans to Legal Rules* (Oxford: Oxford University Press, 2002) p. 26.
27 Bleeker, A., "Does the Polluter Pay? The Polluter Pays Principle in the Case Law of the European Court of Justice", *European Energy and Environmental Law Review* (2009), December, 289–306.
28 Humphreys, M., *Sustainability in European Transport Policy* (London: Routledge, 2010) Chapter 3.
29 Krämer is one commentator who is particularly interested in the precise meaning of the principle, and compares the different language versions of the Treaty of Rome in the search for the meaning that the Court of Justice would use: Krämer, L., *EC Treaty and Environmental Law* (London: Sweet and Maxwell, 1995) p. 56.
30 Humphreys, M., 2010 (n 28).
31 Ibid.
32 Article 174(2) para. 1, the Maastricht Treaty 1992.
33 All these costs have been identified in treaties, regulatory statutes, and academic literature. see Schwartz, P., 2010 (n 3) pp. 248–250.

*The polluter pays principle* 77

Internalisation facilitates the inclusion of external effects in economic calculation and corrects misallocations, while assuring the rational management of resources.[34] The emissions standards and targets are set by reference to the amount of emission reduction achievable based on specific technological choices.[35]

For example, the principle applies through the setting of corporate fuel economy targets or standards by a responsible authority limiting each vehicle's environmental impact, which the car manufacturer must meet or exceed, and failure to do so leads to the payment of a fine.[36] Also, feebates have been used to increase the rate at which consumers would purchase cars equipped with a catalytic converter, and the fees collected may be used to subsidise fuel-efficient purchases.[37] Energy standards are used to encourage firms to shift away from carbon-intensive production toward the use of cleaner fuels. Renewable energy incentives are the most effective and specifically targeted stimulus to decarbonise the economy in numerous Member States of the EU.[38] Finally, support for renewable energy in the EU does not constitute state aid prohibited under the Treaty.[39]

The polluter pays in economic regulation is most visible in the EU system for greenhouse gas (GHG) emission allowance trading (EU ETS) in order to promote reductions of GHG emissions in a cost-effective and economically efficient manner.[40] The EU uses ETS to meet obligations under the Kyoto protocol to the Climate Change Convention. It is the largest multinational GHG emissions trading scheme, allowing regulated entities to use carbon credits and carbon projects to meet obligations under the Protocol.[41]

Legislation has been introduced implementing the 2030 Climate and Energy package agreed in 2014,[42] by which EU Member States are to bring into force the

---

34 Tietenberg, T.H., "Economic Instruments for Environmental Regulation" *Oxford Review of Economic Policy* (1990) 6, 17, at 18.
35 See Stewart, R.B., "Economic Incentives for Environmental Protection: Opportunities and Obstacles", in Revesz, E. *et al* (Eds.), *Environmental Law, the Economy and Sustainable Development* (Cambridge: Cambridge University Press, 2000) p. 171 at 175.
36 See Directive 2009/30/EC of 23 April 2009 amending Directive 98/70/EC as regards the specification of petrol, diesel, and gas-oil, and introducing a mechanism to monitor and reduce greenhouse gas emissions: OJ L 140/88. Note that Firms that exceed their fuel economy requirements can sell credits associated with that additional fuel economy to firms that do not meet the standard in a given year.
37 Directive 2009/30/EC of 23 April 2009, ibid.
38 See Directive 2009/28/EC of The European Parliament and Of the Council of 23 April 2009 on the promotion of the use of energy from renewable sources and amending and subsequently repealing Directives 2001/77/EC and 2003/30/EC OJ EU, L 140/16.
39 Case C-379/98 *Preussen Elektra, G v Schhleswag AG* [2001] ECR I-2099 and below at section 2.3.2 of this chapter.
40 Directive 2003/87/EC of the European Parliament and of the Council of 13 October 2003 establishing a scheme for greenhouse gas emission allowance trading within the Community and amending Council Directive 96/61/EC (25 October 2003, OJ L 275, p. 32 as amended).
41 Directive 2003/87/EC (2003) 275.
42 See Article 2(1) of the draft Directive 2009/29.

laws, regulations, and administrative provisions necessary to comply by deadline for transposition (i.e., by end of 2018).[43] In this cap-and-trade system, firms can buy and sell the certified emission allowances through a tradable quota system, or via variable emissions reduction credits and transferable market permit systems based on their polluting needs.[44] The effectiveness of the principle is seen in the very high level of compliance with the EU ETS rules in the aviation sector.[45] Also, the principle is further applied by way of sanction, through prohibition on the selling of allowances where the installations are non-compliant with the system requirements.[46]

The Carbon Capture Storage instrument is an innovative polluter pays principle instrument but a peculiar method that seeks to reduce GHG emissions to mitigate climate change.[47] In the Carbon Capture Storage regime, the cost is in the pollution prevention and control – the operation and maintenance of the carbon dioxide storage facility. They tend to transfer the owner/operator responsibility for the carbon dioxide storage facility to pay for carbon dioxide pollution. The EU ETS has been amended to encourage investment in Carbon Capture Storage to reduce carbon dioxide emissions for Member States and the EU.[48] Some States have adopted regulatory instruments providing financial incentives for Carbon Capture Storage investments and the long-term liability costs associated with it.[49]

There are also non-market based incentive instruments applying the polluter pays principle. These include mainly subsidies and financial assistance. Governments may provide financial or other form of economic assistance to low-emitting activities or technology application as an incentive to motivate a particular environmentally beneficial outcome. These can take the form of tax credit, tax breaks, or other forms of financial assistance. In such cases the cost

---

43 The European Commission Proposal for a Directive of the European Parliament and of the Council amending Directive 2003/87/EC to enhance cost-effective emission reductions and low-carbon investments of 15 July 2015 (COM(2015) 337 final) 2015/148 (COD) setting out the draft EU emissions trading scheme legal framework for the fourth trading period as from 2020.
44 The scope of Directive 2003/87/EC has been broadened from 1 January 2013 to include certain sectors of the chemicals industry (see Annex 1 of Directive 2009/29).
45 Note that aircraft operators responsible for more than 99.5 per cent of aviation emissions covered under the EU ETS complied including more than 100 commercial aircraft companies based outside EU, which operated flights within the EEA.
46 See www.emissions-euets.com/directive-200387ec-of-the-european-parliament-and-of-the-council-of-13-october-2003-establishing-a-scheme-for-greenhouse-gas-emission-allowance-trading.
47 See Report of the Interagency Task Force on Carbon Capture and Storage August 2010 p.7 (CCS Report).
48 Council Directive 2009/29/EC (supra note 18) 140.
49 Also Directive 2009/31/EC of the European Parliament and of the Council of 23 April 2009 on the geological storage of C02 and amending Council Directive 85/337/EEC, European Parliament and Council Directives 2000/60/EC, 2001/80/EC, 2004/35/EC, 2006/12/EC, 2008/1/EC and Regulation (EC) No 1013/2006.

is not borne by the polluter but by the taxpayer.[50] Similarly, 'aid and payments' are incentive mechanisms used as a bargaining instrument for buying from the polluter the right to pollute. Subsidies as incentives have grown to be popular in countries seeking the deployment of energy technologies, which indirectly reduces GHG emissions.[51]

Without doubt, there is extensive and comprehensive representation of the polluter pays principle in legal instruments and administrative standards and case law. It is now useful to illustrate how the polluter pays principle is integrated, in practice, into selected EU economically driven policy areas – transport, agriculture, competition, and state aid. The result could also mean that full integration into the priorities of the various policy areas might demonstrate that environmental protection is being attributed a more significant role when contrasted with conflicting economic interests.

*Transport policy*

In the field of transport, the Commission has already provided for the comprehensive integration of environmental concerns, and, in particular, pollution control, into its policy agenda.[52] Although not explicitly referring to the polluter pays principle, the 2008 Commission Communication entitled "Greening Transport" is the starting point of the new wave of measures for the internalisation of external costs, setting out a mode and impact-specific strategy covering all modes of transport.[53]

In the road sector, the Commission has promoted the internalisation of external costs through measures such as minimum taxes for motor fuel;[54] the incorporation of a carbon dioxide component into the registration and annual circulation taxes for cars;[55] and the revision of the Eurovignette Directive.[56]

In the maritime sector, the Commission has confirmed its obligation to include shipping in the EU's emissions trading scheme.[57] An obligation which is in line with the EU's 2009 ETS law which states that if there was no global solution

---

50 Schwartz, P., 2015 (n 4).
51 Ibid.
52 For further discussion of how the polluter pays principle interacts with EU transport policy, see Humphreys (n 142).
53 Communication from the Commission to the European Parliament and the Council: Greening Transport, COM(2008) 433 final of the 8 July 2008, section 3.1.
54 Council Directive 2003/96/EC of 27 October 2003 restructuring the Community framework for the taxation of energy products and electricity, OJ L 238 of the 31 October 2003.
55 Proposal for a Council Directive on passenger car related taxes, COM(2005) 261 final of the 5 July 2005.
56 Directive 2011/76/EU of the European Parliament and of the Council of 27 September 2011 amending Directive 1999/62/EC on the charging of heavy goods vehicles for the use of certain infrastructures, OJ L 269/1 of the 14 October 2011.
57 Ibid.

to maritime pollution in the International Maritime Organisation by the end of 2011, the Commission must act unilaterally.[58] It is also hoped that by internalising external costs in maritime transport, this will have a positive impact on the use of inland waterway transport, a mode with a much greater level of energy efficiency.[59]

Lastly, in the aviation sector the Commission has put forward several proposals to internalise external costs, the most prominent of which is the proposal to include carbon dioxide emissions in the emissions trading scheme. Such a programme would allow airlines to sell or bank surplus allowances, provided their emissions levels fall under their allowances. Alternatively, if they exceed their emissions allowance, the programme would require them either to take measures to reduce their emissions or to buy additional allowances from the market. Since the start of 2012, emissions from all flights within the European Economic Area are included in the emissions trading scheme, with exemptions for operators with low emissions. Steps to include in the emission trading scheme flights to and from non-EEA countries have been suspended.[60] The application of the EU Aviation Directive to non-EU airlines aims to resolve market competitiveness resulting from pricing carbon.[61]

According to the, then, EU's Climate Action Commissioner, Connie Hedegaard, the approach enshrined in the emissions trading scheme reflects the design and purpose of the polluter pays principle.[62] Despite this, the approach has also been subject to criticism surrounding the grandfathering of the common allocation method, whereby allowance is allocated on the basis of historical emissions, thereby providing more free allocation to the highest emitting entities. According to some, this practice is, in essence, contrary to the polluter pays principle.[63]

---

58 Directive 2009/29/EC of the European Parliament and of the Council of 23 April 2009 amending Directive 2003/87/EC so as to improve and extend the greenhouse gas emission allowance trading scheme of the Community, OJ L 140/63 of the 5 June 2009.
59 Greening Transport (n 151) 3.1.
60 European Commission, Climate Action, "Reducing Emissions from the Aviation Sector", 4 September 2012, http://ec.europa.eu/clima/policies/transport/aviation/index_en.htm accessed 30/10/2012
61 Meltzer, J., "Climate Change & Trade: The EU Aviation Directive & the WTO", *Journal of International Economic Law* (2012) 15, 111, 118–119.
62 European Commission, Hedegaard, C., "Time to Get Serious About Aviation Emissions", European Commission, 31 May 2011, see http://ec.europa.eu/commission_2010-2014/hedegaard/headlines/articles/2011-05-31_01_en.htm
63 For contrasting views on the compatibility of the polluter pays principle with the practice of grandfathering see: Nash, J., "Too Much Market? Conflict Between Tradable Pollution Allowances and the 'Polluter Pays' Principle", *Harvard Environmental Law Review* (2000) 24, no. 2, 1–59; and Woerdman, E., Clò, S. and Arcuri, A., "Chapter 5 – Emissions Trading and the Polluter-Pays Principle: Grandfathering and Over-Allocation", in Faure, M. and Peeters, M., *Climate Change and European Emissions Trading: Lessons for Theory and Practice* (Cheltenham: Edward Elgar, 2008).

It seems that, from an interpretation and application perspective, the internalisation of external costs is an approach that pervades a large part of transport policy and legislation whereby it is recognised that pollution must be paid for – at some level at least – in order to achieve sustainable environmental and economic development. Trouble may lie, however, in the enforcement of these standards, and whether the sanctions for failure to pay are sufficient to incentivise change. Moreover, whether imposing such standards at an EU-level is sufficient to make a real, substantial imprint on the impact of pollution on the environment worldwide is doubtful. Certainly, from this perspective, the EU-level efforts seem symbolic at best.

*Common agricultural policy*

Although not initially designed as an environmentally friendly policy,[64] the EU's common agricultural policy (CAP) has since acknowledged the need to use principles, and in particular the polluter pays principle, to integrate environmental protection into everyday farming practices.[65] This is in recognition of the fact that agricultural practices and the environment are intertwined, with the former being capable of having both a positive and negative impact on the latter and *vice versa*. Therefore, to ensure integration of environmental concerns, farmers are required to respect those common rules and standards, which form part of the cross-compliance regime.[66] These rules and standards represent the reference level up to which the costs for complying with these obligations have to be borne by the individual farmer, in line with the polluter pays principle.[67] Non-compliance is subject to sanctions.[68]

This practice has been reinforced by the Community Guidelines for State Aid for Environmental Protection and Energy.[69] The Guidelines make clear that, on

---

64 Grossman, M.R., "Agriculture and the Polluter Pays Principle: An Introduction", *Oklahoma Law Review* (2006) 51, no. 1, 19.
65 Agriculture and the Environment: Introduction, European Commission, Agriculture and Rural Development, 07/03/2012, http://ec.europa.eu/agriculture/envir/index_en.htm last accessed 29/10/2012
66 Council Regulation (EU) 1307/2013 of 17 December 2013 establishing rules for direct payments to farmers under support schemes within the framework of common agricultural policy and repealing Council Regulation (EC) No 637/2008 and Council Regulation (EC) No 73/2009 see Commission Delegated Regulation (EU) No 640/2014 of 11 March 2014 supplementing Regulation (EU) No 1306/2013 with regard to the integrated administration and control system and conditions for refusal or withdrawal of payments and administrative penalties applicable to direct payments, rural development support and cross-compliance.
67 Agriculture and the Environment (n 162).
68 Cross-compliance, European Commission, Agriculture and Rural Development (2012), http://ec.europa.eu/agriculture/envir/cross-compliance/index_en.htm
69 Communication from the Commission, "Guidelines on State Aid for Environmental Protection and Energy", OJ C 200/1 of the 26 June 2014.

the one hand, state aid may be used to enable a full internalisation of costs when the level of environmental protection undertaken goes beyond usual farming practice and is, thereby, higher than the mandatory EU standards. On the other hand "respect for the 'polluter pays principle' [. . .] through environmental legislation ensures in principle that the market failure linked to negative externalities will be rectified. Therefore, state aid is not an appropriate instrument and cannot be granted insofar as the beneficiary of the aid could be held liable for the pollution existing under Union or national law".[70]

The interplay between the CAP and other policies – such as the Common Fisheries Policy – and the integration of environmental protection through the polluter pays principle is also a key issue for the Commission.[71] The coherence and inter-linkage of policies is integral to the furthering of the EU environmental agenda, among other things, no matter what the specific priorities in the policies may be.[72] Such integration of environmental concerns across EU policies is recognised in various cross-cutting frameworks such as the Water Framework Directive;[73] the Marine Strategy Framework Directive;[74] and the Soil Thematic Strategy.[75]

Also, Directive 2004/35/EC, by establishing a framework for environmental liability based upon the polluter pays principle, demonstrates a clear example of the implementation of the principle by the European Commission in the field of agriculture.[76] In Annex III of the Directive, some agricultural activities are included in those which entail an immediate or imminent threat of environmental damage, thus engaging strict liability.[77] Having said this, Grossmann highlights that by stating that the Member States may allow an operator not to bear the cost of remedial actions, providing they satisfy certain conditions, Article 8(3) and (4) of the Directive seem contrary to the purpose of the polluter pays principle.[78]

---

70 Paragraph 44 Communication from the Commission, "Guidelines on State Aid for Environmental Protection and Energy", OJ C 200/1 of the 26 June 2014.
71 See the five fundamental principles of good governance in European Commission, 'European Governance: A White Paper', 25 July 2001, COM(2001) 428 final.
72 See the 'Governance Argument' in Kingston, S., "Integrating Environmental Protection and EU Competition Law: Why Competition Isn't Special", *European Law Journal* (2010) 16, no. 6, 795.
73 Directive 2000/60/EC.
74 Directive 2008/56/EC.
75 Strategy for Soil Protection (n 65); Proposal for a Directive of the European Parliament and of the Council establishing a framework for the protection of soil and amending Directive 2004/35/EC, COM 92006) 232 final of the 22 September 2006 and Report from the Commission to the European Parliament, the Council, the European Economic and Social Committee and the Committee of the Regions – The Implementation of the Soil Thematic Strategy and Ongoing Activities, COM(2012) 46 final of the 13 February 2012.
76 Directive 2004/35/EC.
77 Ibid., Article 3(1).
78 Grossman, M.R., "Agriculture and the Polluter Pays Principle: An Introduction", *Oklahoma Law Review* (2006) 51, no. 1, 25.

This brief analysis, however, reveals clear CAP support for the integration of principles such as the polluter pays through its operations, and relies heavily upon it for its legitimisation. When the futures of both agriculture and the environment are so interdependent, efforts must not only be made to ensure that pollution of the environment is paid for, but also to encourage proactive environmental conservation through compensation.

*Competition and state aid*

Some European Commission decisions have indicated an inclination to exempt, from the controls of competition law, those agreements that contribute to EU environmental policy. In *DSD*,[79] the Commission granted an exemption on the grounds that the exclusivity agreement at issue, despite generating economies of scale, gave "direct practical effect to [the] environmental objectives" set out in a Directive on Packaging Waste,[80] reasoning that "the exclusivity clause in the Service Agreements contributes to improving the production of goods and to promoting technical or economic progress".[81] Having said this, some authors have identified competition law as one area of economic prioritisation which often evades the Court's increasing preponderance for environmental protection.[82] However, whether this position is tenable in the long term is less certain, in the context of the varying priorities in competition law, particularly since the financial crisis of 2008, but perhaps more especially in view of the growing understanding that a *laissez faire* approach will undermine the economic stability of the not-so-future generations.

The matter is as equally vague regarding the application of the polluter pays principle. Competition has, according to some, the "inherent propensity to waste resources",[83] and, as such, plays a significant role in the exacerbation of environmental concerns. If applied, the polluter pays principle could hold certain restrictions and distortions of competition outside the scope of application of Articles 101(1) and (2) TFEU, provided they are necessary to ensure the internalisation of environmental costs.[84]

Article 101(3) provides the necessary legal basis to justify anti-competitive agreements from the Article 101 prohibition. The application of this exemption requires the exercise of discretion by the Commission and relevant Member State authorities, who must balance the interests of fair and open competition with

---

79 DSD, [2001] OJ L 319/1, 143–145.
80 Directive 94/62 [1994] OJ L 365/5.
81 DSD (n 79) 146.
82 See Kingston, S., *Greening EU Competition Law and Policy* (Cambridge: Cambridge University Press, 2012).
83 Vedder, H., "Competition Law and Environmental Protection in Europe – Towards Sustainability?" *Europa Law Publishing* (2003) 59.
84 Ibid., 430.

environmental protection proportionately.⁸⁵ However, whether this balance is actually conducted in a way that reflects the rhetoric behind the importance of integrating environmental concerns is subject to some doubt. In fact, many argue that the Commission's approach is far more economically oriented and consumer-welfare driven.⁸⁶

Certainly, if one looks at the recent documents guiding competition law and policy and its implementation, the polluter pays principle is nowhere to be seen and, at best, only passing reference is made to the objective of environmental protection as a whole.⁸⁷ This could demonstrate a clear division between the interpretation and application of the principle, and its actual enforcement in day-to-day decision-making. Having said this, in the recent EU Competition Law Rules Applicable to Antitrust Enforcement, guidance on the application of Article 101(3) to seemingly anti-competitive measures provides that environmentally efficient gains are capable of outweighing the restrictive effects of competition.⁸⁸

Contrast this rather half-hearted integration of environmental protection interests within the competition law framework under the foundational provisions of Article 101 and 102 TFEU with that of state aid policy and an entirely different approach emerges. As mentioned, the 2014 Guidelines on State Aid permit State subsidies to support efforts by undertakings which go beyond the standards required under the polluter pays principle. This explicit integration highlights the clear distinction between state aid control and the rest of competition policy. Although prohibited in principle, it is argued that state aid exemptions are "premised on a recognition that markets may not always work properly left alone – due, for example, to the presence of externalities – and may need some intervention from the state to work more effectively".⁸⁹ How this differs from the reality of competition, however, is not clear.

---

85  Vedder, H. (n 83) 433.
86  For more on this, see Kingston, S. (n 169) 780.
87  No mention of either the integration of environmental protection or the polluter pays principle are made in the following competition law documents: Commission White Paper on Modernisation of the Rules Implementing Articles 85 and 86 of the EC Treaty, Commission Programme No 99/027, OJ C 132/1 of the 12 May 1999; Commission Notice, Guidelines on Vertical Restraints, OJ 291/1 of the 13 October 2000; Council Regulation (EC) 1/2003 of 16 December 2002 on the implementation of the rules on competition laid down in Articles 81 and 82 of the Treaty, OJ L 1/1 of the 4 January 2003; Communication from the Commission, Notice, Guidelines on the application of Article 81(3) of the Treaty, OJ C 101/97 of the 27 April 2004; Communication from the Commission – Guidance on the Commission's enforcement priorities in applying Article 82 of the EC Treaty to abusive exclusionary conduct by dominant undertakings, OJ C 45/7 of the 24 February 2009; DG Competition, Antitrust Manual of Procedures – Internal DG Competition Working Documents on procedures for the application of Articles 101 and 102 TFEU, March 2012, http://ec.europa.eu/competition/antitrust/antitrust_manproc_3_2012_en.pdf
88  See 329. Environmental Standards, Example 5 in EU Competition Law Rules Applicable to Antitrust Enforcement, Volume 1, 1 December 2011, http://ec.europa.eu/competition/antitrust/legislation/handbook_vol_1.pdf
89  Kingston, S. (n 82) 780.

## Critical review of polluter pays approaches to policy

The polluter pays principle is a good illustration of the integration of economic consideration in environmental decision-making to address the regional problem of pollution. Also the idea of charging pollution costs to parties responsible on the argument of efficiency, equity and cost-effectiveness continues to appeal.[90]

There is evidence to suggest that the EU institutions are increasingly interpreting the polluter pays principle as an essential mechanism when developing legislation and policy in a variety of areas which might result in environmental degradation or social harm. There is also evidence to suggest that the Court is taking an increasingly environmentally friendly position when balancing economic with environmental and/or social interests. The implementation of the polluter pays principle appears to vary, depending largely upon the policy field concerned and the extent to which the integration of environmental concerns can, or should, take place. This is no more present than in the field of competition and state aid law and policy, where the integration of environmental concerns through the polluter pays principle differs greatly.

Alternatively, when looking at policy areas such as agriculture or transport, although explicit reference to the polluter pays principle remains limited, the aim of internalising external costs – up to a reasonable and politically palatable level – is a general theme. This is all done with the aim of supporting and incentivising the creation of sustainable systems, capable of supporting themselves in lieu of State or EU funding. There is also a greater reliance on cross-sectoral integration, an approach which is in line with the concept of good governance. More specifically, this approach reflects the aim of coherence, whereby policies must be interlinked, working together to reconcile economic, environmental, and social interests in order to pursue the general EU agenda of sustainable development.

The analysis of the variety of make-the-polluter-pay economic approaches demonstrate that the concept and scope of 'environmental costs' and 'polluter' has diverged so much that while the main focus continues to be on 'costs', it is not always the polluter's costs, or an endeavour to make the polluter pay.[91]

Economic regulation via the polluter pays principle by way of process and product taxes, effluent charges, or the EU emissions trading scheme and emissions crediting, can provide an invaluable revenue stream for governments, which could help reduce the total cost of pollution control to society. Compliance has increased with aviation, and energy standards and costs of complying with the requirements of pollution standards have lowered and products are redesigned in order to comply with waste packaging and recycling laws.

Various polluter pays principle implementation methods see technology as the miracle solution to environmental problems and so rely on economic incentives to encourage adaptation to technology and further investment in the development

---

90 Schwartz, P., 2015 (n 4) 47–8.
91 Schwartz, P., (2015) 447.

of new technologies. Yet the connection between the cost of technology, market competitiveness, productivity, consumption, and environmental pollution remain strange bedfellows, which contradicts the assumption technological solutions will solve all.[92] The economic underpinning of the polluter pays dealings have nurtured a meaning of 'environmental' or 'pollution' cost' or 'polluter' to mean financial gains or other benefit from the business of pollution at a cost to the environment and consumers.

In comparison with the precautionary principle, analysed in Chapter 4, there does seem to be significant evidence to suggest that precaution as expressed in the precautionary principle is capable of being interpreted and applied by the Court in a way which will favour the greater integration of environmental, social, and economic interests. There is also evidence that, when considering the triad, the Court will often tip the balance in favour of social and – increasingly – environmental interests. This could indicate a significant step in EU case law, one which might encourage the institutions to drive forward a more integrated sustainable development agenda, safe in the knowledge that, provided the balance is right, it will be upheld by the Court.

Despite this, the precautionary principle remains contentious. Criticism is founded on the principle's reliance on "sound science in the assessment of risk".[93] As de Sadeleer describes, "the difficulty is that by leaving the realm of rational certainty, precaution necessarily gives rise to controversy and its practical application to conflict".[94] In other words, the principle itself and its support of the sustainable development agenda could be undermined if the scientific predictions upon which economic interests are set aside never materialise.[95]

Nonetheless, taking the polluter pays principle and the precautionary principle together demonstrates how the EU and its institutions can both interpret and enforce the interests of economic development and environmental protection and social welfare in EU law. This, in turn, demonstrates evidence for, and support of, a growing acceptance of the sustainable development agenda, especially in the face of competing – and, in recent years, extremely dominant – economic interests. It reinforces the role of sustainable development as a general principle that can be incorporated through its obligations of result than as an overarching general principle in its own right with limited procedural impact.

Thus, while the general dimension of the polluter pays principle is orientated towards addressing pollution, its consequential environmental protection biases cannot be overlooked, nor can its broad array of policy implications for trade, investment, competition, and development, economic, and social issues. These functions become very important in analysing the polluter pays principle because

---

92 Schwartz, P., (2010) (n 3) 447–448.
93 A good discussion is von Schomberg, R., "The Precautionary Principle and Its Normative Challenges", in Fisher, E. *et al.* (Ed.), *Implementing the Precautionary Principle: Perspectives and Prospects* (Cheltenham: Edward Elgar, 2006) Chapter 2.
94 de Sadeleer, N., 2005 (n 7) 125.
95 Wirth, D., cited Atapattu, S.A., *Emerging Principles of International Environmental Law* (Ardsley: Transnational Publishers, 2006) Chapter 3, pp. 277–278.

they represent the basis upon which polluters assume the responsibility to bear the cost in respect of pollution regulation for environmental protection.

## Conclusion

This analysis in this chapter has argued that the polluter pays principle can capably transpose sustainable development through EU law, policy, and practice. Indeed sustainable development, which in the EU legal order is associated closely with the development of environmental law and policy, and is built on a framework of principles and the polluter pays, is a good illustration of the integration of economic consideration in environmental decision-making to address the regional problem of pollution.

The chapter finds that the EU institutions are increasingly interpreting the polluter pays principle as essential mechanisms when developing legislation and policy in a variety of areas, which might result in environmental degradation or social harm. The analysis also reveals that the Court of Justice is taking an increasingly environmentally friendly position when balancing economic with environmental and/or social interests.

Economic regulation via the polluter pays, through process and production taxes, effluent charges, or the EU emissions trading scheme and emissions crediting, can provide an invaluable revenue stream for governments, which could help reduce the total cost of pollution to the environment and control to society. Compliance has increased with aviation, and energy standards and costs of complying with the requirements of pollution standards have lowered and products are redesigned in order to comply with waste packaging and recycling laws.

In the analysis of specific policy areas such as transport, agriculture, and competition sectors, although explicit reference is made to the polluter pays principle, the emphasis remains limited to the aim of internalising external costs. The internalisation of external costs is an approach that pervades a large part of transport policy and legislation. This is done with the aim of supporting and incentivising the creation of sustainable systems, capable of supporting themselves in lieu of State or EU funding. The road, marine, and aviation sectors bear this evidence. There is need for policy makers to consider more thoughtfully, whether the sanctions for failure to pay 'costs' are sufficient to incentivise change.

The policy analysis also uncovers a rather half-hearted integration of environmental protection interests with that of competition policy. But the explicit integration of state aid control does permit state subsidies to support efforts by undertakings, which go beyond the standards required under the polluter pays principle. This fact distinguishes state aid from the rest of competition policy.

Despite the resounding transposition and integration of the polluter pays – and precaution – principles in EU law and policy and practice, it is not alone conclusive evidence of the EU's approach to sustainable development on a grander scale. There is need to examine the further fundamental subsidiary elements of sustainable development, namely public participation including access to information, and access to justice in environmental matters, which are the subjects of the next chapter.

# 6 Public participation and access rights in EU law

Sustainable development, in EU law and policy, is closely associated with the development of environmental law and policy, and closely intertwined with the framework of principles that largely is environmental law in the EU. The previous two chapters examined two of these principles – the precautionary principle and the polluter pays principle – and demonstrated that they can capably transpose sustainable development through EU law, policy, and practice to address environmental protection and the economic aspect promoting sustainability. This chapter analyses the third key principle set to achieve environmental policy objective, under the social dimension of sustainable development: the right to public participation in the decision-making process. It examines the EU system for promoting public participation, namely by placing sustainable development alongside the fundamental rights – economic and social rights – and freedoms enshrined in the Charter that must be balanced with environmental protection. The Aarhus Convention on Access to Information, Public Participation, and Access to Justice in Environmental Matters is analysed by way of a specific example on the protection of rights in relation to sustainable development. This chapter illustrates the various policy and legislative measures enacted by the EU to incorporate the Convention's provisions into EU law, especially the more contentious 'access to justice' element. The relationships between the Charter and the European Convention on Human Rights and Fundamental Freedoms and the relationship between the Court of Justice and the European Court of Human Rights will also be borne out. It argues that in addition to the guarantees of rights in EU treaties and legislation, the promotion of procedural rights could take place through administrative and deliberative processes. One question to determine is whether, if at all, the EU's approach to the Aarhus Convention is representative of its wider approach to the principle of sustainable development in the EU agenda as a whole.

## Public participation principle and sustainable development

The principle of public participation as an element of the third dimension of sustainable development was expressed in Principle 10 of the Rio Declaration, which states that:

> Environmental issues are best handled with the participation of all concerned citizens, at the relevant level. At the national level, each individual shall have

appropriate access to information concerning the environment that is held by public authorities . . . and the opportunity to participate in decision-making processes. States shall facilitate and encourage public awareness and participation by making information widely available. Effective access to judicial and administrative proceedings, including redress and remedy, shall be provided.

The participation principle derives from the Environmental Impact Assessment (EIA) procedure,[1] and from other spheres of general environmental decision-making, such as environmental planning. The latter parallel path ushers in the broader developmental perspective of sustainability that includes 'Good Governance' or 'environmental Human Rights' aspects.[2] A further application of participation inferred in Rio Principle 10 represents as a distinct element of sustainable development in regulation of economic activities, addresses participation in a narrow and specific context of regulating *activities* for social and environmentally sustainable development, and appreciates in an immediate local context.[3]

The ILA identified public participation, access to information, and access to justice in environmental decision-making as three key components of achieving effective sustainable development.[4] In particular, these components contribute to the "greening" of the decision-making process with the intention of enabling sustainable development issues to be incorporated into policy and legislation at all levels of governance.[5]

The Rio Declaration formulation makes participation a matter for 'all concerned citizens' for effective determination of environmental issues. It places emphasis of the national level participation, where the relevant public authorities must make available environmental information.[6] It goes beyond the public influencing of environmental decisions, to implementation, and enforcement actions. It may involve citizens, government processes, corporations, and organisations. The relevant citizens or entities should be able to compel the release of information, seek restoration or reclamation, obtain an injunction against damaging or wrongful activity, or receive compensation.[7]

Due to their increasingly recognised importance, the three elements – otherwise known as "access rights" – were assembled to realise 'good environmental governance', namely the understanding that where governmental decision-making in the field of environmental law or policy fails to uphold these access rights, the outcomes

---

1 Note that the participatory requirements portrayed herein could also condition EIA participatory obligations; see Schwartz, P., *Sustainable Development and Mining in Sierra Leone* (Kent: Pnuema Spring, 2006) pp. 95–98.
2 See supra chapter 1, p. 17.
3 Schwartz, P., 2006 (n 1) p. 99.
4 See ILA New Delhi Declaration of Principles of International Law Relating to Sustainable Development 2002 (ILA/NDD) (see also supra chapter 2, note 20).
5 Ibid.
6 Schwartz, P., 2006 (n 1) p. 100.
7 Ibid.

of any decision-making are more likely to be "environmentally damaging, developmentally unsustainable, and socially unjust".[8] It was this Principle and the underlying understanding that sustainable development requires the involvement of all stakeholders that later laid the groundwork for the Aarhus Convention on Access to Information, Public Participation, and Access to Justice in Environmental Matters.[9]

## The Aarhus Convention on public participation and social justice

The 1998 Aarhus Convention recognises that:

> Adequate protection of the environment is essential to human wellbeing and the enjoyment of basic human rights, including the right to life itself [and asserts that] every person has the right to live in an environment adequate to his or her health and well-being, and the duty, both individually and in association with others, to protect and improve the environment for the benefit of present and future generations.[10]

The Aarhus Convention enshrines the procedural rights necessary to "contribute to the protection of the right of every person of present and future generations to live in an environment adequate to his or her health and well-being".[11] This statement, contained in Article 1 of the Convention, has been heralded as one of the clearest statements in international environmental law of the right to a healthy environment for both present and future generations.[12]

Human rights sentiment aside, the Convention certainly confirmed the importance of people to the environmental decision-making process. In doing so, it codified the need to democratise and increase transparency within decision-making processes by encouraging interaction between the people and governments within a democratic context, something that is of particular relevance to the EU, as will be discussed further below. Article 2 goes on to describe who is entitled to rely on the Convention and divides the rights contained therein into three pillars, largely reflecting the three access rights of good environmental governance mentioned above.[13] The Convention rights are categorised as follows:

---

8   Banisar, D., Parmar, S., de Silva, L. and Excell, C., "Moving From Principles to Rights: Rio 2012 and Access to Information, Public Participation, and Justice", *Sustainable Development Law and Policy* (2011) 12, 8.
9   United Nations Economic Committee for Europe, "Convention on Access to Information, Public Participation in Decision-Making and Access to Justice in Environmental Matters", Aarhus, Denmark, 25 June 1998, www.unece.org/fileadmin/DAM/env/pp/documents/cep43e.pdf
10  See The Aarhus Convention, ibid. (preamble).
11  Article 1 of the Aarhus Convention.
12  Rodenhoff, V., "The Aarhus Convention and Its Implications for the 'Institutions' of the European Community", *RECIEL* (2002) 11, no. 3, 344.
13  Note that the three pillars contained in the Aarhus Convention are not to be confused with the pre-Lisbon pillars which provided the internal structure of the EU.

## Right to information – Pillar 1

The first pillar of the Convention concerns the public's passive and active right to information.[14] This right can be enforced either by a member of the public requesting otherwise unreleased information from the government (passive) or by a government body actively collecting and disseminating information (active).[15] This gives the public a fairly broad right and, in doing so, raises public awareness of environmental concerns and improves the transparency of the decision-making process.[16]

## Procedural rights – Pillar 2

The second pillar of the Convention concerns the right of public participation and encompasses many forms of interaction such as voting, demonstrating, or petitioning.[17] These procedures give members of the public vital opportunities to steer the decision-making process, demand protection of the environment, and improve general understanding and interest in environmental matters.[18] In turn, this greater public involvement strengthens public support for environment-related decisions and enables additional accountability of decision-makers.[19]

## Access to justice – Pillar 3

The third pillar of the Convention focuses on access to justice and gives the Convention its teeth.[20] It is vital to the enforcement of the rights preceding it, especially given the fact that "the environment has no voice of its own".[21] Article 9(1) provides that the review procedure shall enable any person to enforce his or her rights of access to information under Article 4 of the Aarhus Convention. According to Article 9(2) and (3) of the Convention, any member of the public having a sufficient interest or alleging impairment of a right must be ensured access to a review procedure (judicial or by another independent and impartial body established by law) to challenge the substantive and/or procedural legality of any decision concerning the environment.[22] Details for such procedures are not provided in these Articles and it is for national law to determine what constitutes

---

14 Articles 4 and 5 the Aarhus Convention.
15 Fitzmaurice, M., "Note on the Participation of Civil Society in Environmental Matters. Case Study: The 1998 Aarhus Convention on Access to Information, Public Participation in Decision-Making and Access to Justice in Environmental Matters", *Human Rights and International Legal Discourse* (2010) 4, 50.
16 Poncelet, C., "Access to Justice in Environmental Matters – Does the European Union Comply With Its Obligations?", *Journal of Environmental Law* (2012) 24, no. 2, 288.
17 Articles 6 to 8 the Aarhus Convention.
18 Fitzmaurice (n 15) 51.
19 Poncelet (n 16) 288.
20 Article 9 the Aarhus Convention.
21 Kramer, L., "The Environmental Complaint in the EU", *JEEPL* (2009) 6, 13, 25, cited in Poncelet (n 16) 289.
22 Rodenhoff (n 12) 348.

a "person with a sufficient interest" and what constitutes an "impairment of a right", but such national law must follow the objective of giving the public concerned wide access to justice, albeit solely within the scope of the Convention.[23] The Parties to the Convention therefore retain broad discretion regarding the implementation of their obligations under Article 9(3).[24]

From the perspective of sustainable development, the Aarhus Convention provides the opportunity for signatories to legitimise their environmental decision-making processes by ensuring that the public can participate in the negotiation process, access the relevant documents while and once such decisions are made. They can also challenge those decisions, which, they feel, are contrary to their role as advocates of current and future generations' rights to a healthy and sustainable environment. In this way, the three access rights are the means by which people are able to engage with their responsibilities in environmental law and, as such, allow governments to respond to public concerns and demands, build consensus, and improve the acceptance of and compliance with measures designed to promote environmental protection and sustainable development.[25] Ultimately, therefore, the Aarhus Convention is centred on the role of people – both present and future – in environmental protection, the transparency of the relevant decision-making processes, and the accountability of decision-makers themselves.

## Aarhus' access rights in EU law, policy, and practice

The EU has been party to the Aarhus Convention since 2005 and, pursuant to Article 216(2) TFEU, the provisions of the Convention apply to both the EU institutions, including the Commission and Council, as well as the Member States themselves. The decision to incorporate the Convention into the EU legal order was codified in Directive 2005/370,[26] and Regulation 1367/2006 applied the provisions of the Convention to the EU institutions.[27]

Prior to the Convention's incorporation, the EU had already made steps towards greater access rights in environmental decision-making. For example, the Aarhus Convention, and in particular the access rights, featured strongly in the Sixth Environmental Action Programme (EAP) adopted in 2002.[28]

---

23 Ibid.
24 Garçon, G., "The Rights of Access to Justice in Environmental Matters in the EU – the Third Pillar of the Aarhus Convention", *European Food & Feed Law Review* (2013) 2, 79.
25 Banisar *et al.* (n 8) 8.
26 Council Decision of 17 February 2005 on the conclusion, on behalf of the European Community, of the Convention on access to information, public participation in decision-making and access to justice in environmental matters, 17 May 2005, OJ L 124/1.
27 Regulation (EC) No 1367/2006 of the European Parliament and of the Council of 6 September 2006 on the application of the provisions of the Aarhus Convention on Access to Information, Public Participation in Decision-making and Access to Justice in Environmental Matters to Community institutions and bodies, 25 September 2006, OJ L 264/13.
28 Decision No 1600/2002/EC of the European Parliament and of the Council of 22 July 2002 laying down the Sixth Community Environment Action Program, 10 September 2002, OJ L 242/1.

Moreover, the three pillars on access to information, public participation, and access to justice in environmental matters largely correspond to three of the five principles listed in the 2001 Commission White Paper on Governance, namely openness, participation, and accountability.[29] The remaining two principles in the White Paper are effectiveness and coherence.[30] Although the policy tools suggested in the White Paper had no legally binding effect on the EU institutions or Member States, their inclusion at such an early stage was indicative of the EU's recognition of the role that the public plays in effective environmental governance.

In the run up to the adoption of the Convention into the EU legal order, it nonetheless became clear that further changes were needed to the Union's existing legislation to enable fully the incorporation of the three pillars into all relevant areas of EU law. One such change came with the adoption of Directive 2003/4 on Public Access to Environmental Information,[31] which revoked a predecessor directive.[32] Focusing specifically on the first pillar of the Convention, Article 3(1) of Directive 2003/4 states that:

> Member States shall ensure that public authorities are required, in accordance with the provisions of this Directive, to make available environmental information held by or for them to any applicant at his request and without his having to state an interest.

Also in relation to the first pillar, the EU has gone further than the Convention in its interpretation of certain provisions. The Convention was designed to enable minimal harmonisation, and therefore set only the minimum standards to be achieved. In view of this, the EU has used its powers to offer greater protection than the Convention itself. Article 2(1) of Directive 2003/4 outlines the scope of the term 'environmental information' and goes beyond the provisions in the Convention by adding other pieces of information to the definition. This broader interpretation of 'environmental information' has been further reinforced by Court of Justice case law. For example, in *Stichting Natuur en Milieu*, the Court found that a procedure for authorisation of a plant protection product fell within the term. This broad interpretation has been, to a large extent, accepted and adopted by Member State national courts and authorities such as national ombudsmen.[33]

---

29 See the five fundamental principles of good governance in European Commission, "European Governance: A White Paper", 25 July 2001, COM(2001) 428 final.
30 Ibid.
31 Directive 2003/4/EC of the European Parliament and of the Council of 28 January 2003 on public access to environmental information and repealing Council Directive 90/313, 14 February 2003, OJ L 41/26.
32 Council Directive 90/313/EEC of 7 June 1990 on the freedom of access to information on the environment, 23 June 1990, OJ L 158/56.
33 Case C-266/09 *Stichting Natuur en Milieu* [2010] ECR I-13119. See further Report from the Commission to the Council and the European Parliament on the experience gained in

Despite this, the Court has curtailed the scope of application of this right in general, and in *WWF-EPP v Council* the Court found that "the concept of document must be distinguished from that of information". As such, the Community institutions are only obliged to disclose information held in the form of a formal document, as opposed to "any information in written, visual, aural or electronic or any other material form".[34]

The right of access to information has also been included in the Charter of Fundamental Rights. Article 42 of the Charter states that:

> any citizen of the Union, and any natural or legal person residing or having its registered office in a Member State, has a right of access to documents of the institutions, bodies, offices and agencies of the Union, whatever their medium.[35]

Prior to the Lisbon Treaty, this inclusion in the Charter is unlikely to have had much impact on the protection of this first access right.

However, since 2010 the Charter has been legally binding both on the Member States and EU institutions and, as such, is increasingly considered by parties and the Court. In his opinion to the case *Sweden v. Commission*, Advocate General Poiares Maduro highlighted the fundamental nature of the right of access to information as enshrined in Article 42 of the Charter, stating that:

> This protection of the right of access under ever higher norms has been accompanied by a development in its substance. We have gone from a situation of a mere favour being granted to the individual by the institutions in the exercise of their discretionary power to one of a true subjective, fundamental right granted to the individual. [. . .] With the introduction of Article 255 EC by the Treaty of Amsterdam, [now Article 15(3) TFEU] access to documents of the institutions has become a subjective right granted to "any citizen of the Union, and any natural or legal person residing or having its registered office in a Member State". That right of access, moreover, is of the nature of a fundamental right, as confirmed by the fact that it was reproduced in Article 42 of the Charter of Fundamental Rights.[36]

Thus, the right to information under the first pillar of the Convention is interpreted more broadly in EU law than originally provided for in the Convention,

---

the application of Directive 2003/4/EC on public access to environmental information, 17 December 2012, COM(2012) 774 final, 5.
34 Case T-264/04 *WWF-EPP v. Council of the European Union* [2007] ECR II-911.
35 Pedersen, O.W., "European Environmental Human Rights and Environmental Rights: A Long Time Coming?" *The Georgetown International Environmental Law Review* (2008–2009) 21, 108.
36 Opinion of Advocate General Poiares Maduro delivered on 18 July 2007 in Case C-64/05 P *Kingdom of Sweden v Commission of the European Communities and Others* [2007] ECR I-11389, 40.

and is widely incorporated into the EU legal order as a fundamental right. Despite this, the Court has adopted a pragmatic approach to its interpretation and, as such, the right is not limitless. This curtailment of the right may be intended to protect certain political and economic decisions, which, despite infringing the general right of access to information, are overridden by interests of security.

Directive 2003/35 also aimed to enable better integration of the second pillar of the Convention into EU law. However, as with the right of access to information, prior to the adoption of the Convention into the EU legal order, instruments were already in place that required public participation in decision-making processes, such as Directive 2001/42 on the Assessment of the Effects of Certain Plans and Programs on the Environment.[37] Directive 2001/42 stipulates that:

(i) draft plans and programmes must be made available to the public before they are adopted;
(ii) the public must be given an opportunity to comment on such plans and programmes; and
(iii) the final plan or programme must take into account public consultations.[38]

Add to this both Directive 2000/60, which establishes a framework for Community action in the field of water policy (paragraph 46), and the amended Directive 2011/92 on Public Participation in Environmental Impact Assessments (paragraphs 16–21 and Article 11),[39] and it becomes clear that, when Directive 2003/35 was adopted, it was more of a procedural necessity than a reform of the standards enabling public participation in EU environmental decision-making. This did not mean, however, that the EU ceased to encourage further implementation of the right. In Regulation 1367/2006, the EU expressly extended the scope of the previous Regulation 1049/2001 on public access to European Parliament, Council, and Commission documents, by providing for public participation in the preparation, modification, and review of plans or programmes relating to the environment.

The third pillar of the Convention on access to justice is by far the most controversial of the three, posing the most difficulties in terms of incorporation. In view of this, discussion of its role in EU law will be the focus of the following sections, which will examine, in greater depth, the EU's attempts to protect this right in the EU legal order.

---

37 Directive 2001/42/EC of the European Parliament and of the Council of 27 June 2001 on the assessment of the effects of certain plans and programmes on the environment, 21 July 2001, OJ L 197/30.
38 Dellinger, M., "Ten Years of the Aarhus Convention: How Procedural Democracy Is Paving the Way for Substantive Change in National and International Environmental Law", *Colombia Journal of International Environmental Law & Policy* (2012) 23, 329.
39 See Directive 2000/60/EC of the European Parliament and of the Council of 23 October 2000 establishing a framework for Community action in the field of water policy, OJ L 327/1, 21 December 2000; and Directive 2011/92/EU of the European Parliament and of the Council of 13 December 2011 on the assessment of the effects of certain public and private projects on the environment, 28 January 2012, OJ L 26/1 (as amended).

### Application of 'access to justice' rights in the EU

As described separately by Pederson and Poncelet, the EU has adopted a piecemeal approach to access to justice in environmental matters, introducing amendments and incorporating provisions into a number of existing pieces of legislation over the years.[40] For example, Directive 2003/4 adds specific access to justice provisions, which were not present in the previous Directive 90/313 relating to the refusal of access to information.[41] This Directive requires Member States to provide access to an independent and impartial body established by law in cases where the right of access to environmental legislation has been violated.[42] Directive 2003/35, in addition to detailing the right to public participation in EIA decision-making, removes all ambiguity surrounding the right to address national courts where the right of participation has not been respected.[43] Directive 2004/35 on Environmental Liability confers specific rights on private persons to access particular administrative legal review procedures intended to enable the accountability of decision-makers and to ensure that environmental damage – or threats thereof – are remedied or prevented.[44]

Moreover, in Regulation 1367/06 on the application of provisions of the Aarhus Convention, the EU has incorporated provisions intended to subject EU institutions to the Aarhus Convention by enabling the internal review of administrative acts adopted by EU authorities.[45] It allows NGOs to request an internal review and, if such a request is turned down, the decision and reasons for refusal have to be communicated in written form. This provision has the potential to widen the scope of standing before the Court of Justice as written reasons arguably fall within the definition of a "decision" under Article 230 TFEU, potentially making them amenable to judicial review.[46]

However, the extent to which these above-mentioned measures actually enable the right of access to justice is limited. For example, according to Poncelet, Regulation 1367/06 is restricted both in terms of *ratione personae* and *ratione materiae* and, as such, has little added value to the implementation of access

---

40 See Pedersen (n 35) 105–106; and Poncelet (n 16) 289–290.
41 See Directive 2003/4/EC (n 31); and Directive 90/313/EEC (n 32).
42 Article 6(1) of Directive 2003/4/EC, ibid.
43 Directive 2003/35/EC of the European Parliament and of the Council of 26 May 2003 providing for public participation in respect of the drawing up of certain plans and programmes relating to the environment and amending with regard to public participation and access to justice Council Directives 85/337/EEC and 96/61/EC, 25 June 2003, OJ L156/17.
44 Directive 2004/35/CE of the European Parliament and of the Council of 21 April 2004 on environmental liability with regard to the prevention and remedying of environmental damage, OJ L 143/56 30 April 2004.
45 Regulation 1367/2006 (n 27).
46 Pedersen (n 35) 108.

to justice rights in the EU legal order.[47] The first reason given for this limited impact is that Article 10 of the Regulation excludes individuals from the right to bring an application for internal review, a provision which seems contrary to the purposes of Article 9(3) of the Convention which confers access rights on "members of the public".[48] Secondly, the requirement in Article 11 that the applicant must show that the contested measures have legally binding and external effects is not a requirement foreseen by Article 9(3) of the Convention.[49] Rather than covering a wide range of administrative and judicial procedures, this need for 'legally binding effect' will exclude measures such as decisions taken in the course of infringement proceedings and Environment Action Programmes.[50] Thirdly, according to the definition of 'administrative act' in Article 2 of the Regulation, the administrative act concerned must be taken under environmental law. Despite being at first glance a reasonable requirement based on pre-established case law and the primary and secondary objectives of legislation, such a requirement may exclude measures where the objective is not environmental protection *per se*, but nonetheless contribute to the impairment of ecosystems.[51] Fourthly, any request for review of a refusal to conduct an internal review is restricted by the fact that it must be conducted under Court of Justice standing requirements which, as will be discussed in further detail below, are unduly obstructive to the objective of access to justice.[52]

Furthermore, unlike for the first two pillars of the Convention, there is no one measure under EU law which confers a right of access to justice in case of breach of environmental law. In 2008, the Commission submitted a proposal for a directive on access to justice in environmental matters intended both to promote compliance and to ensure consistency across the EU Member States by harmonising national *locus standi* requirements.[53] This minimum harmonisation was considered particularly important given the varying accessibility of national courts throughout the EU and the transnational dimensions of many environmental problems.[54]

As elaborated by Pánovics, among the various ways to qualify for standing, two extreme positions can be identified. The first is a restrictive approach, whereby

---

47 Poncelet (n 16) 303 and 307.
48 Ibid., 304.
49 Poncelet (n 16) 305.
50 Ibid.
51 de Sadeleer, N., *Commentaire Megrét Environnement et Marché Intérieur* (Editions de l'Université de Bruxelles 2010) 187, cited in Poncelet (n 16) 306.
52 Pallamaerts, Dr M Compliance by the European Community with its Obligations on Access to Justice as a Party to the Aarhus Convention, Institute for European Environmental Study, June 2009, 6.
53 See COM(2003) 624 final.
54 Pánovics, A., "The Need for an EU Directive on Access to Justice in Environmental Matters", *Studia Iuridica Auctoritate Universitatis Pecs* (2010) 147, 146. See also Milieu, L., "Inventory of EU Member States", *Measures on Access to Justice in Environmental Matters* (2007) 21, available at http://ec.europa.eu/environment/aarhus/study_access.htm

an individual only has standing in cases which concern him or her directly and privately. The second is a "more generous, expansive approach, where *locus standi* does not depend on the connection between the subject and interest pursued at all".[55] It is his view that the approaches of most EU Member States sit somewhere between these two extremes; however, "there has been a general – albeit slow and heterogeneous – tendency among them to move from the first position to the latter in cases concerning the environment".[56] This phenomenon is aggravated by the fact that the Court of Justice has been criticised for insufficiently enabling access to justice by operating an unduly restrictive test for legal standing.

Moreover, in 2013, the EU commissioned several expert group meetings on access to justice in environmental matters, and the findings of the synthesis report prepared by Professor Chris Backes of Maastricht University indicated that the implementation of Article 9(3) (and Article 9(4)) across the Member States was divergent, random, and inconsistent.[57] One of the options discussed in the report was to pass the original proposal for a directive harmonising access to justice in environmental matters or to introduce a new proposal, addressing previous issues. However, despite the obvious need for harmonisation in this area, no harmonising legislation exists. Some Member States argue that such a measure would add little value, that their commitments under the Aarhus Convention do go far enough to protect access to justice rights, and that the subsidiarity principle precludes the EU from legislating on this matter.[58]

Nonetheless, the Commission continues to recognise the potential deficit in access to justice in environmental matters, reiterating in its 7th EAP the importance of "effective access to justice in environmental matters and effective legal protection, in line with the Aarhus Convention and recent case law of the Court of Justice of the European Union".[59] More specifically, the Commission stated that the programme would ensure that by 2020, national provisions on access to justice would reflect the case law of the Court of Justice, and that non-judicial conflict resolution mechanisms would be made available in order to reach amicable solutions in the field of environmental law and policy.[60]

However, whether the Court of Justice can truly be the standard bearer for greater access to justice in environmental matters is up for debate. Although the

---

55 Pánovics (n 54) 144.
56 Ibid.
57 European Commission, DG Environment "The Aarhus Convention: Commission Expert Group Meetings relating to access to justice in environmental matters", 11 April 2014, http://ec.europa.eu/environment/aarhus/experts_groups.htm
58 Kramer, L., "The Environmental Complaint in the EU", *JEEPL* (2009) 6, 13, 25, cited in Poncelet (n 16) 290–291.
59 Such as in Article 62 of the 7th EAP – Decision of the European Parliament and of the Council on a General Union Environment Action Programme to 2020 "Living well, within the limits of our planet", Decision 1386/2013/EU.
60 Proposal for a Decision of the European Parliament and of the Council on a General Union Environment Action Programme to 2020 "Living well, within the limits of our planet", 29 November 2012, COM(2012) 710 final, 60 and 63.

Court of Justice has taken it upon itself to address this gap in the law, it has done it inconsistently. It is to this case law approach that the discussion now turns.

### Access to justice case law

The Aarhus Convention has taken an increasingly important role before the Court of Justice, with a range of cases demonstrating "the new and broad contexts in which the Convention is at least considered".[61] However, as Poncelet argues:

> [T]here is a dichotomy in the Court's approach to access to justice in environmental issues. On the one hand, the Court has attempted to fill the legislative gap by requiring national courts to relax their rules and grant EU citizens effective redress. On the other hand, the EU Courts themselves remain largely inaccessible to individuals seeking to protect the environment.[62]

In relation to the interpretation and implementation of the third pillar of the Convention in the Member States, the Court of Justice has often applied the rule generously to enable access to justice for the individual concerned. In cases such as *Janecek v Freistaat Bayern*, the Court found that certain environmental directives were capable of conferring specific rights upon individuals, on which they may rely before their national courts.[63] This case concerned Directive 96/62/EC on ambient air quality assessment and management,[64] which requires Member States to draw up action plans indicating the measures to be taken in the short term where there is a risk that air quality limit values and/or alert thresholds will be exceeded. The Court found that, where there was such a risk, a person directly concerned can require the competent authorities to draw up the action plan.

In relation to public awareness of the right to access justice, the Court found in *Commission v Ireland* that Ireland had not fulfilled its obligation under the

---

61 See Eckes, C., "Environmental Policy 'Outside-In': How the EU's Engagement With International Environmental Law Curtails National Autonomy", *German Law Journal*, 13 (2012) 1165, in which she refers to cases concerning information about the trading of emission allowances under the Emissions Trading Scheme (for example case C- 524/09 Ville de Lyon [2010] ECR I-14115) and cases concerning information on the precise location of mobile phone base stations (for example, case C-71/10 Information Commissioner [2011] ECR I-7205). These cases, according to Eckes, demonstrate that the potential relevance of the Aarhus Convention extends to information that is relevant for economical transactions and security.
62 Poncelet (n 16) 287.
63 See Case C-237/07 *Janecek v Freistaat Bayern* [2008] ECR I-6221, cited in Jans, J., "Harmonisation of National Procedural Law via the Back Door? Preliminary Comments on the ECJ's Judgment in *Janecek* in a Comparative Context", in Bulterman, M., Hancher, L., McDonnel, A. and Sevenster, H. (Eds.), *Views of European Law From the Mountain* (Alphen aan den Rijn: Kluwer Law International, 2009) p. 267, cited in Poncelet (n 16) 292.
64 Council Directive 96/62/EC of 27 September 1996 on ambient air quality assessment and management, OJ 1996 L 296/55 (as amended).

third pillar of the Convention as it had failed to inform the public adequately of the availability of judicial review for relevant environmental measures. According to the Court, the mere availability on the internet of rules and decisions does not ensure, in a sufficiently clear and precise manner, that the public concerned is in a position to be aware of its rights on access to justice in environmental matters.[65]

Furthermore, the Court widely interpreted the rules on access to justice in *Djurgården-Lilla Värtans Miljöskyddsförening* v *Stockholms kommun*, in which it considered Directive 85/337 on the assessment of the effects of certain public and private projects on the environment – the EIA Directive. Here the Court had to consider the legality of a Swedish measure which reserved the right to bring an appeal solely to environmental protection associations which have at least 2,000 members. This minimum membership requirement meant that only two Swedish NGOs were eligible.[66] In her opinion to this case, Advocate General Sharpston stated that "any restriction whose effect is to hinder rather than to facilitate access to administrative and judicial procedures for environmental organisations must [. . .] evidently, be rejected".[67]

While the Court confirmed that it is for national law to determine the conditions for access to justice for NGOs, it held that these national rules must ensure "wide access to justice".[68] The Court also found that, although a national law may require that an environmental protection association have a minimum number of members, the number required cannot be fixed at such a level that it runs counter to the objective of access to justice under the Convention.[69] Accordingly, the measure was in breach of Article 10a of Directive 85/337.[70]

Advocate General Sharpston also gave an Opinion in *Bund für Umwelt und Naturschutz Deutschland, Landesverband Nordrhein-Westfalen eV v Bezirksregierung Arnsberg*. She found that the EIA Directive should be interpreted in a manner such that environmental associations may argue in front of a national judge on behalf of the environment and that the provisions upon which associations may rely on to access the courts include even those intended "to serve the interests of the general public alone rather than those which, at least in part, protect the legal interests of individuals".[71] In its judgement in this case, the Court

---

65 Case C-427/07 *Commission v. Ireland* [2009] ECR I-6277.
66 Case C-263/08 *Djurgården-Lilla Värtans Miljöskyddsförening v Stockholms kommun genom dess marknämnd* [2009] ECR I-9967.
67 Opinion of Advocate General Sharpston in Case C-263/08 *Djurgården-Lilla Värtans Miljöskyddsförening v Stockholms kommun genom dess marknämnd* [2009] ECR I-9967, cited in Poncelet (n 16) 293.
68 Case C-427/07 The European Commission vs. Ireland [2009] ECR I-6277, 45.
69 This is a position supported by the Compliance Committee in Compliance Committee, Aarhus Convention, 14 June 2005, Compliance by Belgium, ACCC/C/ 2005/11 (Belgium), www.unece.org/env/pp/compliance/Compliancecommittee/11TableBelgium.html
70 Case C-263/08 *Djurgården-Lilla Värtans Miljöskyddsförening v. Stockholms kommun* [2009] ECR I-9967.
71 Opinion of Advocate General Sharpston delivered on 16 December 2010 in Case C-115/09 *Bund fur Umwelt und Naturschutz Deutschland v Bezirksregierung Arnsberg* [2011] ECR I-3673, cited in Poncelet (n 16) 293.

found that a legislative act which does not comply with the Directive's requirements or "which does no more than simply 'ratify' a pre-existing administrative act", can be challengeable before a national court or another independent and impartial body as to its substantive or procedural legality. This, the Court found, was necessary to avoid the possibility that Article 9 of the Aarhus Convention lost "all its effectiveness".[72]

Then, in *LZ VLK v Ministry of Environment*, the Court considered whether an environmental protection association may be a 'party' to administrative proceedings concerning, in particular, the granting of derogations to the system of protection for species (such as the brown bear) listed in Annex IV(a) to the Habitats Directive.[73] According to the Court, Article 9(3) of the Aarhus Convention could not be interpreted in such a way as to make it, in practice, impossible or excessively difficult to exercise rights conferred by EU law, as such an interpretation would be contrary to the objective of the Convention.[74] Nonetheless, the Court felt that it could not confer direct effect on Article 9(3) of the Convention, as it remained "for the courts of those Member States to determine, on the basis of national law, whether individuals could rely directly on the rules of that international agreement relevant to that field".[75]

Thus, through case law, the Court has adopted a teleological approach to the doctrine of *'effet utile'* by interpreting provisions of EU legislation so as to give effect to the obligations under the Aarhus Convention.[76] However, although the Court has ruled favourably on the right of access to justice generally, the *locus standi* requirements for individuals wishing to access the Court of Justice itself in such cases is less generously interpreted.

Access to the Court of Justice for individuals and NGOs has been elusive, partly due to the fact that the *locus standi* requirements laid down in Article 263 TFEU are notoriously strict. The requirement of "direct and individual concern" in Article 263(4) TFEU, as interpreted by the seminal *Plaumann* case,[77] constitutes the main stumbling block for applicants. This, in turn, has had damaging effects on the ability for individuals and NGOs to enforce their rights under environmental law before the Court.

---

72 The European Union Aarhus Centre, 'Access to Justice under the Environmental Impact Assessment Directive and the Aarhus Convention', www.clientearth.org/aarhus-centre/news/access-to-justice-under-the-environmental-impact-assessment-directive-and-the-aarhus-convention-1675
73 Council Directive 92/43/EEC of 21 May 1992 on the conservation of natural habitats and of wild fauna and flora, 22 July 1992, OJ L 206/7.
74 Case C-240/09 *Lesoochranárske zoskupenie VLK v. Ministry of Environment* [2012], [2012] ECR I-1255.
75 Eckes, C., "Environmental Policy 'Outside-In': How the EU's Engagement With International Environmental Law Curtails National Autonomy", *German Law Journal* (2012) 13, 1166.
76 Poncelet (n 16) pp. 292–293.
77 Case 25/62 *Plaumann & Co. v Commission of the European Economic Community* [1963] ECR 95.

Case C-321/95P *Greenpeace v Commission* is symbolic in this respect, as it demonstrates the failure of the Court to apply the same standards to itself as it has since applied to national courts in the Member States. In this case, the Court of Justice upheld the decision of the General Court that an association formed for the protection of the collective interests of a category of persons could not be considered to be directly and individually concerned so as to satisfy the Article 263(4) TFEU requirement. As a consequence, Greenpeace was not entitled to bring an action for annulment where its members could not do so individually.[78] Little has changed since this case and, despite occasional efforts by the Court to deviate from the restrictive *Plaumann* rules, such as in *Jégo-Quéré*,[79] the Court has confirmed that it will require an amendment of the TFEU before the law on standing can change. This was confirmed in paragraph 45 of the *UPA* case.[80]

Arguably, EU standing requirements are not in line with the spirit of the Convention. Indeed, the Aarhus Convention Compliance Committee has repeatedly emphasised that a broad interpretation of the Convention should be the presumption, not the exception.[81] The Aarhus Convention Compliance Committee controls parties' compliance with the Convention and produces non-binding decisions interpreting the application of its provisions. In 2011 it was asked to decide whether the standing requirement of "individual concern" before the EU Courts was in compliance with the Aarhus Convention. Despite showing great deference to the Court, it reached a rather critical conclusion, especially regarding the Court's general adherence to the third pillar of the Convention. It found that:

> [W]ith regard to access to justice by members of the public, the Committee is convinced that if the jurisprudence of the EU Courts, as evidenced by the cases examined, were to continue, unless fully compensated for by adequate administrative review procedures, the [EU] would fail to comply with Article 9, paragraph 3 and 4, of the [Aarhus] Convention.[82]

In view of this, the Aarhus Convention Compliance Committee recommended that "a new direction of the jurisprudence of the EU Courts should be established

---

78 Case C-321/95P *Greenpeace v Commission* [1998] ECR I-1651.
79 Case T-177/01 *Jégo-Quéré v Commission* [2002] ECR II-2365.
80 Case C-50/00P *Unión de Pequeños Agricultores v Council of the European Union* [2002] ECR I-6677.
81 See Andrusevych, A., Alge, T. and Clemens, C. (Eds.) *Case Law of the Aarhus Convention Compliance Committee (2004–2011)*, 2nd edition (RACSE, Lviv, 2011), available at www.unece.org/fileadmin/DAM/env/pp/Media/Publications/ACCC_Jurisprudence_Ecoforum_2011.pdf cited in Poncelet (n 16) p. 300.
82 Economic Commission for Europe, 'Meeting of the Parties to the Convention on Access to Information, Public Participation in Decision-making and Access to Justice in Environmental Matters: Findings and Recommendations with regard to communication A CCC/C/2008/32 (Part I) concerning compliance by the European Union', adopted 14 April 2011, ECE/MP.PP/C.1/2011/4/Add.1, 88.

in order to ensure compliance" and "that all relevant EU institutions within their competences take the steps to overcome the shortcomings reflected in the jurisprudence of the EU Courts in providing the public concerned with access to justice in environmental matters".[83]

Although the EU's standing requirements could be seen as violating the access to justice provisions in the Aarhus Convention, it is worth noting that every EU citizen has the right to bring a complaint before the European Ombudsman or to send a petition to the European Parliament. However, neither of the options brings with it the possibility for legally binding decisions and, for this reason, proper and consistent application of the third pillar by the EU institutions, including the Court, is paramount.[84] Furthermore, even if *locus standi* requirements are overcome, judicial review by the Court of Justice is not only lengthy, but also restricted by the limited availability of injunctive relief.[85]

Failure to achieve such access to justice risks undermining the objectives of the Aarhus Convention as a whole. Any substantive right, to have meaning, must be accompanied by the ability to enforce that right and, if the obligations in the Convention are implemented without enforcement or review, then the likelihood of the EU institutions achieving fully integrated sustainable development is slim.

## Critical review of access rights approach to EU sustainability policy

Public participation encourages transparency, public pressure, and, thereby, the accountability of decision makers. However, this element of the principle does come with the important caveat of whether the public chooses to enforce those rights or not. Indeed, in many areas of EU action there is a significant gap between the framework for public participation and the utilisation of that right within the framework.

Nonetheless, limited engagement in opportunities for public participation does not negate the importance of the right itself. Access to information acts as a check on decision-making by bringing into the public domain documents which might otherwise have been kept from view. And access to justice enables individuals to challenge the application of decisions in view of the objectives of environmental protection and sustainable development.

The EU has gone further than the Aarhus Convention in its interpretation of certain provisions relating to information access and has used its powers to offer greater protection than the Convention itself, broadening the scope of the definition of environmental information. In terms of public participatory rights, these had already existed in the EU prior to the recognition of Aarhus rights. The Aarhus Convention thus represents more of a procedural necessity than a reform

---

83 Ibid., 97.
84 Pedersen (n 35) p. 107.
85 Pallamaerts (n 52) pp. 6–7.

of the standards enabling public participation in EU environmental decision-making. Nonetheless, EU regulation substantially extended the scope of public access to European Parliament, Council, and Commission documents, and participatory influences on plans and programmes.

Certainly, strengthening procedural rights, access to information, public participation, and access to justice will help promote sustainable development as this chapter argues. However, as with environmental protection, the case law to date contains little, if any, reference by the Court to sustainable development – either as an objective or as a general principle. Therefore, it seems that for the present at least the interpretation of Article 11 TFEU remains at the political level and is not yet a general principle that the CJEU is willing to rely upon in order to review the validity of Union law or policies.[86] Yet, how long this will remain the case is debateable. Is it still reasonable to consider the 'greening' of human rights law and the right to information and to participate in decision-making as sufficient protection?

Perhaps a more thorny issue on the application of Aarhus in EU system is the third pillar on access to justice. Indeed, the EU added specific access to justice provisions, to include access to an independent and bodies in cases of violations, the right to address national courts, which undermine participatory rights, and on private persons to access particular administrative legal review procedures. However, the extent to which these above-mentioned measures actually enable the right of access to justice is limited.

The Court of Justice widely interpreted the rules on access to justice under the EIA Directive regarding the effects of certain public and private projects on the environment. Unlike the Convention first two pillars, there is no one measure under EU law which confers a right of access to justice in case of breach of environmental law, *per se*. This engenders varying standards for accessibility in national courts throughout the EU and in dealing with transnational environmental problems. It has been criticised for insufficiently enabling access to justice by operating an unduly restrictive test for legal standing for individuals seeking to protect the environment. Generally, the court has ruled favourably on the right of access to justice, but has been less generous with its interpretation on the *locus standi* requirements for individuals wishing to access the Court of Justice itself.

Currently, individuals or environmental interest groups have limited opportunity to challenge certain measures at EU-level. They can seek judicial review, rely on the preliminary reference procedure, or make a formal complaint to the Commission. But each of these procedures come with their own limitations, such as standing, delays, and potentially prohibitive legal expenses.[87] Surely such limited opportunities are, in the long-term, untenable, and greater recognition of sustainable development by the Court must eventually emerge. In some cases such as application of international agreements, the court could not confer direct effect

---

86 Horspool, M., Humphreys, M. and Wells-Greco, M., *European Union Law*, 9th edition (Oxford: Oxford University Press, 2016) p. 136.
87 Boyle, A.E. and Anderson, M.R., *Human Rights Approaches to Environmental Protection* (Oxford: Clarendon Press, 1998) 121–122.

to EU legislation differing to national law to determine the affordability of access. This difference of the court to national authorities ties in with the Rio Declaration emphasis on the national level participation, where the relevant public authorities must make available environmental information and access to justice for citizens.

For the meantime, however, it is worth considering the importance of the Aarhus Convention to the EU outside the enforcement of the access rights. According to Getliffe, the Aarhus Convention "sums up the ethos of proceduralisation" by enabling greater democratisation and transparency in decision-making, something which is of great importance to the EU.[88] Public participation, in particular, plays a vital role in this movement towards greater democracy; Article 42 of the Aarhus Declaration stating that:

> An engaged, critically aware public is essential to a healthy democracy. By helping to empower individual citizens and environmental NGOs to play an active role in environmental policymaking and awareness raising, the Aarhus Convention will promote responsible environmental citizenship.[89]

The EU has long been criticised for its 'democratic deficit,' to the extent that some have posited that it does not meet the democratic structure standards it expects of others.[90] Thus, "the ideological underpinnings of proceduralisation are attractive to the EU as a means of indicating a commitment to reducing the democratic deficit".[91] As such, the Aarhus Convention and the rights enshrined therein serve a further purpose in EU law, namely the legitimisation of the EU legislative agenda.

It is worth noting, EU citizen has the right to bring a complaint before the European Ombudsman or to send a petition to the European Parliament; albeit these options lack the possibility for legally binding decisions to test the consistency of applying the third pillar by the EU institutions.

## Conclusion

This analysis of the EU system on public participation alongside the fundamental rights reveals that there is a successful incorporation of the Rio Declaration Principle 10 and the Aarhus Convention provisions into EU law promoting social aspect of sustainability. The Aarhus Convention focus is on people, transparency,

---

88 Getliffe, K., "Proceduralisation and the Aarhus Convention: Does Increased Participation in the Decision-Making Process Lead to More Effective EU Environmental Law?" *Environmental Law Review* (2002) 4, 101.
89 Ibid., 108.
90 Beck, U., *Politik der Globalisierung* (Frankfurt am Main, 1998) cited in Demmke, C., *The Secret Life of Comitology or the Role of Public Officials in EC Environmental Policy* (European Institute of Public Administration, 1998), www.eipa.nl/eipascope/98/scop-3/secret-comitology.htm cited in Getliffe (n 88) 108.
91 Getliffe, K., "Proceduralisation and the Aarhus Convention: Does Increased Participation in the Decision-Making Process Lead to More Effective EU Environmental Law?", *Environmental Law Review* (2002) 4, 108.

and accountability. It enables and empowers the public to be informed of and to participate in environmental decision-making and to challenge relevant decisions, which, they believe, are contrary to the interests of environmental protection.

The chapter finds that there are various policy and legislative policies, documents, and measures enacted or undertaken by the EU transposing or applying the Aarhus provisions directly of relatively toward social sustainability in environmental decision-making. Certainly, with regard to the first and second pillars and their interpretation by the Court, the EU has demonstrated significant willingness to enable greater access to information and participation of the public.

However, gaps in consistency still exist, especially in relation to the implementation of the Convention's third pillar, with seemingly double standards being imposed by the Court of Justice. In particular, the apparent willingness to incorporate and enforce this right is undermined by the need for EU rules on legal standing to be relaxed and national rules on access to justice to be harmonised.

Access to justice for enforcement is the "teeth" of the Aarhus Convention. Removing such access to justice through restrictive standing rules does not necessarily prevent the subsidiary elements enshrined in the Aarhus Conventions from guiding EU administrative and deliberative decision-making, but there remains limited means of enforcement in the event of breach. In effect the approach tends to guarantee the application of the principle of sustainable development, albeit at the "weaker" end of impact; especially if the emphasis rests on judicial enforcement as opposed to legislative, administrative, and deliberative processes enhancing public participation rights. Invariably, EU's approach to the Aarhus Convention is representative of its wider approach to the principle of sustainable development in the EU agenda as a whole.

It is desirable therefore that there is development in the law to enable greater access to justice in environmental matters at the EU level for several reasons: First, access to justice is an essential instrument in a democratic society to effectively challenge violations of the law. It constitutes the backbone of the rule of law, which the EU seeks to uphold. Secondly, without proper access to justice, EU institutions and Member States will never be properly accountable for their actions under the first two pillars. And thirdly, failure to enforce fully such rights enshrined in the Aarhus Convention sets an arguably dangerous precedent for the EU's general approach to sustainable development.

Policy makers should also consider that such a development cannot be achieved unless the EU is successful in garnering the support of its Member States, to harmonise legislation on access to justice in environmental matters before national courts. They should also work to review the treaty requirements on standing before the Court of Justice to facilitate access to justice at the EU level.

As 'masters of the treaties' only the Member States have the power to expand access to EU courts by amending Article 230 of the Treaty and, arguably, the pressure for EU Member States to act in this way is likely to increase following the Aarhus Convention Compliance Committee decisions.[92]

---

92 Ibid., 7.

# 7 Sustainable development in EU external relations

Sustainable development has been established in the previous chapters as an international principle with primary relevance for regulating economic activities for environmental protection alongside the competing need for ensuring economic and social sustainability. Sustainable development has been shown to be capable of application through sub-principles: the precautionary principle, the polluter pays principle, and the principles of public participation and access to justice. These sub-principles have been applied in wide-ranging areas of EU law and policy to address the environmental, economic, and social dimensions of sustainability.

As sustainable development is an international concept, by its very nature, it requires a global approach for it to be fully achieved. It is generally accepted that external action by the EU in the field of sustainable development is equally as important as internal action. Its credibility has had more bearing as a player in discussions about environmental protection and, to a lesser extent, sustainable development. The goal of this chapter is therefore to locate sustainable development in EU external relations, bringing out as much as possible relevant areas where the EU's efforts promote the three dimensions of sustainability through the sub-principles.

One of such areas of focus is an area closely linked to sustainable development: climate change. Climate change is global in nature and is widely recognised as an issue which must be addressed on a global and international level. The discussion here will first consider why sustainable development is an international issue for the EU and will then question whether the EU's approach to date has been effective in encouraging third countries to adjust their approach to sustainable development, and whether it is necessary for the EU to alter course to ensure that the agenda is properly promoted worldwide. This is followed by an examination of the external legal and policy approach to sustainable development taken in relation to key actors and competitors on the international stage, namely the WTO, the US, China, Russia, India, and Brazil. The approach in the WTO and in these countries will further inform what is understood by sustainable development in the EU and the speciality of sustainable development's status in EU law and policy. This, in turn, can allow conclusions to be drawn on the fate of similar efforts made in relation to sustainable development, and the challenges that the EU might have to overcome in order to achieve its goals.

## Sustainable development as an international issue for the EU

The perspective of the EU is that the promotion of sustainable development to the wider world helps both the EU and the Member States address those issues which pose a threat, directly or indirectly, to their internal stability. Since both the sources and the impact of unsustainable development do not respect state or regional borders, these threats can come in various shapes and guises. Air pollution is one of the most apparent threats emerging from environmental degradation and requires the intervention of balanced and sustainable development on an international scale. Despite being one of the EU's key policy interests, air pollutant concentrations among the EU Member States frequently exceed the legally binding air quality limits set by the EU Air Quality Directives.[1] However, non-conformity within the EU only scratches the surface of the wider problem, primarily that some of the world's largest air polluters – China, the United States, India, and Russia – are outside of the EU's immediate control. The environmental protection imperative in the precautionary principle becomes immediately relevant in the EU's approach to this problem *vis-a-vis* other international actors. Therefore, in order to enable lasting change, the EU must enlist the cooperation of other key actors in the fight against further environmental degradation.

Another threat to the EU is the potential impact that sustainable development can have on the economy. If the EU is to push for more sustainable trade practices, the standards set are developed balancing the sustainability aims with the aim of maintaining competitiveness. Cooperation with non-Member States enables the EU to develop standards that do not place the European Economic Area market at too much of a disadvantage when competing with other national or regional markets less concerned with promoting sustainable practices. Here again a case could be made for the application and promotion of the polluter pays principle as the economic tool for promoting sustainability by a market-oriented approach using economic instruments, incentives, and cost internalisation, including through technology development and innovation of best available technology.

If used correctly, sustainable development can also be used to the EU's advantage when promoting change. Technological innovation and modernisation in the economy could not only advance environmental objectives but also signify a competitive advantage, providing an incentive for third parties to act. For example, in developing new technology for sustainable and renewable energy resources, the Union could become less dependent on fossil fuels and gain "a first-mover advantage on energy technologies that it could later export".[2] This,

---

1 European Environment Agency, "Air Pollution", www.eea.europa.eu/themes/air/intro
2 European Commission, Joint Research Centre – EDGAR, "$CO_2$ Time Series 1990–2011 Per Capita for World Countries", 17 April 2013, http://edgar.jrc.ec.europa.eu/overview.php?v=CO2ts_pc1990-2011

in turn, could spark further competition on a global scale and signify a move towards more sustainable practices by competing economic entities.³

Certain side effects of unsustainable development can also have a significant impact on the EU's internal security. Natorski and Surrallés provide one such example, namely the depletion of non-renewable natural resources, which has resulted in growing concerns over the global access to energy.⁴ Greater appreciation of threats of this kind emerged in the EU during the 2000s, when the world demand for energy peaked. As a consequence, there emerged a growing dependency on unstable regions where the most important oil and gas reserves are concentrated. This dependency made the EU vulnerable to energy crises such as that in 2006 when Russia closed the gas pipelines to its neighbouring countries. Moreover, natural catastrophes, accidents, war, and terrorist attacks have all affected the global energy infrastructure and fuelled uncertainty surrounding the capacity of producers to satisfy the growing demand. These developments provided a stark reminder to the EU of its reliance on neighbouring countries which have their own political agendas and which perhaps do not benefit from stable political systems or good governance.⁵ In response, the Commission has since recognised that a reduction in greenhouse gas emissions (GHGs), increased energy efficiency, and shifted towards renewable energy as essential means of ensuring a more limited reliance upon imported fossil fuels and greater internal security for its Member States.⁶

Another potential security risk resulting from the impact of climate change is desertification. Conflicts over scant resources like water could not only cause instability in regions bordering the outlying EU Member States, but also lead to a mass migration of 'climate refugees'.⁷ This growing understanding of the potential of climate-related security risks, and the resulting need to engage in international cooperation to address them, has led the EU to recognise climate change as a key security issue in the 2008 review of the European Security Strategy 2003:⁸

> In 2003, the ESS already identified the security implications of climate change. Five years on, this has taken on a new urgency. In March 2008, the High Representative and Commission presented a report to the European Council which described climate change as a "threat multiplier". Natural

---

3 For more, see Can Schaik, L. and Schunz, S., "Explaining EU Activism and Impact in Global Climate Politics: Is the Union a Norm- or Interest-Driven Actor?" *Journal of Common Market Studies* (2012) 50, no. 1, 176.
4 Natorski, M., Surrallés, A.H., "Securitizing Moves to Nowhere? The Framing of the European Union's Energy Policy", *Journal of Contemporary European Research* (2008) 4, no. 2, 71.
5 Ibid., 71–77.
6 See, for example, the Commission Communication, "An Energy Policy for Europe", COM(2007) 1 final of the 10 July 2007.
7 Schaik and Schunz (n 3) 177.
8 European Union, "A Secure Europe in a Better World – European Security Strategy", 12 December 2003.

disasters, environmental degradation and competition for resources exacerbate conflict, especially in situations of poverty and population growth, with humanitarian, health, political and security consequences, including greater migration. Climate change can also lead to disputes over trade routes, maritime zones and resources previously inaccessible.[9]

When combined, all of these potential threats to EU stability mean that it has long been necessary for the EU to promote sustainable development beyond its borders. Yet, the external promotion of sustainable development has also provided much needed justification of the 'added value' of the EU in times of increasing Euro-scepticism. Following the 2004 and 2007 enlargements, the two negative votes in referenda on the Constitutional Treaty, and the impact of the financial crisis on the stability and credibility of the Eurozone, the EU was left in a relatively weak position. The UK referendum on EU membership can be seen as the latest expression of angst about the EU even if it, conversely, leads to a reinvigoration of sentiment within the EU for the remaining States after the UK's departure. Certain policies, therefore, provided an opportunity for the EU to focus on more concrete projects where the institutions could demonstrate their credibility as a regional and international power.[10] Climate change and, more broadly, the objective of sustainable development, have provided such opportunities since the adoption of the Lisbon Treaty.

Nonetheless, authority on matters of environmental protection and sustainable development will be short-lived if the EU does not actually succeed in enabling change at a global level. As described in the previous chapters, by recognising sustainable development as a general principle, one that can be integrated into many, if not all, relevant areas of Union competence, the EU is already demonstrating in its internal policy-making a certain level of leadership by example. However, this alone is not enough. If the EU does not also seek to encourage international cooperation, the efforts at both the EU and Member State level will be significantly undermined.

## The EU's presence in the international arena: on climate change

Climate change, which is closely linked to sustainable development, is widely recognised as an issue which must be addressed on a global scale. According to Ottavio Quirico:

> [The world is made up of an] interrelated web of ecosystems, including the atmosphere, and thus constitutes a 'global common' – that is, a resource

---

9 European Commission, "Report on the Implementation of the European Security Strategy – Providing Security in a Changing World", 11 December 2008, S407/08, 5.
10 Schaik and Schunz (n 3) 179.

which is difficult or impossible to exclude others from enjoying, but that is degraded by common use.[11]

To combat climate change, it is necessary to establish a sustainable level of greenhouse gases through stringent emissions control.[12] Yet, as the EU is, at the time of writing, the third largest emitter, responsible for 10 per cent of global emissions, it cannot act alone.[13] Therefore, since the 1970s the EU has moved to the fore of leadership in international climate change.

The UN Conference on the Human Environment held in Stockholm in 1972 is widely recognised as representing the seminal moment in EU leadership. But, it was not until the 1990s that the EU really gained momentum in combating climate change as an actor "morally predestined to exercise global environmental leadership".[14] Although at this point in time the United States was still the key source of innovative environmental policy, "it was becoming apparent that the United States was fast abdicating this role".[15] Thus, from this point onwards the EU proceeded by "laying out bold unilateral goals, vigorously supporting the Kyoto Protocol and pushing hard for an ambitious post-2012 successor agreement".[16]

The pinnacle of the EU's leadership came in 2002, when it successfully rounded up enough followers for the Kyoto Protocol to enter into force.[17] Later, the EU became the first party to the United Nations Framework Convention on Climate Change (UNFCCC) to put concrete GHG reductions on the table which went beyond the expiration of the Kyoto commitments in 2012. At the same time, it also pledged to boost its use of renewable energy by 2020. By committing to these ambitious projects, the EU established itself as the frontrunner in environmental protection efforts and, in this way, attempted to demonstrate to other actors that building a low-carbon economy could be compatible with energy security, economic growth, and competitiveness. Moreover, by making such demands of its Member States, the Union placed itself in a position where it

---

11 Quirico, O., "Disentangling Climate Change Governance: A Legal Perspective", *Review of European Community and International Environmental Law* (2012) 21, no. 2, 93.
12 Ibid.
13 Olivier, J., et al., "Trends in Global Co$_2$ Emissions – 2016 Report", http://edgar.jrc.ec.europa.eu/news_docs/jrc-2016-trends-in-global-co2-emissions-2016-report-103425.pdf
14 See European Council, "Presidency Conclusions, European Council, Dublin 25 and 26 June 1990", SN 60/1/90, 27, cited in Vanden Brande, E., "Chapter 7 – Green Civilian Power Europe", in Orbie, J. (Ed.), *Europe's Global Role: External Policies of the European Union* (Aldershot: Ashgate, 2008) p. 161.
15 Vogler, J., "The European Contribution to Global Environmental Governance", *International Affairs* (2005) 4, no. 81, 836.
16 Parker, C.F. and Karlsson, C., "Climate Change and the European Union's Leadership Moment: An Inconvenient Truth?" *Journal of Common Market Studies* (2010) 48, no. 4, 928.
17 A key part of this success was the EU's support for Russian WTO membership and an EU – Russian energy deal that would nearly double the price of Russian natural gas by 2010, for more see Parker & Karlsson (n 16) 929.

could credibly ask others to act in a similar manner, proof of which can be seen in the subsequent emission trading schemes set up in Australia, New Zealand, and Japan, and attempted in the United States.[18]

This effort was taken a step further in 2012, when the EU agreed in principle to a deal which linked the EU emission trading scheme (ETS) with Australia's new carbon market system from 2015.[19] Efforts are ongoing to widen the scheme to include South Korea, China, Switzerland, and California. If successful, this will create the biggest carbon market in the world, significantly slowing down $CO_2$ emissions and climate change,[20] and demonstrating what can be achieved by EU leadership in sustainable development.

Despite its success, EU leadership also gave rise to internal divergences. When working out the finer details of the ETS scheme, the French presidency had to negotiate various compromises. For instance, newer EU Member States insisted on the right to catch up and bridge the economic gap with the older, western EU Member States, entailing an expectation that they would grow and that the growth could threaten climate change.[21] Alternatively, Germany and Italy demanded that the auctioning of allowances be phased in more slowly and, if a satisfactory international agreement was not achieved, that exposed industries received up to 100 per cent of their emissions allowances for free in order to guard against 'carbon leakage'.[22]

Lastly, the eight Central and Eastern European Countries (CEECs) – a recognised grouping of the EU of Member States who acceded en bloc in 2004 – had to be allocated a further 2 per cent of funding on top of the schemes already in place.[23] And, even when eventually agreed upon, the emission-trading scheme was still not enough to place the EU on a sufficiently strong footing at the 2009 Copenhagen Conference for it to advocate successfully its agenda. Instead, many of the goals that the EU outlined for the conference went unachieved – the most prominent of which being the desire to retain the legally binding architecture

---

18 See, for example: President Obama's Waxman-Markey bill, which would have created the American Clean Energy and Security Act of 2009, providing for a national cap-and-trade system reducing 2005 emission levels by 17 per cent by 2020, 42 per cent by 2030, and 83 per cent by 2050. Although accepted by the House of Representatives, the bill was later defeated in the Senate; see also the Australian Clean Energy Bill (2011); the New Zealand Climate Change Response (Emissions Trading) Amendment Act (2008); and the Japanese voluntary ETS. See also Parker and Karlsson (n 16) 939–940.
19 European Commission, "International Climate Market: Pathway Towards Linking EU and Australian Systems", ec.europa.eu, http://ec.europa.eu/clima/policies/ets/linking/index_en.htm#australia
20 Carroll, D., "Emissions Trading – the EU's Path to Becoming a 'global actor'?" *Public Service Europe*, 29 August 2012, www.publicserviceeurope.com/editor-blog/173/emissions-trading-the-eus-path-to-becoming-a-global-actor
21 Parker and Karlsson (n 16) 934–935.
22 The practice whereby companies relocate production to countries with less restrictive emission constraints.
23 Parker and Karlsson (n 16) 935–936.

established by the Kyoto Protocol when forming its successor agreement.²⁴ Instead, the United States, China, India, Brazil, and South Africa met privately on the last night of the conference and decided upon a document which dropped the reference to a 'legally binding' outcome of future climate negotiations. The EU, having been side-lined in these meetings, had to accept the deal.²⁵

Although at the Durban and Doha climate change conferences – in 2011 and 2012 respectively – the EU succeeded in ensuring that all Parties would support a roadmap towards a multilateral, rule-based legal framework,²⁶ the difficulties encountered at Copenhagen highlight some of the inherent, internal challenges that the EU will likely always encounter when acting as one entity in international negotiations. Undoubtedly, in any international forum, the EU has more clout when it speaks with one voice. However, coordinating and effectively taking into account the position of the current twenty-eight Member States – and soon to be twenty-seven before further possible enlargements – with the States at differing levels of economic and political development is a monumental task in a field as contentious as climate change.²⁷ This is further complicated by the shared competence of the EU in the field of environmental policy and the resulting ambiguous division of labour between the EU and the Member States in negotiations,²⁸ with both EU institutions and Member State governments sometimes represented. Also, with the expansion of the EU comes a growth in the scope, variety, and depth of its policy agenda, thus making the task of joining up these agendas an increasingly complicated process. Some even argue that intrinsic to these challenges is the difficulty in reconciling the EU's "historic commitment to economic development with its new concern to protect the environment", a theme which runs throughout this book.²⁹ From this perspective, leadership in climate change is " 'symbolic politics' [and that] when it comes to implementation the results are far behind the rhetoric".³⁰ Indeed, success in reducing carbon emissions has been limited, and progress towards a more ambitious post-Kyoto agreement has been stunted. The Paris Climate Accord, agreed within the United Nations Framework Convention on Climate Change in December 2015, is being ratified both by the EU and its Member States, out of a total of 194 signatory states, plus the EU. The Paris Accord includes a mechanism "to contribute to the

---

24 Dimitrov, R.S., "Inside UN Climate Change Negotiations: The Copenhagen Conference", *Review of Policy Research* (2010) 27, no. 6, 810.
25 Ibid.
26 Maljean-Dubois, S. and Wemaëre, M., "After Durban, What Legal Form for the Future International Climate Regime", *Carbon & Climate Law Review*, no. 3, 2012, 189–190.
27 Vogler (n 15) 841.
28 Ibid., 839.
29 Baker, S., Kousis, M., Richardson, D. and Young, S., "Introduction: The Theory and Practice of Sustainable Development in EU Perspective", in Baker, S., Kousis, M., Richardson, D. and Young, S. (Eds.), *The Politics of Sustainable Development: Theory, Policy and Practice within the EU* (London: Routledge, 1997) 28–29.
30 Vanden Brande, E., "Chapter 7 – Green Civilian Power Europe", in Orbie, J. (Ed.), *Europe's Global Role: External Policies of the European Union* (Aldershot: Ashgate, 2008) 173–174.

mitigation of greenhouse gases and support sustainable development",[31] and is due to start in 2020.

Although, at the time, the EU's intentions may have seemed promising, when examining progress to date, it seems that its efforts to instigate change have been more aspirational than effective. This could well be an unintentional outcome, but it is on this note that the discussion turns to the efforts made by the EU in promoting sustainable development to the wider world, and whether this endeavour has a similar fate.

## EU promoting sustainable development

The EU demonstrated leadership by example in the field of climate change by setting ambitious targets, which went above and beyond those established by international agreements. Due to the tightly bound relationship between sustainable development and climate change, such leadership could be seen as a means by which the EU has sought to develop the general sustainable development strategy.

Yet, in recent years, the EU has also singled out sustainable development as an objective and, potentially, a principle to be promoted externally by various means. Although the EU promotes sustainable development to its Member States and institutions through its own policy and legislative initiatives, it has also come to recognise the external impact that certain internal policies can have on third parties. The 2001 Sustainable Development Strategy acknowledges the importance of mitigating the potential negative impact of internal policies on the sustainable development efforts of non-EU countries through a high degree of policy coordination.

According to the strategy, if sustainable development within the EU involves 'exporting' problems to other areas then, by definition, it is not genuinely sustainable.[32] This sentiment was reinforced in the February 2002 Commission Communication, which explicitly refers to the external dimension of sustainable development and highlights six key areas of action: harnessing globalisation; making trade contribute further to sustainable development; fighting poverty and promoting social development; improving the coherence of EU policies; encouraging better governance at all levels; and financing sustainable development.[33] In 2005, the Commission published a review of the EU's efforts to address the external dimensions of these six trends in which it noted that:

> It is essential to show European leadership along twin internal and external tracks. This requires an integrated approach and reflects the fact that with

---

31 Paras 6.4–6.7.
32 Adelle, C., Hertin, J. and Jordan, A., "Sustainable Development 'Outside' the European Union: What Role for Impact Assessment", *European Environment* (2006) 16, 57–58.
33 European Commission Communication, "Towards a global partnership for sustainable development", COM(2002) 82 final.

globalisation and increasing interdependence between issues, the EU can only deliver fully on its key internal priorities if it succeeds at the same time on the world scene. Equally, the EU's ability to reflect its global commitments in all its policies is crucial if it is to turn words into deeds, maintaining its credibility as a world leader in the field of sustainable development.[34]

The importance of addressing the external impact of EU internal policies was further highlighted in 2003 by then EU Environment Commissioner, Margot Wallstrom, who warned that the Union's credibility "will suffer if unsustainable trends persist, or if [its] policies have detrimental impacts outside the EU".[35] Thus the effort of addressing the external impact of internal policies became important for the EU not only in terms of encouraging sustainable development on a grander scale, but also in maintaining its position as a credible world leader.

For some, this is a success, as the link made between internal affairs and the external dimensions of sustainable development sets it apart from other political entities such as the United States.[36] However, for its impact on sustainable development to be truly felt, the EU must also directly target sustainable development practices in third world countries through its external relations. The foundation for promoting sustainable development through the EU's external policy can be found in EU legislation and policy. Regulation EC/2493/2000 first dealt specifically with the integration of the environmental dimension in developing countries.[37] Article 21 TEU obliges the EU to promote sustainable development through external relations, stating that its external policies must pursue the objective of "foster[ing] sustainable economic, social and environmental development of developing countries, with the primary aim of eradicating poverty". The Treaty-based authority for action in the EU's external – i.e., international – sphere is clear and the external dimension of the EU's sustainable development agenda thereby has a sound legal basis. The seventh Environmental Action Programme, adopted in 2012, reiterates the EU's role in the wider world and states that the Rio+20 outcomes on sustainable development must be reflected in the internal and external policy priorities of both the Union and its Member States.

The explicit inclusion of sustainable development objectives in external policy is not the only means by which the EU can promote change. As mentioned above, the EU has often acted on the part of its Member States when drafting, negotiating, and ratifying multilateral environmental agreements (MEA) in the

---

34 European Commission Communication, "The 2005 Review of the European Sustainable Development Strategy: Initial Stocktaking and Future Orientations", COM(2005) 97 final of 9 February 2005, 6.
35 Adelle, Hertin, and Jordan (n 32) 57–58.
36 See, for example, Vogel, D., *The Hare and the Tortoise Revisited.* In: *Environmental Policy in the EU: Actors, Institutions and Processes*, 2nd edition (London: Earthscan, 2005).
37 Regulation EC/2493/2000 of the European Parliament and of the Council of 7 November 2000 on measures to promote the full integration of the environmental dimension into the development process of developing countries, OJ L 288/1.

field of climate change. This authority has been extended to sustainable development and other related policies. The EU has a vested interest in ensuring that key international environmental agreements are adopted worldwide as many of the priority areas for environmental protection and sustainable development are dependent on international implementation. The 6th EAP recognises the importance of the EU's success in this area, containing a specific provision for the ratification, compliance, and enforcement of all MEAs relating to the environment where the Union is a party. The EU is a party to many MEAs relating to a variety of matters pertaining to improved environmental protection and sustainable development, including several MEAs that emerged as a consequence of the 2002 conference on the environment entitled the *World Summit on Sustainable Development*. Despite this, the implementation of these agreements has fallen short of initial expectations. The world summits such as the Copenhagen Conference in 2009 represent another example of where the EU has been unable to bring secure agreement to its agenda, suggesting that it struggles to fulfil its full potential as a leader and negotiator on the international stage.

Nevertheless, the EU takes a multi-pronged approach to influencing third parties. For some time the EU's approach to external relations has been categorised as the exercise of soft, rather than hard power. According to Nye, "soft power" is the power to influence other countries without either force or money, instead drawing those people who – by "admiring its values, emulating its example, aspiring to its level of prosperity and openness – want to follow it".[38] It is also argued by some that the EU promotes change as a "normative power", a term coined by Ian Manners.[39] According to Manners, the EU upholds a collective identity based upon its "ideational impact" which provides it with an "ability to shape the conceptions of 'normal' in international relations".[40] Manners identified five core and four subsidiary values which contribute to the EU's normative presence and, "it is in projecting these values, and in promoting the establishment of related norms for the governance of international behaviour, that the EU might be said to exercise normative power".[41] One of the four subsidiary values is sustainable development[42] and, by promoting this value, the EU can take its leadership in the field further through the dissemination of norms and standards to external actors.[43]

---

38 See Nye, J., "Bound to Lead: the Changing Nature of American Power", *American Political Science Review* (1990) 84, 1400; and Nye, J., *Soft Power: The Means to Success in World Politics* (New York: Public Affairs, 2004).
39 See Manners, I., "Normative Power Europe: A Contradiction in Terms?" *Journal of Common Market Studies* (2002) 40, 235–256.
40 Ibid., 238–239.
41 Bretherton, C., and Vogler, J., *The European Union as a Global Actor*, 2nd edition (London: Routledge, 2006) 42.
42 Manners (n 39) 242.
43 Vogler (n 15) 836.

One example where the EU's normative power in promoting sustainable development is particularly prominent is in its enlargement policy.

> It is the Commission's view that, in the long term, enlargement 'may in fact be the biggest single contribution to global sustainable development that the EU can make', allowing new members to leapfrog traditional stages of development and upgrade environmental protection, social development and economic growth by adopting some 300 legislative acts constituting the Union's 'environmental acquis'.[44]

In exercising normative power, the EU has used the promise of enlargement as a means of encouraging political and economic reforms amongst aspiring members.[45] The conditionality mechanism in the accession process has also allowed Union membership to be dependent on the implementation by the candidate country of the Copenhagen criteria and the *acquis communautaire*, including the various commitments to encourage sustainable development.[46] From the point of view of the EU, this not only satisfies its Treaty obligation to 'promote' sustainable development but also, by extending its borders, allows it to exercise greater leverage vis-à-vis other dominant actors.

This scope of normative influence is further reinforced by agreements with third countries covered by the European Neighbourhood Policy (ENP). Through the ENP, the EU offers neighbouring countries to the east and south a privileged relationship of greater political association, deeper economic integration, and increased mobility for people and workers. However, the extent of these relationships is determined by the "mutual commitment [by both parties] to common values".[47] Thus, pursuant to the 2001 Göteborg Conclusions, the agreements are required to include sustainable development as an objective.[48]

The result of these efforts under enlargement and ENP policy is that the EU is able to distance itself from other dominant countries and assert itself as an alternative, credible global power, which places core values and norms before its own self-interests. This, in turn, conceptualises other dominant players as the Union's 'other'.[49] Yet, whether this is actually the case again relates to the extent to which these values and norms are enforced. Although candidate countries covered by

---

44  Ibid., 842.
45  Smith, K., "Enlargement and European Order", in Hill, C. and Smith, M. (Eds.), *International Relations and the European Union* (Oxford: Oxford University Press, 2005) p. 271.
46  Schimmelfennig, F. and Sedelmeier, U., "Governance by Conditionality: EU Rule Transfer to the Candidate Countries of Central and Eastern Europe", *Journal of European Public Policy* (2009) 11, no. 4, 663.
47  European External Action Service, "European Neighbourhood Policy: An Overview", http://eeas.europa.eu/enp/
48  Vogler (n 15) 842.
49  Bretherton and Vogler (n 41) 43.

enlargement policy will, to a certain extent, be obliged to follow the EU's lead in promoting sustainable development, the enforcement of sustainable development obligations through ENP agreements is much less certain. Many argue that there is a large gap in expectation between the EU's eastern and southern neighbours and their adherence to the terms of their ENP agreements. Especially in relation to human rights protection, eastern countries are frequently held to much higher standards than their southern counterparts. Perhaps this is because the southern States represent much greater economic potential and this encourages the EU to forgo some of its human rights values in order to enable more effective trade. Or perhaps, because the eastern States are more likely to one-day join the EU, the Union imposes more stringent standards to set them on the road to accession. Either way, if the EU truly wishes to lead the way towards global sustainability, such inconsistency of enforcement in its neighbourhood seems untenable.

Extending further than the neighbouring countries, the EU also seeks to encourage greater sustainable development through trade agreements with third parties. "As the world's largest market, largest exporter, most generous aid donor and largest foreign investor, the EU is well endowed to offer economic, technological and diplomatic incentives",[50] and it is these incentives which allow the EU to enforce standards – such as sustainable development – on trading partners.

Since the early 1990s, the EU's trade agreements have included a 'human rights clause' requiring the parties to respect human rights and democratic principles. More recently, however, they have also included clauses or chapters on 'sustainable development', which contain obligations on negotiating parties to respect international labour and environmental standards. The sustainable development sections incorporated into these agreements are not simply a matter of discretionary foreign policy, they are mechanisms that, in theory, enable the EU to comply with its obligations under the EU Treaty.[51] The importance the sustainable development obligations represent to the EU is demonstrated by the fact that in the EU–India free trade agreement currently in negotiation, the chapter on sustainable development is among the potential stumbling blocks that could stall the conclusion of an agreement otherwise greatly beneficial to both parties.[52]

The first of the EU's free trade agreements to make reference to the objective of sustainable development was the 1993 EU–Hungary Europe Agreement. Since then, the term has been incorporated to varying extents in trade agreements with countries all over the globe. Sustainable development chapters are now found

---

50  Parker and Karlsson (n 16) 928–929.
51  Bartels, L., "Human Rights and Sustainable Development Obligations in EU Free Trade Agreements", University of Cambridge Faculty of Law Research Paper, no 24/2012, at 16–17.
52  Gstöhl, S., "The Common Commercial Policy and Political Conditionality: 'Normative Power Europe' Through Trade", *Egmont Institute of International Relations – Studia Diplomatica* (2010) LXIII, no. 3, 7–8.

in the 2008 EU–Cariforum agreement,⁵³ the 2010 EU–Korea agreement,⁵⁴ and the 2012 EU–Central America,⁵⁵ the EU–Peru/Colombia agreements,⁵⁶ and the 2016 EU–Canada Comprehensive Economic and Trade Agreement (CETA).⁵⁷ The EU is now seemingly committed, as a matter of policy, to including these provisions in future trading agreements.⁵⁸

Bartels distinguishes between the different obligations imposed on third parties in the sustainable development chapters, citing the EU–Central America Agreement as a typical example:

> The parties affirm their commitments to the ILO core labour principles and to certain multilateral environmental agreements; and they also undertake to 'effectively implement' the fundamental ILO Conventions referred to in the ILO Declaration of Fundamental Principles and Rights at Work of 1998. Beyond this, the parties undertake not to lower their levels of protection to encourage trade of investment, or to fail to effectively enforce their labour and environmental legislation in a manner affecting trade or investment between the parties; and they undertake that they will 'strive to ensure' that their laws and policies provide for and encourage appropriate but high levels of labour and environmental protection and that they will 'strive to improve' these laws and policies.⁵⁹

However, the scope and level of the obligation imposed varies depending on the agreement. For example, the principle of sustainable development was given an unusually broad definition in the 2008 Cotonou Agreement, which states that:

> respect for all human rights and fundamental freedoms, including respect for fundamental social rights, democracy based on the rule of law and transparent and accountable governance are an integral part of sustainable development, whose pillars – economic development, social development and environmental protection – are interdependent and mutually reinforcing.⁶⁰

---

53 European Union, "Economic Partnership Agreement between the CARIFORUM States, of the one part, and the European Community and its Member States, of the other part", OJ L/289/I/3, 30 October 2008.
54 European Union, "Free Trade Agreement between the European Union and its Member States, of the one part, and the Republic of Korea, of the other part", OJ L/127, 14 May 2011.
55 European Commission, DG Trade, "EU-Central America Association Agreement", http://trade.ec.europa.eu/doclib/press/index.cfm?id=689
56 European Commission, DG Trade, "Trade Agreement between the European Union and Columbia and Peru", http://trade.ec.europa.eu/doclib/press/index.cfm?id=691
57 http://ec.europa.eu/trade/policy/in-focus/ceta/index_en.htm
58 Bartels (n 51) 11.
59 Ibid.
60 Ibid., 10–11.

Similarly, the sustainable development obligations are specifically monitored by a variety of bodies, the influence of which differs depending on the agreement. The Trade and Development Committee established by the EU–Cariforum agreement has a broad mandate to discuss sustainable development issues including those lying outside the clause in the agreement. But the Trade and Sustainable Development Board in the EU–Central America agreement has a mandate only to oversee the implementation of the sustainable development chapter.[61] As is the case in the EU's identity as a normative power, the inconsistency in the standards and monitoring bodies imposed in the agreements raises concerns regarding the EU's willingness and ability to enforce sustainable development obligations. In the recent trade agreements that have been concluded, it is notable that "none of the agreements admit the possibility of violating the 'principle of sustainable development'. Rather [. . .] the agreements contain provisions on cooperation as well as concrete obligations to respect and 'strive' to improve multilateral and domestic labour and environmental standards".[62]

Certainly, when looking at the enforcement of the human rights obligations contained in EU trade agreements, there has been a somewhat chequered success. Not only is the EU setting different standards depending upon the country and the economic interests concerned, but it has also consistently favoured positive measures over negative ones when securing better human rights protection in third countries, with the suspension of a trade agreement seeming to be a measure of last resort. For example, according to Gstöhl, the Generalized System of Preferences (GSP) has been extended, without distinction, to human rights violators.[63] The EU has operated the GSP since 1971 and, with this autonomous trade measure, has granted developing countries non-reciprocal duty-free access or tariff reductions for a wide range of products. Special incentives were granted to countries respecting certain labour standards. In 2005 the EU introduced an integrated special incentive arrangement (GSP+) for sustainable development and good governance, which provides supplementary benefits in terms of duty-free access to all the products covered by the general GSP. However, the application of the conditionality contained in these agreements has been very inconsistent, with any decision to remove trade preferences seemingly requiring persistent and serious breaches of labour standards, beyond those required for condemnation by the ILO.[64] Furthermore, the European Parliament has repeatedly called on the Commission to show greater rigour in implementing GSP+ by suspending preferences for countries, which seriously and systematically breach fundamental social rights. Yet, in response, the Commission reiterates its preference for a

---

61 Ibid., 14.
62 Ibid., 11.
63 Gstöhl (n 52) 2–12.
64 For example, in 2013, the ILO criticised the Uzbekistan government for allowing child labour to be used in its cotton trade. Despite this, the EU continues to allow Uzbekistan to benefit from preferential import duties for its cotton exports to the EU.

cooperative approach and "does not want the social provisions to be enforced or linked to sanctions or punitive measures".[65]

But what would happen if the agreement turned out to have negative effects on sustainable development, either in terms of labour standards or in terms of environmental protection? The EU would have little power to withdraw from the commitments that contribute to this situation. Nor could it take coercive steps with a view to enforcing the other country's own obligations. This, arguably, could leave the EU compromised, whereby its trade practices openly contradict the sustainable development agenda it proclaims itself to follow, both internally and externally. According to Bartels, this lack of enforcement power does not matter since:

> the EU is required merely to pursue the objectives of sustainable development and the eradication of poverty. So long as the EU does not act in a manner that has a high likelihood of contradicting these objectives, it is unlikely to fall foul of this obligation.[66]

## Sustainable development and key actors on the international stage

Many international organisations and countries have contributed to the expansion of sustainable development worldwide by providing a forum within which actors can discuss their sustainability-related challenges and solutions or they play a remarkable leadership role, and contribution in the field of environmental, economic, and social change. The discussion following will focus on the role that international organisations and other key actors can play in sustainable development. It will examine the World Trade Organization (WTO), the United States, China, Russia, India, and Brazil. These together provide an interesting point of comparison to contextualise the EU's approach.

### *The World Trade Organization (WTO)*

The WTO started life primarily as an economic and trade entity, and has subsequently had to adapt to encourage greater environmental protection and sustainable development.

As an international economic organisation comprised of 150 member governments, the WTO plays a key role in the global economy, administering various trade agreements including the General Agreement on Tariffs and Trade (GATT). Since the establishment, WTO has recognised the role of sustainable development in international trade. For various reasons, it considers itself well placed to couple economic and trade incentives with sustainable and environmentally friendly

---

65  Gstöhl (n 52) 8.
66  Bartels (n 51) 17.

development. One such reason is the impact – both positive and negative – that trade liberalisation has on the environment. From a positive perspective, trade liberalisation can help to ensure that resources are used effectively, by encouraging more resource-efficient technology and by generating the money to pay for it.[67] Conversely, it can also facilitate unsustainable economic activity through the increase in deregulation, which weakens the ability for countries to enforce rules that set certain environmental and labour standards.[68]

Since the 1990s the WTO has recognised the explicit link between sustainable development and the disciplined opening of new markets. In the preamble to the Marrakesh agreement establishing the WTO, the members called for an expansion of global trade "in accordance with the objective of sustainable development".[69] The WTO views sustainable development and trade liberalisation as 'mutually supportive'.[70]

This clearly gives the WTO the mandate both to contribute to the prevention of environmental degradation and to use trade to encourage the development and use of resources in a sustainable and equitable way.[71] Consequently, the WTO has established various policy mechanisms through which it aims to incorporate sustainable development, and its various components, into international trade.[72] Such mechanisms include the WTO Agreement on Trade-Related Aspects of Intellectual Property Rights, established to provide a framework for an intellectual property system that promotes access to and the dissemination of green technologies.[73] Also, the WTO Agreement on Technical Barriers to Trade and the WTO Agreement on the Application of Sanitary and Phytosanitary Measures both provide the scope for WTO members to implement regulatory measures designed to protect the environment and impose disciplines, which ensure that such measures are not unnecessary restrictions on international trade.[74] The WTO Committees on Trade and Development and Trade and Environment were also

---

67 Brack, D., Chatham House, "The World Trade Organization and Sustainable Development: A Guide to the Debate", *Energy, Environment and Development Programme*, BP 05/03, 7.
68 Ibid., 2.
69 The Marrakesh Agreement, cited in McNamee, D., "Climate Change, the Kyoto Protocol, and the World Trade Organization: Challenges and Conflicts", *Sustainable Development Law and Policy* (2005–2006) 6, 41.
70 Decision on Trade and Environment',14 April 1994, GATT Secretariat, in *The Results of the Uruguay Round of Multilateral Trade Negotiations, the Legal Texts* (WTO, UK, Cambridge University Press, 1999) 411 (hereinafter the Legal text) ; Preamble, 4; WTO, Doha Ministerial Declaration, para. 6, WT/MIN(01)/DEC/1, 20 November 2001; Doha Ministerial Declaration, Preamble.
71 Johnson, E., "The Interface Between Trade, Investment and Sustainable Development: Implications for India", *Macquarie Journal of International and Comparative Environmental Law* (2005) 2, 41.
72 See World Trade Organization, "Harnessing Trade for Sustainable Development and a Green Economy", p. 3.
73 Ibid., 4.
74 See World Trade Organization, "Harnessing Trade for Sustainable Development and a Green Economy", p. 4.

established to review the relationship between development or environmental protection and trade rules and to identify possible reforms.

These policy initiatives, though intended generally to support sustainable development, are quite limited. Even now, neither of the two above-mentioned WTO committees has come to concrete conclusions. Instead, the most significant progress has occurred in the development of WTO rules by the organisation's dispute-resolution bodies. Environmental regulations imposed by a member of the WTO are often challenged under the most-favoured nation or national treatment provisions in the GATT Agreement. Article XX of the GATT provides exceptions to these obligations, including exceptions for those measures "necessary to protect human, animal or plant life or health" (Article XX(b)) or "relating to the conservation of exhaustible natural resources" (Article XX(g)). Nonetheless, the Chapter of Article XX adds another condition to be satisfied, namely that the measure is not applied in a manner "which would constitute a means of arbitrary or unjustifiable discrimination between countries where the same conditions prevail, or a disguised restriction on international trade".[75]

Recent dispute settlement cases have led to a number of significant reinterpretations of these rules, including the applicability of the sustainable development commitment in the Marrakesh agreement to the relevant paragraphs of Article XX of the GATT.[76] However, there appears to be some inconsistency in the interpretation by the Court, leading to further doubts as to whether the WTO is really the appropriate forum for promoting sustainable trade. For example, determination of what is 'necessary' under Article XX(b) of GATT is ultimately up to the WTO. And, although the interpretation is meant to be based on 'science', this still raises concerns about "the competence of the WTO in determining the necessity of environmental protection measures, given that the general expertise of the organisation is in the field of trade, rather than sustainable development or science".[77] These concerns have been exacerbated by the fact that, until recently, WTO panels and appellate bodies have interpreted the general exceptions of Article XX extremely narrowly.[78] Indeed, in the Brazil-Retreaded Tyres dispute,[79] the appellate body decided that it was for individual nation States to determine which environmental measures should be employed. This can be contrasted with the panel's earlier decision in the Thailand-Cigarettes dispute,[80] where it was

---

75 This was confirmed by the WTO panel in the US-Gasoline dispute (Appellate Body Report, United States – Standards for Reformulated and Conventional Gasoline WT/DS58/AB/R (adopted 6 November 1998); see also Felicity Deane, "The WTO, the National Security Exception and Climate Change" CCLR (2012) 2, 155.
76 Brack (n 68) 7.
77 Johnson, E. (n 71) 46.
78 McNamee, D., "Climate Change, the Kyoto Protocol, and the World Trade Organization: Challenges and Conflicts", *Sustainable Development Law and Policy* (2005–2006) 6, 42.
79 Appellate Body Report, Brazil – Measures Affecting Imports of Retreaded Tyres, WT/DS332/AB/R (17 December 2007).
80 Panel Report, Thailand – Restrictions on Importation of and Internal Taxes on Cigarettes, BISD 37S/200 (7 November 1990).

concluded that there must be no alternative to the measure that a member could reasonably be expected to employ for Article XX to apply.[81] Furthermore, under paragraph (g) of Article XX, the panel in the Canada-Unprocessed Herring and Salmon dispute[82] determined that while a trade measure did not have to be necessary or essential for the conservation of an exhaustible natural resource, it had to be primarily aimed at the conservation of an exhaustible natural resource to be considered as 'relating to' conservation within the meaning of Article XX(g).[83]

One of the most contentious trade–environment debates concerns process and production methods (PPMs), many of which are environmentally unsustainable.[84] During the 1990s, a series of cases seemed to imply that trade discrimination towards PPMs could not be applied on the basis of environmental protection. In the tuna-dolphin dispute,[85] the panel found that such trade restrictions could only be adopted within the contracting party's jurisdiction and only for the resource in question (i.e., tuna).[86] However, more recently, WTO rulings suggest that such discrimination can be allowed under the right circumstances. In the shrimp-turtle case,[87] the Panel found that the commitment to sustainable development in the preambular language of the Marrakesh Agreement could have an influence on the interpretation of Article XX GATT.[88] As a consequence, a United States embargo on imports of shrimp caught in a way which killed endangered species of sea turtles could be justified under Article XX(g).[89] Crucial to this decision was the definition of sub-paragraph (g), which the appellate body argued was not 'static' but rather 'evolutionary' and should be interpreted in view of the "contemporary concerns of the community of nations about the protection and conservation of the environment".[90]

---

81 Deane, F., "The WTO, the National Security Exception and Climate Change", *CCLR* (2012) 2, 152.
82 GATT Panel Report, Canada – Measures Affecting Exports of Unprocessed Herring and Salmon, GATT BISD 35S/ 98 (22 March 1988).
83 Deane, F., "The WTO, the National Security Exception and Climate Change", *CCLR* (2012) 2, 153–154.
84 Brack (n 68) 7–8.
85 GATT Panel Report, United States – Restrictions on the Import of Tuna, DS21/R – 39S/155, (3 September 1991). This was again confirmed in 2012, when the WTO panel found that dolphin-friendly labels on tins of tuna constituted a barrier to Mexican products which did not have these labels, see Appellate Body Report, United States – Measures Concerning the Importation, Marketing and Sale of Tuna and Tuna Products, AB-2012-2 (16 May 2012).
86 Cordonier Segger, M., "The Role of International Forums in the Advancement of Sustainable Development", *Sustainable Development Law and Policy* (2009–2010) no. 4, 16.
87 Appellate Body Report, United States – Import Prohibition of Certain Shrimp and Shrimp Products, WT/DS58/AB/R (12 October 1998).
88 However, in this case, the measure was nonetheless ruled invalid as a result of the discrimination between the parties to which it applied.
89 Brack (n 68) 7–8.
90 Deane (n 84) 154.

Moreover, the WTO has shown that it has sufficiently developed its approach to be able to distinguish between trade restrictions which are put in place in a genuine attempt to adhere with the objective of sustainable development and those which are implemented under the guise of sustainable development, but which actually are intended to promote national industry. In 2014, the WTO examined restrictions which were imposed by the Chinese government on the exportation of rare earth elements, which are used in technological devices. Although accounting for 90 per cent of global production, the Chinese government chose to limit exports in an effort to reduce pollution and conserve resources. Despite this, the WTO dispute resolution mechanism found that "the overall effect of the foreign and domestic restrictions [was] to encourage domestic extraction and secure preferential use of those materials by Chinese manufacturers", thereby dismissing the sustainable development argument put forward by the Chinese government.

Further to the exceptions included in Article XX, some argue that the exceptions provided under Article XXI on measures relating to national security can also be extended to encompass climate change measures.[91] Although the WTO has not yet reached the point of explicitly authorising trade restrictive measures which have the aim of promoting sustainable development in the name of national security, a move in this direction would certainly reflect the growing appreciation (such as that in the EU's Security Strategy) of the potential security threat environmental degradation can pose to modern-day society and the importance of sustainable development to mitigate it.

There is no doubt that international trade plays a vital role in promoting sustainable development across the world. Yet, in view of the above, it seems that the WTO still has some way to go before it succeeds in establishing a consistent and balanced approach to sustainable development in trading relationships. The various policy mechanisms established to promote sustainable practices are, in theory, a great step. But the committees established to review them provide little inspiration for further development. Moreover, case law to date illustrates a move towards protecting the environment where possible and fair, although the overall approach taken by the WTO panels and appellate body remains far from clear-cut. It is worth noting here that organisations like the WTO are arguably under an obligation to evolve along with human society. Therefore, the fact that the text of Article XX was drafted in 1948 and has not been amended since could mean that it is unsuitable to address the current threats and necessary exceptions to international trade.[92]

In the Doha Ministerial Declaration, adopted at the start of the recent trade negotiations, the WTO reaffirmed its commitment to the objective of sustainable development. It states that it is "convinced that the aims of upholding and safeguarding an open and non-discriminatory multilateral trading system, and acting

---

91  For more on climate change at the exception under Article XXI see Deane (n 84) 151.
92  Deane (n 84) 158.

for the protection of the environment and the promotion of sustainable development can and must be mutually supportive". Yet, after years of negotiation, at the 9th WTO Ministerial Conference, agreement was found on the first set of issues. However, the main outcome of the conference was the Trade Facilitation Agreement, which, once implemented, could help remove environmentally harmful, trade-distortionary measures and promote greater access to environmental goods and services at a cheaper cost.[93] Despite this, many issues remain to be agreed. Therefore, for the time being at least, sustainable development as an objective in the WTO remains at the mercy of out-dated legislation, ineffective policy mechanisms, and inconsistent dispute resolution.

## Other key actors' role in sustainable development

### The United States

Until recently, the United States (US) has been the key economic, political, and diplomatic actor on the international stage. While its status is, perhaps, in decline, the US still plays a remarkable leadership role, and makes a significant leadership contribution in the field of environmental, economic, and social change. Consequently, its approach to sustainable development is worth some discussion, as it could form an influential basis for other developed countries.

The US Constitution makes no reference to the phrase "sustainable development" but at both a policy and legislative level there is recognition of the concept. The US is currently the second largest emitter of greenhouse gases and, in an effort to address this, the Obama administration attempted to incorporate various measures to reduce $CO_2$ emissions. Before his election into office in 2009, President Obama promised to implement an economy-wide cap-and-trade system. However, two attempts – the Waxman-Markey and the Kerry-Lieberman bills – both failed to deliver on this promise.[94] Subsequently, the Obama administration's focus was on the Environmental Protection Agency, which in 2012 won an appeal which found that GHGs are a danger to the public and that the Agency therefore has the right to regulate them.[95] The first few months of the Trump administration have seen a change in tone, with, in particular, an announcement in June 2017 that the US will withdraw from the 2015 Paris Climate Accord, but the Trump administration has not to date been a model of clarity, and it is difficult to assess the impact on US policy outside of the sphere of political announcements.

Efforts at the regional level to establish ETS-type schemes have been spearheaded by the Regional Greenhouse Gas Initiative, which has resulted in

---

93 WTO Harnessing Trade Report (n 75) 1.
94 Bossley, L., "Dealing With Reality", *Journal of World Energy Law and Business* (2012) 5, no. 4, 363.
95 Ibid.

initiatives such as the California Cap-and-Trade Program, the enforceable obligation of which started in January 2013.[96] Further to this, as of 2014 and according to the US Environmental Protection Agency, 31 States had GHG inventories 25 States had climate change action plans.[97]

In the field of environmental protection more generally, there are two principal federal statutes: the Clean Air Act (CAA) and the Clean Water Act (CWA). Each statute demonstrates an entirely different approach to the tension that exists between environmental and economic interests, thus giving some indication of the US's varied approach to sustainable development. On the one hand, the CAA regulates air emissions from stationary and mobile sources and provides that minimum standards of environmental quality must be met regardless of the economic consequences and costs. On the other hand, the CWA establishes the basic structure for regulating discharges of pollutants and reflects greater ambivalence, mandating environmental protection only to the extent that it is affordable.[98]

Other pieces of legislation require a greater balancing of the costs and benefits of environmental action. The National Environmental Policy Act established the first broad national framework for environmental protection and takes a regulatory approach that is information-based. It requires an agency to consider the anticipated adverse environmental impacts of a proposal before taking action. However, the impact of this obligation is mitigated by the fact that, according to the Supreme Court, the agency concerned has no obligation to modify its proposal once it has adequately considered the environmental impacts of its proposed action.[99]

The Endangered Species Act is designed "to provide a means whereby the ecosystems upon which endangered species and threatened species depend may be conserved, [and] to provide a program for the conservation of such endangered species and threatened species".[100] Since its inception, the ESA has developed to become one of the most powerful pieces of environmental legislation in the US. Initially enacted as a largely symbolic gesture following the first Earth Day and the voter attack on the Dirty Dozen – the twelve senators with the worst environmental records during the 1970s – citizen activist groups increasingly relied on the legislation to challenge un-environmentally friendly development. Following the Court's pro-environmental protection decision in *Hill*,[101] Congress reviewed

---

96 See California Government, "Cap-and-Trade Program", www.arb.ca.gov/cc/capandtrade/capandtrade.htm
97 See EPA, "Greenhouse Gas Inventories", http://epa.gov/statelocalclimate/state/state-examples/ghg-inventory.html#all and EPA, "Climate Change Action Plans", www.epa.gov/statelocalclimate/local/local-examples/action-plans.html#all
98 Healy, M.P., "The Sustainable Development Principle in United States Environmental Law", *Journal of Energy and Environmental Law* (Summer 2011), 23–27.
99 Ibid., 28.
100 U.S. Fish and Wildlife Service, "Endangered Species Act of 1973 as amended through the 108th Congress", section 2, 5(b).
101 *Tennessee Valley Authority (TVA) v. Hill*, 437 U.S. 153, 174 (1978).

the degree to which the ESA should provide unconditional protection for endangered species and, as a consequence, enacted several amendments which diluted the substantive requirements of Section 7 of the Act. The Endangered Species Committee was also established to adjudicate requests for exemptions and to provide relief in favour of development, but only when the developmental benefits "clearly outweigh" the harm to the environment.[102]

Looking at these examples, US environmental law appears to be quite varied in its interpretation of sustainable development, especially when balancing economic and environmental interests. Ranging from protection of the environment at all costs to protection of the environment only when convenient, this inconsistency of legislative approach may cause great future uncertainty when deciding whether the regulatory regime should protect health and the environment over economic development, or provide for a balancing of the two.[103] Furthermore, the evolution of legislation such as the ESA demonstrates that the earliest legislation in the US was driven by public pressure, seemingly the reverse of the top-down approach of EU environmental and sustainable development policy.

In relation to trade, the approach seems to be more consistent. The Trade Act of 2002 identifies sustainable development as one of the many goals to be achieved in any bilateral, regional, or multilateral trade and investments. Furthermore, Congress, when reviewing the Act, identified a number of environmental and sustainable development objectives to be pursued by the US whilst negotiating such agreements.[104] The environmental provisions established in the North Atlantic Free Trade Agreement (NAFTA) and the side agreement (the North Atlantic Agreement on Environmental Cooperation) have both served as the general baseline for all environmental provisions contained in subsequent trade agreements, providing that where there is an inconsistency between the NAFTA

---

102 Healy (n 99) 30.
103 Ibid., 35.
104 Namely: to ensure that trade and environmental policies are mutually supportive and to seek to protect and preserve the environment and enhance the international means of doing so, while optimizing the use of the world's resources; to seek provisions in trade agreements under which parties to those agreements strive to ensure that they do not weaken or reduce the protections afforded in domestic environmental and labour laws as an encouragement for trade; to ensure that a party to a trade agreement with the United States does not fail to effectively enforce its environmental laws, through a sustained or recurring course of action or inaction, in a manner affecting trade between the parties, while recognizing a party's right to exercise discretion with respect to investigatory, prosecutorial, regulatory, and compliance matters and to prioritise allocation of resources for environmental law enforcement; to strengthen the capacity of U.S. trading partners to protect the environment through the promotion of sustainable development; to reduce or eliminate government practices or policies that unduly threaten sustainable development; and to seek market access, through the elimination of tariffs and non-tariff barriers, for U.S. environmental technologies, goods, and services. See Kennedy, K.C., "The Status of the Trade-Environment-Sustainable Development Triad in the Doha Round Negotiations and in Recent U.S. Trade Policy", *Indiana International and Comparative Law Review* (2009), 539–40.

and trade provisions in environmental agreements listed under the NAFTA, the environmental trade agreements will prevail.[105]

Although the four free trade agreements were negotiated in 2007 with Colombia, Panama, Peru, and South Korea all contained enhanced environmental and sustainable development provisions mandated by the Bipartisan Agreement on Trade Policy concluded between Congress and the White House, all other parties to free trade agreements have their own obligations. Parties to agreements concluded with the US must adopt, maintain, and implement all relevant multilateral environmental treaties including, *inter alia:* the Montreal Protocol on Ozone Depleting Substances; the Inter-American Tropical Tuna Convention; and the International Whaling Convention. However, as bold as this latter obligation may seem, Kennedy highlights two significant qualifications that substantially narrow its effect:

> First, in order to establish a violation of this commitment, the complaining Party must show that the responding Party's failure to fulfil an obligation under one of the covered [multilateral environmental agreements] has been 'through a sustained or recurring course of action or inaction'. Second, the sustained or recurring course of action or inaction must be 'in a manner affecting trade or investment between the Parties'. In other words, if the violation occurs outside the trade or investment context, then it cannot be the subject of a complaint.[106]

In relation to Bilateral Investment Treaties, no such agreement contained any provisions on the environment until 2005, when the Uruguay-US Treaty was concluded, which stated that nothing in the Treaty could "be construed to prevent a Party from adopting, maintaining, or enforcing any measure otherwise consistent with this Treaty that it considers appropriate to ensure that investment activity in its territory is undertaken in a manner sensitive to environmental concerns".[107] However, as in the case of free trade agreements concluded with the US, such provisions lack both incentives to comply and mechanisms to measure enforcement and the extent of progress towards sustainable development.

According to this interpretation of the provisions in both free trade agreements and Bilateral Investment Treaties, it seems that the US approach closely reflects that of the EU. Despite imposing quite high standards in the rhetoric of the agreement, there is limited enforcement of sustainable development obligations. This perspective is reinforced by the fact that the US has never broken a trade agreement based on the other contracting party's non-compliance with

---

105 Kennedy (n 105) 537–540.
106 Kennedy (n 105) 540–544.
107 See Article 12(2) of the Treaty between the United States of America and the Oriental Republic of Uruguay Concerning the Encouragement and Reciprocal Protection of Investment, 2006.

obligations relating to, for example, human rights.[108] As with the EU, this carrot-but-no-stick approach risks undermining the credibility of not only the trade or investment agreement itself, but also the United States.

In view of this, it seems that sustainable development has not yet really penetrated the US legislature, which can be identified as still being stuck in 'economy versus environment' mode. Primary amongst its economic concerns is how the US fares against China, its most important global competitor, and it is here that the discussion turns to the next key player in international affairs.[109]

## China

Despite still being categorised as a developing country, by 2005, China had become the world's second-largest economy. This growth was significant in aiding its transition from a 'backbencher' in international politics to one of the most dominant economic and political players.[110] However, as China's economy grew, so too did its environmental footprint, and, in 2007, it surpassed the United States to become the world's largest emitter of GHGs.[111] As a consequence, China is in a very interesting and fast-evolving situation, one worth considering from the perspective of what the sustainable development agenda of the future will be. China's approach to sustainable development is also of interest because of the various internal challenges that it has to overcome, including: a large population in poverty, which by some estimates amounts to more than 122 million people; a complex and diverse geographical and geological environment; and severe, diverse, and frequent natural disasters.[112] Add to this a growing social demand for stable energy supplies in the country; encroaching deserts in the north; and the intermittent closure of factories in the south due to lack of water, and the need to develop sustainable practices is clear.

According to the Chinese National Report presented to the Rio+20, the country has been incorporating sustainable development into national strategies since 1996.[113] However, it was not until the 2000s that there seemed to be any significant steps forward in promoting sustainable development, the most prominent of which can be found in the field of energy policy. Over the past decade, China has become the world's largest producer of hydropower, solar, and wind power;

---

108 Tsogas, G., "Labour Standards in the Generalised Systems of Preferences of the European Union and the United States", *European Journal of Industrial Relations* (2000) 6, no. 3, 365.
109 Carlane, C., "The Glue That Binds the Straw That Broke the Camel's Back? Exploring the Implications of U.S. Reengagement in Global Climate Change Negotiations", *Tulane Journal of International and Comparative Law* (2010) 19, 122.
110 Ibid., 122–124.
111 Tabou, A. and Lemoine, M., "Willing Power, Fearing Responsibilities: BASCIC in the Climate Negotiations", *CCLR* (2012) 3, 197.
112 "The People's Republic of China National Report on Sustainable Development", 2012, p. 5.
113 Ibid., 2.

for instance by the end of 2011, wind power accounted for 45GW of generation capacity, more than in the US.[114] It has also made some steps towards greater marine and forest protection.[115] Furthermore, the State Environmental Protection Administration has been upgraded to the Ministry of Environmental Protection, affording the body a more prominent status within the hierarchy of the national government.[116]

In 2012 the first steps were made toward a domestic cap-and-trade system for emissions, the National Development and Reform Commission announcing its 'Tentative Measures for the Administration of Voluntary Greenhouse Gasses Emissions Reduction Trading'. These measures envisaged seven pilot schemes, the first commencing in Shenzhen and Shanghai in 2013, then later in Beijing and Guangdong. Signalling a prelude to China-wide fixed caps, the potential size of such a system would make the EU emission trading scheme "pale to insignificance".[117] It would also provide an interesting example for other major players in the global market, as the system envisaged encouraging different sectors or regions to compete with each other to reduce carbon intensity and, as all winners and losers are likely to be Chinese, any transfer of money would remain within the Chinese economy.[118] Furthermore, a successful emission trading scheme in China would significantly impact upon the wider world. If China were to remain outside of the global climate regime, the international community would be faced with problems of international emissions leakage, a global race to the bottom would occur, and energy intensive operations would be outsourced from areas subject to emissions regulation to areas, such as China, where no such regulations exist.[119]

Additionally, in 2013, the Ministry of Environmental Protection enacted two new policies which would, for the first time, directly affect heavily polluting industries in China. The first was a trial programme making environmental liability insurance mandatory. The second was a proposal for stricter emission limits with which industries would have to comply in 47 major Chinese cities.[120] Two further separate programmes – a limit on energy use and a direct energy consumption tax – are also planned.[121] The Chinese government has agreed a £180 billion anti-pollution plan, partly in response to the revelation that pollution in China was found to reduce life expectancy in the north by five years. Despite this, the

---

114 Lacy, P., "Is China the Global Game-Changer for Sustainability?" *The Guardian*, 27 January 2012, www.guardian.co.uk/sustainable-business/china-development-renewables-sustainability
115 The People's Republic of China National Report (n 418) 4.
116 Carlane (n 110) 129–130.
117 Bossley (n 95) 362.
118 Ibid.
119 Carlane (n 110) 124.
120 Baker and McKenzie, "Environment, China – Client Alert: China Issues New Environmental Insurance Requirements and Limits on Emissions", April 2013, 1.
121 Bossley (n 95) 362.

Ministry of Environmental Protection, the body in charge of these initiatives, faces its own problems having been described by its own Minister as one of the four worst government departments in the world.[122]

Although steps have been taken which not only address high levels of emissions in China and are likely to be intended to improve air quality for China's neighbours as well, China's approach to sustainable development has its critics. The approach is particularly criticised for being fragmented, with differing levels of implementation across its various provinces. According to Carlane this is partly because Chinese law-making is very top heavy, with environmental legislation being drafted by the central government in ambiguous terms in order to provide local agencies with considerable breadth in their interpretation and implementation.[123] Having said this, such an approach is hardly surprising given the country's vast territory and the varying geological environments across its thirty-four provinces. Furthermore, issues exist regarding the interrelation between the country's economic growth, poverty, and environmental degradation. Poverty alleviation requires economic development, which puts further pressure on the fragile ecosystem. Equally, protection of the environment and other natural resources can prevent low-income regions from emerging from poverty.[124]

There is also an interesting comparison to be drawn between the different rationales of China and the EU behind their choice to promote sustainable development internally. As opposed to the 'moral obligation' declared by the EU, China takes a more pragmatic stance. One of the key priorities of the Chinese regime is to avoid social unrest. Thus, in order to respond to incidences of environmental crises or shortages of energy supply, the Chinese government has decided to take action. The avoidance of social unrest is also reflected by the fact that Chinese environmental law is non-participatory. Unlike the EU's obligations under the Aarhus Convention, "citizen participation [in China] is neither included in the law-making process nor welcome in the implementation or enforcement stages".[125]

Thus it seems that China is beginning to consider how development interests can be aligned with sustainable growth and better environmental protection. Some even argue that China could "provide the beginnings of a solution for scaling sustainability and decoupling growth from environmental impact" and make the step between rhetoric and action.[126] This commitment has been backed up

---

122 Phillips, T., "China's Environment Ministry 'one of four worst departments in world' ", *The Telegraph*, 9 July 2013, www.telegraph.co.uk/news/worldnews/asia/china/10168806/Chinas-environment-ministry-one-of-four-worst-departments-in-world.html
123 Carlane (n 110) 129.
124 Zhang, J., "Is Environmentally Sustainable Economic Growth Possible in China?" *The Diplomat*, 10 January 2013, http://thediplomat.com/china-power/is-environmentally-sustainable-economic-growth-possible-in-china/
125 Bossley (n 95) 362.
126 Lacy, P., "Is China the Global Game-Changer for Sustainability?" *The Guardian*, 27 January 2012, www.guardian.co.uk/sustainable-business/china-development-renewables-sustainability.

by significant energy investment, with $51 billion (approximately £33 billion) in new renewable energy projects in 2010 alone and almost $1.6 trillion (approximately £1 trillion) allocated for strategic sectors in the period 2012-2017.[127] Despite this, the country still has significant hurdles to overcome, and a political perspective which suggests sustainable development objectives may be set aside in the interests of reducing poverty and stabilising nation-wide growth.

*Russia*

The next point of comparison is Russia. Russia has been witness to significant internal growth and is frequently now discussed in conjunction with Brazil, India, and China as a member of a group of large countries experiencing rapid growth, a group with its own name: BRIC. Yet the country presents unique issues which are highly relevant to the future of the global sustainable development agenda, and it is therefore worthy of further examination. First, as the largest country in the world, with one-fifth of the world's forests and the highest level of energy intensity, Russia controls the environmental dynamics of not just the Northern hemisphere, but the entire planet.[128] Despite this, the country is well known for its environmentally harmful activities, ecological disasters, and widespread industrial pollution of the water and air. Secondly, the country has a significant number of social challenges to overcome which are closely related to its recent history as a State emerging from an extended period of communist party rule, with a vast divide between the rich and poor and an inherent lack of trust towards the State and its officials.[129]

In relation to climate change, Russia's position was laid out in the Presidential Statement on the 2009 Russian Climate Doctrine, later adopted by governmental degree in 2011. The statement maintains that:

> [p]olitical decisions on climate and regulations based on them should focus on the long-term interests of the Russian Federation . . . [and t]he choice of economic instruments contributing to lower man-made greenhouse gas emissions . . . will be determined on the basis of their effectiveness with the help of Government and private financing mechanisms.[130]

In view of these statements, the responsibility for developing an emissions trading scheme was considered to be a primarily economic effort and was thus placed in the hands of the Ministry of Economic Development.[131] This, arguably, points towards a primarily economic focus on climate change efforts, with limited inclusion of environmental or social interests.

---

127 Ibid.
128 Karghiev, V., Helio International, "Energy and Sustainable Development in the Russia Federation", *Sustainable Energy Watch* (2005–2006), 18.
129 Crotty, J. and Hall, S., "Environmental Awareness and Sustainable Development in the Russian Federation", *Sustainable Development* (2012), 2, 311–320.
130 Bossley (n 95) 363–364.
131 Ibid.

This approach is replicated to a certain extent in the Russian approach to sustainable development more generally. Russia is a signatory to Agenda 21 and the Rio Convention and has approved a series of legislative acts with the stated aim of implementing the provisions of Agenda 21 domestically. Despite this, Oldfield and Shaw argue that Russia struggles to promote sustainable development due to its interpretation of the term. As discussed earlier in this book, the major feature of the Bruntland definition is that "continued economic growth is attainable in conjunction with environmental improvement and that, furthermore, a synergistic relationship can exist between the two". Yet, as Oldfield and Shaw illustrate, when the term is directly translated into Russian, it means 'stable' or 'steady development', thus losing the ecological connotations of the word 'sustainable'. This, in turn, might explain the economic focus of sustainable efforts, such as that taken in the emissions trading scheme mentioned above. Nonetheless, the term is often expanded in official documents to emphasise the balance between socio-economic and environmental interests thereby indicating that although the term might be 'lost in translation', Russia's official interpretation of sustainable development appears to overlap to a considerable extent with Western understandings of the concept. In fact, certain policy documents emphasise the need for sustainable development through continued economic growth and increased environmental regulation. The Main Directions of the Long-term Socio-economic Development of Russia (2000–2010), which was put together by a number of leading environmental organisations, produced a draft 'ecological doctrine', which focused on areas such as the efficient use of natural resources and the development of an effective civil society. Later versions of the doctrine compiled by scientists and government officials concentrated on the need for more effective management of legislative and economic systems to ensure the sustainable development of society.[132] In view of this, it certainly seems that, at a rhetorical level at least, there appears to be a genuine attempt to integrate all three pillars of sustainable development into the Russian policy agenda, although perhaps with a greater emphasis on economic interests.

However, there are concerns about the extent to which this rhetoric is put into practice. For Oldfield and Shaw, the official stance is largely influenced by the desire to appease the international community and to avoid ostracising Russia at the international level.[133] Moreover, on assuming the presidency for the first time in 2000, President Putin engaged in various efforts which seemed directly contradictory to the policy documents being produced, including promoting more heavy and extractive industries by removing barriers to the exploitation of Russia's mineral wealth. This was to encourage the economic recovery of the

---

132 For more on this, see Oldfield, J.D. and Shaw, D.J.B., "Revisiting Sustainable Development: Russian Cultural and Scientific Traditions and the Concept of Sustainable Development", *Area* (2002) 34, no. 4, 394–395.
133 Ibid.

country – or what some have termed a 'dirty recovery'.[134] To enable this further, Putin also abolished the Ministry for Environmental Protection, merging it into Russia's Ministry for Natural Resources, thus making environmental protection subordinate to natural resource extraction.[135] Lastly, and perhaps in response to 'colour revolutions' in other post-Soviet States, a weakening of civil society in Russia has happened in what was already a challenging place for the rule of law. The influence of civil society on environmental and sustainable development decision-making has correspondingly made this increasingly difficult. For example, Putin established a law which "placed restrictions on donations from foreign NGOs to all Russian groups, including the environmental movement, and compelled all NGOs to engage in lengthy registration procedures".[136]

In recent years Russia has been undergoing a complex and difficult transition. Uncertainties surrounding the country's future may translate into worldwide uncertainties about the future well-being of the global environment. Therefore, while Russia's official commitment to sustainable development is seemingly clear, precisely how the concept is understood and enforced is by no means guaranteed. Crotty and Rodgers argue that the primary means by which the government has attempted to enforce its rhetoric on sustainable development is through market mechanisms and, although not without fault, these mechanisms can prove helpful in encouraging sustainable development in countries like Russia where economic incentives are the most effective to impose.[137] Russia typifies an inconsistent approach to sustainable development and does not demonstrate a full and balanced integration of all three pillars of the concept.

## *India*

India is a richly diverse country. It is home to about 8 per cent of the world's biodiversity and has within its territory four biodiversity hotspots: namely the Eastern Himalaya, Indo-Burma, Western Ghats and Sri Lanka, and Sundaland regions.[138] However, as another BRIC country, India has experienced rapid economic growth which, despite lifting many out of poverty, has been accompanied by the depletion of natural resources and degradation of the environment.[139]

India's approach to sustainable development over the past 40–50 years can be divided into four phases. The first phase was characterised by the country's efforts to establish and reinforce the policy and legal basis for sustainable development in

---

134 Crotty and Rodgers (n 130) 179.
135 See Bobylev, S., "Is Russia on an Unsustainable Development Path?", *Problems of Economic Transition* (2005) 47, 6–21 and Bykov, A., "Natural Resource Nanagement", *Problems of Economic Transition*, 47, 7–17.
136 Crotty and Rodgers (n 130) 179.
137 Ibid.
138 Indian Ministry of Environment and Forests, "Sustainable Development in India: Stocktaking in the Run Up to Rio+20", (2011), 59.
139 Ibid., 53.

its constitution.[140] Following the 1972 Stockholm Conference, the 42nd amendment to the Constitution of India was made, incorporating Article 48A.[141] This Article declared the protection and improvement of the environment and the safeguarding of forests and wildlife as part of the Directive Principles of State Policy. Also, Article 51A(g) imposes a fundamental duty upon Indian citizens to "protect and improve the natural environment, including forest, lakes, rivers and the wildlife, and to have compassion for living creatures".[142] The Supreme Court of India has since upheld the effect of these two articles, stating that the "cumulative effect of Articles 48A and 51A(g) seems to be that the state as well as the citizens are now under constitutional obligation to conserve, protect and improve the environment, with every generation owing a duty to all succeeding generations to develop and conserve the natural resources of the nation in the best possible way".[143] During this phase, India also enacted primary environmental legislation addressing a number of issues, including: the Wildlife (Protection) Act (1972); the Water (Prevention and Control of Pollution) Act (1974); the Water (Prevention and Control of Pollution) Cess Act (1977); the Forest Conservation Act (1980); and the Air (Prevention and Control of Pollution) Act (1981).[144]

The second phase emerged from the aftermath of the Bhopal disaster in 1984.[145] Both the National Environment Tribunal Act (1995) and the National Environment Appellate Authority Act (1997) were enacted to enable cases for liability and compensation to be brought by victims of pollution and other environmental damages. These have been since been repealed and replaced by the new National Green Tribunal Act of 2010.[146] The Environment (Protection) Act was also enacted and encompassed three key objectives: the protection of the environment; the improvement of the environment; and the protection of human beings, other living creatures, plants, and property from hazardous materials or activity.[147] Moreover, at this time, Supreme Court judgments continued to further the objectives of sustainable development in a relatively progressive manner, recognising that principles such as the precautionary principle, the polluter pays principle, and intergenerational equity could all fall under Article 21 of the Indian Constitution on the right to life.[148]

---

140 Sustainable Development in India (n 139) 2.
141 Ibid., 25–26.
142 Ibid., 25–26.
143 *State of Tamil Nadu v. Hind Store*, AIR 1981 SC 711.
144 Sustainable Development in India (n 139) 25–26.
145 The Bhopal disaster is considered by many as the world's worst industrial disaster. Although the exact cause of the disaster is still in debate, a gas leak exposed 500,000 people to the highly toxic methyl isocyanate gas and resulted in the deaths of thousands. Further to the loss of life and devastation to the local community, the full extent of which remains unclear, the leak resulted in pollution of the soil and groundwater in the surrounding area.
146 Sustainable Development in India (n 139) 27.
147 Ibid.
148 See *Indian Council for Enviro-Legal Action v. Union of India* (AIR 1996 SC 1446) and *Vellore Citizens' Welfare Forum v. Union of India* (AIR 1996 SC 2715) cited in Sustainable Development in India (n 139) 27.

The third phase was characterised by India's accession to the WTO in 1995. A strong focus was therefore placed on reconciling economic with environmental and social interests. Of particular concern was the country's energy consumption, especially its heavy reliance on coal and its vast imports of oil.[149] Consequently, legislation such as the Energy Conservation Act was enacted in 2001 to promote the more sustainable use and production of energy.[150] Also, the Electricity Act (2003) was introduced, which requires State Electricity Regulatory Commissions to specify a percentage of electricity that the electricity distribution companies must procure from renewable sources such as wind.[151]

Finally, the fourth phase symbolises greater civil society engagement which has sought to establish a legal regime that is socially just and equitable.[152] The phase gained particular momentum after the introduction of the Right to Information Act in 2005 "which has the objective of promoting transparency and accountability in the working of public authorities".[153] The phase has also been witness to the enactment of the National Environment Policy (2006). This is a key policy document for sustainable development in India which recognises that the most reliable foundation for environmental conservation is to ensure that people have better lives from the act of conservation of natural resources than they would from environmental degradation.[154] It is this understanding of a fully integrated approach which has been upheld by the Supreme Court of India, which stated that "coordinated efforts of all concerned would be required to solve the problem of ecological crisis and pollution. Unless we adopt an approach of sustainable use, the problem of environmental degradation cannot be solved".[155]

During this most recent phase, there has also been a growing understanding of the impact of climate change on the future of the country. The different ecological and climatic zones in India make the country extremely susceptible to the impacts of climate change.[156] This is exacerbated by the fact that it is home to over 1.2 billion people, many of whom depend directly upon climate-sensitive sectors and natural resources.[157] It is also recognised that, in addition to an increase in natural disasters, climate change could have several damaging consequences for the country, including: a greater number of increasingly severe droughts and floods; a decrease in the yield of crops as temperatures increase; a rise in sea levels

---

149 Sustainable Development in India (n 139) 59.
150 Ibid., 27–28.
151 Ibid., 20.
152 Ibid., 27–28.
153 Ibid., 27–28.
154 Ibid., 2–3.
155 See *Karnataka Industrial Development Board* (2006) 6 SCC 321, cited in Rustomjee, S., "Global Environmental Law and India", *International Journal of Legal Information*, (2009) 36, no. 2, 348.
156 Sustainable Development in India (n 139) 59.
157 Sathaye, J., Shukla, P.R. and Ravindranath, N.H., "Climate Change, Sustainable Development and India: Global and National Concerns", *Current Science* (2006) 90, no. 3, 318.

which will displace those populations in coastal zones; and an increase in the number of States and regions which become hot-spots for malaria.[158]

Yet, despite having an energy system that relies primarily on coal, its per capita share of global $CO_2$ emissions is relatively small, recorded as being 1.6 tonnes in 2011, compared to 17.3 in the US and 8.57 in the EU.[159] Moreover, under the principle of common but differentiated responsibilities, developing countries such as India do not have binding commitments to reduce GHG emissions. Nonetheless, India's has come to recognise the role it must play. Therefore, in 2008 the Prime Minister of India launched the National Action Plan on Climate Change, which was published to identify measures that promote Indian development objectives "while also yielding co-benefits for addressing climate change effectively".[160] It outlines eight national initiatives for addressing sustainable development and climate change, one being the Jawaharlal Nehru National Solar Mission. This initiative envisages establishing India as a global leader in solar energy by setting an ambitious target of 20,000 MW of solar power by the year 2022.[161] Another initiative is the National Mission for Enhanced Energy Efficiency, responsible for the 'Perform Achieve and Trade' mechanism and with the aim of rewarding energy efficiency in seven energy-intensive industrial sectors.[162] Later, at the Copenhagen Conference in 2009, India went further and declared its commitment to voluntary mitigation actions to reduce emissions intensity by 20–25 per cent by 2020 in comparison to the 2005 level (excluding the agriculture sector).[163] Then, in 2011, India's Prime Minister approved the National Mission for a Green India, which aims to double India's afforested land by 2020, thereby enabling its forests to absorb 50–60 million tonnes of CO2 annually, offsetting about 6 per cent of India's annual emissions.[164]

When considering the above, it is fair to conclude that India has taken a reasonably proactive stance to sustainable development, enacting a multitude of laws that integrate all three pillars of sustainable development. Yet, again, enforcement of this legislation is where India falls behind. Transitioning to a more sustainable development pathway requires considerable financial support and current sources of revenue at state or local levels are limited. As a consequence, these levels of government have been largely dependent on the assistance of the central government to finance their sustainable development efforts, which leads to greater delays and red-tape.[165] The courts, it seems, are ready to protect environmental

---

158 Ibid., 318–319.
159 Joint Research Centre, EDGAR (Emission Database for Global Atmospheric Research), "CO2 Time Series 1990–2011 Per Capita for World Countries", 23 May 2013 http://edgar.jrc.ec.europa.eu/overview.php?v=CO2ts_pc1990-2011
160 The Center for Climate and Energy Solutions, "Summary: India's National Action Plan on Climate Change", June 2008, www.c2es.org/international/key-country-policies/india/climate-plan-summary
161 Sustainable Development in India (n 139) 20.
162 Bossley (n 95) 364.
163 Sustainable Development in India (n 139) 66.
164 Ibid., 18.
165 Ibid., 46.

interests wherever possible; however, their enforcement of sustainable development principles is limited by the lack of expert knowledge and training in the relevant fields.[166]

Furthermore, despite its legislative and policy efforts, the attitude of the Ministry of Environment and Forests towards the government's climate change and sustainable development obligations seems to be frustrated at best. For example, according to their official website, "[m]ost mitigation of GHG emissions in developing countries leads to diversion of resources, earmarked for development, to meeting a global environmental problem for which such countries are not responsible".[167] This latter statement raises an issue which is of great concern for many developing countries, namely that they should not have to pay for the emissions which have accumulated as a result of the industrialisation of developed countries. In their eyes, such payments would only inhibit their own development, as the Ministry's website states itself:

> India has contributed very little to these emissions, and even now emits just 4% of the global emissions with 17% of the world's population. Emissions from any point in the world has equal effect on the global climate, and even if India were to completely reduce its emissions to zero by going back to the stone age, it would hardly make any difference to the impacts of climate change on India (or anywhere else).[168]

It is not the intention of this section to debate whether the Indian Ministry of Environment and Forests is correct in saying the above. Rather, it is included to demonstrate that although significant and noteworthy efforts have been made on paper, substantial hurdles remain.

### *Brazil*

Brazil is the fifth largest land mass in the world with the sixth largest economy and a population of almost 200 million. In terms of relevance to environmental protection and sustainable development, Brazil plays an extremely important role. Firstly, the country's territory contains about 60 per cent of the Amazon, which covers approximately 50 per cent of the country and accounts for about a third of the world's surviving tropical forests,[169] and is home to vast biodiversity.[170] As a consequence, the country has had a substantial environmental responsibility and, to respond to this, Brazil has introduced a variety of legal instruments to combat

---

166 Rustomjee (n 156) 350.
167 Indian Ministry of Environment and Forests, "Frequently Asked Questions on India and Durban Platform", http://moef.nic.in/modules/others/?f=durban-faqs
168 Ibid.
169 Kellman, J.E., "The Brazilian Legal Tradition and Environmental Protection: Friend or Foe", *Hatings International and Comparative Law Review* (2001–2002) 25, 147.
170 StratosInc, "Brazil Case Study: Analysis of National Strategies for Sustainable Development", June 2004, 2.

environmental degradation. For example, Brazil's 1981 National Environmental Policy has the following aims: to protect and enhance the existing environment; to reclaim the damaged environment; and to ensure sustainable socioeconomic development.[171] The 1988 Constitution of the Federative Republic of Brazil also devotes a full section to the environment, providing a guarantee for a healthy and stable environment to all Brazilian citizens.[172] The 1998 Law of Environmental Crimes is a critical piece of legislation, imposing fines of up to $50 million and jail sentences for crimes ranging from illegal logging to industrial pollution.[173] Lastly, the Brazilian Agenda 21, signed in 2002, is a comprehensive strategy for sustainable development.

Secondly, Brazil demonstrates one of the greatest levels of environmental awareness in the developing world. A survey released by the Brazilian research firm IBOPE showed that 94 per cent of all Brazilians are concerned about the environment.[174] The Brazilian city of Curitiba has also received a lot of attention due to the exemplary moves it has made to reduce carbon dioxide emissions through a coordinated emission reduction plan which actively integrates all three pillars of sustainable development. Furthermore, almost half of all the energy consumed in Brazil comes from renewable sources with 75 per cent of the energy consumed being hydroelectric.[175]

Thirdly, despite having such a high share of renewable energy, the practice of deforestation in the country has been a significant contributor to GHG emissions.[176] Not only does the process of deforestation produce a lot of carbon emissions, but also the reduction in forest coverage reduces the amount of $CO_2$ which can be absorbed from the air. Forest fires – usually started by farmers to make the land available for agriculture – have also contributed significantly to deforestation, even when the 12,000 square miles of forest cut down every year to create grazing land, if left undisturbed, would produce about ten times as much food in terms of fruit, game, and fish.[177] Such practices were heavily criticised by the international community for damaging one of the world's most precious forests. Yet, for some time, the country was highly protective of its sovereignty over the rainforest and even refused to discuss the effect of deforestation in international climate change meetings.

However, recently there has been a notable shift in attitude. During the Copenhagen conference, President Lula emphasised Brazil's commitment to reducing GHG emissions and even declared that they would financially support

---

171 Kellman (n 170) 154.
172 See Title III, Chapter VI, Article 225 of the Constituição da República Federativa do Brasil.
173 Kellman (n 170) 156.
174 Barros, P. and do Valle, A., "Rio+20: Why Brazil Is a Country of Contradictions", *The Guardian*, 13 June 2012, www.guardian.co.uk/sustainable-business/rio-20-brazil-sustainable-development-environment
175 Ibid.
176 Sweig, J. E., "A New Global Player: Brazil's Far-Flung Agenda", *Foreign Affairs*, (2010) 89, no. 6, p. 175.
177 Kellman (n 170) 149.

developing countries if necessary.¹⁷⁸ Moreover, immediately after the discussions in Copenhagen, President Lula signed a law which established Brazil's National Plan on Climate Change which outlines a strategy to reduce the average deforestation rate by 70 per cent before the end of 2017.¹⁷⁹ Brazil's actions, both during the Copenhagen conference and since, have demonstrated its capacity as a representative of developing world capable of addressing climate and sustainable development needs, despite not being an economic superpower yet.¹⁸⁰

Despite this, the road to sustainable development has not been easy, and concerns remain regarding the country's ability to implement its environmental standards consistently across the board. Several issues remain, for instance, in the clarity of application of crucial pieces of national legislation. For example, the Constitution divides responsibility for environmental protection between the federal, state, and municipal levels of government. However, the relative power of each level to protect the environment is not obvious.¹⁸¹ This in turn leads to varied interpretation of the general provisions set by the central government, thus leading to divisions and inconsistency of application. Another example is the Law of Environmental Crimes, which had – just six months after being passed – several key articles vetoed. Consequently, language was removed from the law that would have made corporations liable for environmental crimes, leaving the law applicable only to individuals.¹⁸² A final example is the National Sustainable Development Strategy (the Brazilian Agenda 21) which, as a social pact, does not necessarily have any legally binding role over the action of the State.¹⁸³

There are many reasons, which are cited for the seemingly faulty enforcement of legislation. Some, for example, place the blame on the Brazilian legal culture, whereby untrained and inexperienced judges and lawyers have single-handedly prevented the successful enforcement of Brazilian environmental legislation.¹⁸⁴ According to Kellman:

> Brazil's government can pass a multitude of environmental laws, but this legislation means nothing if it is continually ignored in the place where laws are supposed to mean the most – the judiciary. Legal practitioners and decision makers are still deeply engrained with the old way of thinking, under which economic lobbies rule the courts and lawmaking bodies.¹⁸⁵

---

178 Trennepohl, N., "Brazil's Policy on Climate Change: Recent Legislation and Challenges to Implementation", *Carbon & Climate Law Review* (2010) 3, 271.
179 Sweig (n 177) 179.
180 de Paula Domingoa, N., "The Interface Between Climate Change and Trade Regimes Through the Eyes of Brazil", *Florida A & M University Law Review* (2011) 6, no. 2, pp. 240–241.
181 Kellman (n 170) 152–153.
182 Ibid., 156.
183 Stratosinc (n 171) 3.
184 Kellman (n 170) 146.
185 Ibid., 161.

Whether the Brazilian legal culture is really to blame is up for debate. But there does seem to be evidence that the Brazilian government is prioritising economic stabilisation policies at the cost of other priorities such as environmental initiatives, and in particular allowing corporate or agribusiness lobbyists to influence policy and law-making.[186] An example of this can be seen in the recent debate over the Brazilian forestry code. The code, which was approved by the Brazilian congress in May 2012, represented a major step backwards for Brazilian environmental legislation. The aim of some of the law's provisions was to give amnesty to illegal loggers and open several loopholes for the legalisation of further deforestation. After civil society intervention, President Dilma Rousseff partially vetoed the law, which was later passed in October the same year.[187] Moreover, on discovering massive oil reserves 150 miles off its southern coast in 2007, the Brazilian government has since declared its intention to use the revenue from its oil production to fund green development. Nonetheless, many raised their concerns about the potential for corruption and politicisation when placing oil at the heart of Brazil's development.[188]

Both of these examples demonstrate that legitimate concerns still exist regarding the State's true intentions in the field of the environmental protection or sustainable development. Even so, it is important to recognise the significant headway that the country has made in recent years, even if the developments were achieved for economic, rather than environmental or social, reasons.

## Conclusion

The analyses on sustainable development in EU external relations have revealed that the EU has clearly made efforts to introduce sustainable development objectives into its external relations, especially in the area of climate change. Its international efforts on sustainability generally and specifically on climate change together promote the three dimensions of sustainability and are applicable to implement via the precautionary approach, the polluter pays principle and the public participation and access to justice requirements. The findings reveal that in spite of the EU's efforts promoting sustainability in the international arena, the issue of enforcement, as in the EU's internal sphere, remains key and in question.

This reflects the argument made in previous chapters, namely that there is a clear dichotomy between the EU's ambitions and what it is willing and/or able to impose. In this sense, the EU's approach to sustainable development in its external relations appears more as a symbolic Treaty requirement, encouraging the promotion, but not the enforcement, of sustainable development objectives. Its credibility in the international arena will ultimately rest upon how effectively it implements and enforces its sustainable development standards, and

---

186 Stratosinc (n 171) 2.
187 Barros and do Valle (n 175).
188 Sweig (n 177) 179.

implementation and enforcement are needed urgently if the EU truly wishes to assert itself as the leader in the international sustainable development agenda.

Although the EU is not exceptional when it comes to the inconsistent application of political conditionality,[189] it seems that the lack of enforcement could undermine the eventual impact of any genuine carrot-and-stick approach in the future. Moreover, failure to follow through on, for example, the conditions of free trade agreements, could have negative political fallout for the Union. Such an impact could not only be extremely damaging to the credibility of the EU's reputation in the push towards greater, global sustainable development, but also set a dangerous precedent for other countries looking to revert to old habits. In this sense, more than normative or soft power is required for the EU to make real and lasting changes to how third world countries perceive sustainable development and its subsidiary elements.

Even if the EU's ultimate strategic interest is to ensure that emerging sustainable development models in countries both neighbouring the EU and further afield do not damage the Union's economic competitiveness,[190] such inconsistency in the application of political conditionality is risky. It is in Europe's interest to preserve its identity as a leader in sustainable development, but must demonstrate that it is willing and able to maintain this role.[191]

The general conclusions drawn from the previous chapters on the EU's approach toward sustainable development are not at odds with its external competitors. Despite varying efforts to promote sustainable development through legislation, case law, and policy, the EU is not unique in failing to meeting its self-imposed expectations. Indeed, many other countries have similar enforcement hurdles to overcome not to mention their own, specific, political, and social issues. There is the tendency that ultimately economic interests – polluter pays regulation – will prevail over environmental or social ones (precautionary and participatory considerations) in the pursuit of sustainable development. This indicates that, in addition to the incorporation of the subsidiary principles of sustainable development, perhaps the best way to promote sustainable development in a coherent, global manner is through the 'bolting-on' of the principle onto other, more desirable, economic incentives.

What is certain, however, is that while going some way to deal with individual sustainable development issues, disparate and unrelated initiatives around the

---

189 Tsogas finds that the very few countries which the US suspended from its GSP had either governments disliked by the US or minimal trade with it. "If outcomes of trade conditionality of labour standards are in agreement with other policy objectives [. . .] so much the better; if not [. . .] then labour standards are simply ignored". Tsogas, G., "Labour Standards in the Generalised Systems of Preferences of the European Union and the United States", *European Journal of Industrial Relations* (2000) 6, no. 3, 365.
190 Lightfoot, S. and Burchell, J., "The European Union and the World Summit on Sustainable Development: Normative Power Europe in Action?" *Journal of Common Market Studies* (2005) 43, no. 1, p. 91.
191 Vanden Brande (n 30) 170.

world will add to the trend of missed opportunities. This will be increasingly the case if the sustainable development agenda remains a policy gloss on previous unsustainable practices or ultimately economic initiatives. In which case, greater emphasis should be placed on the important role that the EU could and should have in encouraging the protection of sustainable objectives in ways that are innovative, comprehensive, and effective worldwide.

# 8 Conclusion

The sustainable development concept means different things to different people and in different contexts. The concept suggests a reframing of the approach to economic growth, social interaction, and resource use. In some readings, the concept is revolutionary. It appears that, after three decades, the basic philosophies underpinning the concept are largely uncontested, even if there remains a great variation in both the concept's ultimate requirements and in expectations of what implementing the concept will achieve. As a concept, sustainable development is central to the protection of the environment in EU law. It is natural to expect that when a concept is so important to the EU agenda, that concept will establish as a general principle to promote the international sustainability agenda within the EU legal order. But sustainable development in EU law has come up against the challenge of a concept with such flexibility in meaning in terms of what it says about how a standard can be understood in any clear or absolute way that can be applied by a court.

This book set out to consider the role that the concept of sustainable development plays in law and policy in the EU amidst debate over its meanings, being a general principle, a standard, an aspiration, both singularly and collectively. In trying to resist the temptation to consider the concept is meaningless, while finding an appreciable context to test the EU approach to sustainable development, the book constructs a logical analytical framework for understanding the concept and deriving a practical meaning therefrom that ensures its application in regional and domestic legal, policy, and political contexts.

The book thus presents the international concept of sustainable development and some of its key principles. In a critical discourse, it reviews the varying perspectives and contestable meaning and interpretations of the concept, with meaning emerging in different contexts and at different times. Despite the definitional questions, Chapter 2 demonstrates that sustainable development has direct and primary relevance for regulating economic activities for environmental protection, alongside competing need for ensuring developmental sustainability. It finds that sustainable development can be applied through key sub-principles to address the three dimensions and objectives of sustainability – the polluter pays principle, the precautionary principle, and the principle of public participation.

There is an appreciable legal character of sustainable development beyond legislative and judicial processes that may confer obligations relevant for pursuing sustainability to include adjudicatory, administrative, and deliberative processes. The flexibility in the concept allows for the interpretation of its principles – i.e., the precautionary principle, the polluter pays principle, and public participation and access to justice – within legal rules to enhance environmental protection at the global or domestic level.

Through the analytical framework constructed it was possible to examine the application of sustainable development in EU law, policy, and practice through these sub-principles as representing a trajectory of implementation for the three dimensions of sustainability. The analysis set out in this work reveals, in Chapter 3, that the international concept and principle of sustainable development is capable of application at a regional level, within the EU. It shows that sustainable development as having application in wide-ranging areas of EU law and policy, including through the principles of subsidiarity and proportionality. It is in seeing sustainable development as a framework that its true purpose exists.

The EU legal system transposes the sustainable development concept in two main legal paradigms. Firstly, through specific mention of the need to integrate environmental protection requirements into policy areas by Article 11 TFEU. In this context, sustainable development could fit into either of two camps. It either remains a guiding principle, referred to in EU policy and legislative documents as an objective of EU law to be considered and – in theory – followed. Alternatively, it will develop in the case law of the Court of Justice of the European Union as a general principle upon which claims for judicial review of EU and Member State measures can be made.

Whether a general principle of sustainable development exists or is emerging in EU law was examined in Chapter 3. The context of the general principles in the EU legal order as a whole is important. There are limitations to the approach of seeing the concept as a general principle of law, however, not least the fact that no one definition of a general principle exists. Moreover, the existing principles do not necessarily provide an accurate legal structure within which sustainable development can easily sit. Instead, the framework of comparison chosen is that of a spectrum of general principles, ranging from those, which act as a guide to EU decision-making, to those capable of procedural impact.

The second paradigm reveals that the EU system places sustainable development alongside the fundamental rights and freedoms enshrined in the Charter, with which sustainable development has little in common. The inclusion of sustainable development in the Charter suggests its promotion, and its association with fundamental rights of the EU legal order. Here the extent to which the Charter promotes the realisation of sustainable development will depend upon how the Charter will be viewed and used as the relationship between it and the European Convention on Human Rights and Fundamental Freedoms, and the relationship between the Court of Justice and the European Court of Human Rights develop. The instance of the intergenerational equity in the transposition of EU's sustainable development raises issues particularly regarding the lack of mechanism for judicial scrutiny.

It finds that although sustainable development has wide application in EU legal order, a lingering gap remains between the rhetoric of the institutions and the reality of enforcement. Sustainable development will not amount to much if it cannot be enforced either under its own name or by means of one of its component principles. Whichever direction the principle takes in the years to come, this analysis demonstrates the emphasis which should be placed on the principle of sustainable development and the future role it has to play in the legality and judicial scrutiny of EU and Member State measures.

Having established the context and methods of application of international sustainable development in EU law, Chapter 4, 5, and 6 substantively apply the key sub-principles of sustainability to illustrate how these can promote the three dimensions of sustainable development in EU legal order. The precautionary principle can capably transpose sustainable development through EU law, policy, and practice to promote environmental protection. Both the precautionary and protection principles provide an appreciable legal framework in which a general principle of sustainable development could sit.

Although sustainable development and sustainability are rarely referred to by the Court of Justice, the concept's individual elements are deeply embedded within the legal framework for environmental protection. Precaution has increasingly favourable application in EU law and wide implementation in various policy areas. Sustainability also applies in the objective interpretations by the Court of Justice. Together, these ensure a transferable legal framework for promoting the environmental protection dimension of sustainable development through the precautionary principle. The interpretation of the principle in legislation and policy and its enforcement by the Court, the EU institutions, and the national authorities bolsters the legal effect of the principle including on the basis of enforcement. Enforcement as a process itself can be sustainable, by balancing the three competing environmental, economic, and social interests in a way that ensures legal and political credibility. Some of the case law does suggest, in general, ways the re-balancing of economic and environmental protection interests should be attempted.

Similarly, the polluter pays principle can capably transpose sustainable development through EU law, policy, and practice. Indeed sustainable development in the EU legal order is associated closely with the development of environmental law and policy. This allows for the operation of framework of principles within which the polluter pays rests as a good illustration of the integration of economic consideration in environmental decision-making to address the regional problem of pollution. Chapter 5 specifically finds that the EU institutions are increasingly interpreting the polluter pays principle as essential mechanisms when developing legislation and policy in a variety of areas, which might result in environmental degradation or social harm. It also shows that the Court is taking an increasingly environmentally friendly position when balancing economic with environmental and/or social interests.

Economic regulation via the polluter pays principle, through process and production taxes, effluent charges, or emissions trading schemes and emissions crediting, can provide an invaluable revenue stream for governments, which could help reduce the total cost of pollution to the environment and control to society. Compliance has increased with aviation, and energy standards and costs of complying with the requirements of pollution standards have lowered and products are redesigned in order to comply with waste packaging and recycling laws.

However, in the transport, agriculture, and competition sectors, i.e., in specific areas of EU policy, although explicit reference is made to the polluter pays principle, the emphasis remains limited to the aim of internalising external costs. The internalisation of external costs is an approach which pervades a large part of transport policy and legislation. This is done with the aim of supporting and incentivising the creation of sustainable systems, capable of supporting themselves in lieu of State or EU funding. The road, marine, and aviation sectors all demonstrate this focus. There is need for policy makers to consider more thoughtfully whether the sanctions for failure to pay 'costs' are sufficient to incentivise change or to implement sustainability.

The policy analysis also uncovers a rather half-hearted integration of environmental protection interests with that of State Aid policy. But the explicit integration of State Aid control does permit State subsidies to support efforts by undertakings, which go beyond the standards required under the polluter pays principle. This fact distinguishes State Aid from the rest of competition policy, which has an inherent propensity to waste resources.

Despite the transposition and integration of the polluter pays – and precautionary – principles in EU law and policy and practice, there is an ongoing need to test the EU's approach to sustainable development on a grander scale by examining the principle of public participation, access to information, and access to justice in environmental matters. The EU system has successfully incorporated the Rio Declaration Principle 10 and the Aarhus Convention provisions into EU law promoting public participation alongside the fundamental rights to influence social aspect of sustainability.

The Aarhus Convention focus is on people, transparency, and accountability. It enables and empowers the public to be informed of and to participate in environmental decision-making and to challenge relevant decisions, which, they believe, are contrary to the interests of environmental protection. The research finds that there are various policy and legislative initiatives, documents, and measures enacted or undertaken by the EU transposing or applying the Aarhus provisions directly for social sustainability in environmental decision-making. Certainly, with regard to the first and second pillars of the Aarhus Convention, the EU has demonstrated significant willingness to enable greater access to information and participation of the public.

However, gaps in consistency exist, especially in relation to the implementation of the Convention's third pillar, with seemingly double standards being imposed by the Court of Justice. In particular, the apparent willingness to incorporate and enforce this right is undermined by the need for EU rules on standing before the Court to be relaxed and national rules on access to justice to be harmonised.

Access to justice for enforcement is key to the Aarhus Convention. The subsidiary elements enshrined therein guide EU administrative and deliberative decision-making, but with only limited means of enforcement in the event of breach. In effect the approach tends to guarantee the application of the principle of sustainable development, albeit at the "weaker" end of impact; especially if the emphasis rests on judicial enforcement as oppose to legislative, administrative, and deliberative processes enhancing public participation rights. Invariably, the EU's approach to the Aarhus Convention is representative of its wider approach to the principle of sustainable development in the EU agenda as a whole.

It is desirable therefore that there is development in the law to enable greater access to justice in environmental matters at the EU level for several reasons. First, access to justice is an essential instrument in a democratic society to effectively challenge violations of the law. It constitutes the backbone of the rule of law, which the EU seeks to uphold. Second, without proper access to justice, EU institutions and Member States will never be properly accountable for their actions under the first two pillars. And third, failure to enforce fully such rights enshrined in the Aarhus Convention sets an arguably dangerous precedent for the EU's general approach to sustainable development.

Policy makers should also consider that such a development cannot be achieved unless the EU is successful in garnering the support of its Member States, to harmonise legislation on access to justice in environmental matters before national courts. They should also work to review the treaty requirements on standing before the Court of Justice to facilitate access to justice at the EU level. As 'masters of the treaties' only the Member States have the power to expand access to EU courts by amending Article 230 of the Treaty and, arguably, the pressure for EU Member States to act in this way is likely to increase following the Aarhus Convention Compliance Committee decisions.

EU external relationships on sustainable development demonstrate the EU has clearly made efforts to introduce sustainable development objectives into its external relations, especially in the area of climate change. Its international efforts on sustainability generally and specifically on climate change together promote the three dimensions of sustainability and are applicable to implement the precautionary approach, the polluter pays principle, and the public participation and access to justice. In spite of the EU's efforts promoting sustainability in the international arena, the issue of enforcement remains as big an issue in the sphere of external EU relations as it does in the EU's internal sphere.

This reflects the argument made throughout this work, namely that there is a clear dichotomy between the EU's ambitions and what it is willing and/or able to impose. In this sense, the EU's approach to sustainable development in its external relations appears more as a symbolic Treaty requirement, encouraging the promotion, but not the enforcement, of sustainable development objectives. Its credibility in the international arena ultimately rests upon how effectively it implements and enforces its sustainable development standards, and this is needed urgently if the EU truly wishes to assert itself as the leader in the international sustainable development agenda. The lack of enforcement could undermine the eventual impact of any genuine carrot-and-stick approach in the future.

Moreover, it seems impossible to believe that failure to follow through on, for example, the conditions of free trade agreements, would not have negative political fallout for the Union. Such an impact could not only be extremely damaging to the credibility of the EU's reputation in the push towards greater, global sustainable development, but also set a dangerous precedent for other countries looking to revert to old habits. In this sense, more than normative or soft power is required for the EU to make real and lasting changes to how third countries perceive sustainable development and its subsidiary elements.

Even if the EU's ultimate strategic interest is to ensure that emerging sustainable development models in EU and non-EU countries do not damage the Union's economic competitiveness, such inconsistency in the application of political conditionality is risky. It is in Europe's interest to preserve its identity as a leader in sustainable development, but must demonstrate that it is willing and able to maintain this role.

The analysis of other, non-EU states confirms the general conclusions drawn from the previous chapters on the EU's approach toward sustainable development – that despite varying efforts to promote sustainable development through legislation, case law, and policy, it appears that the EU is not unique in failing to meeting its self-imposed expectations. Indeed, many other countries have similar enforcement hurdles to overcome not to mention their own, specific, political, and social issues.

Moreover, it often seems the case that, ultimately, economic interests will prevail over environmental or social ones, even in the pursuit of sustainable development. This indicates that, in addition to the incorporation of the subsidiary principles of sustainable development, perhaps the best way to promote sustainable development in a coherent, global manner is through the 'bolting-on' of the principle onto other, more 'desirable', economic incentives.

However, what is certain is that while going some way to deal with individual sustainable development issues, disparate and unrelated initiatives around the world will add to the trend of missed opportunities. This will be increasingly the case if the sustainable development agenda remains a policy gloss on previous unsustainable practices or ultimately economic initiatives. In which case, greater emphasis should be placed on the important role that the EU could and should have in encouraging the protection of sustainable objectives in a way, which is innovative, comprehensive, and effective worldwide.

On the specific question of whether a general principle of sustainable development exists in EU legal context, and without undermining the potentiality for application of the concept through its sub-principles addressing the three dimensions of sustainability proven so far, it is safe to suggest that sustainability is emerging as a tool in EU law and its form is uncertain. As a general principle, it is not capable of having procedural effect. That being so, certain aspects of the EU legal order have set sustainable development apart, and the sustainable development concept demonstrates the potential to steer decision-making in the EU and to frame the development of policy. Since the evidence pointing toward a general principle of sustainable development remains inconclusive, the concept's component parts have a key part to play, specifically to aid the determination of the role they may have in eliciting an emergent general principle of sustainable development in the EU legal order.

Certain elements of sustainable development add to the emergence of an overarching principle whilst others undermine it. In particular, although the EU appears to have understood that the achievement of sustainable development and its objectives requires both a multi-faceted approach and a radical reappraisal of economic, social, and environmental needs, much of the EU's ambition is not reflected in the implementation, especially in relation to enforcement. This appears to be most prevalent in the promotion of sustainable development outside of the EU and demonstrates an inconsistency of approach, often resulting from limited or diverging political will, which is damaging to both the sustainable development agenda and the EU's global credibility as an advocate of harmonisation and change.

Despite this, it is important to recognise that the EU is not alone in this struggle. In comparison to its counterparts, it has made significant headway in prioritising sustainable development both at home and abroad. In doing so, it has overcome a great deal of the idiosyncrasies, both political and legal, which are inherent to a union of currently twenty-eight Member States. This is representative of the added value that the EU has in using its power – soft, normative, or otherwise – to influence not only its Member States, but also third parties.

Nonetheless, greater efforts are required to achieve, in full, the sustainable development needs and objectives of the EU. In particular, more must be done to address the EU's lackadaisical and inconsistent approach to enforcement, which does little else than dilute the impact of otherwise effective and innovative law and policy. Far better, for example, to openly make free trade conditional on the promotion of sustainable development, than to allow third parties to ignore it with impunity.

The challenge of the concept's flexibility of meaning should not mean that there are no standards to apply and greater consistency in the application of the concept across the EU and in the external plane. There is an opportunity here to discuss and negotiate on what a sustainable development framework means in different contexts as new agreements are negotiated. There is also something in the complex nature of the concept that suggests different approaches to different situations.

Although the EU's approach is one, which, in many cases, is inconsistent and self-serving, perhaps this is precisely what a general principle of sustainable development requires to be implemented. Indeed, to insist on absolutes would be both unsustainable and entirely contrary to the concept's nature and evolution. Rather, a varied approach to application may be required, reflecting the flexibility of the concept's definition and role. Accordingly, perhaps the most effective means by which the EU can achieve sustainable development is to vary its enforcement depending on context. For example, it appears that one way in which sustainable development objectives can be achieved, in the short term at least, is by cloaking them in economic incentives. This approach, if standardised, would be particularly effective when aiming to enforce some of the more controversial elements of environmental protection both at home and abroad.

Notwithstanding the above, what is certain is that sustainable development is just one of many areas where the EU can demonstrate its worth. It can show to Member States and third world countries that economic gain can be partnered with environmental protection and social development and can be done so successfully towards sustainable development applying key sub-principles of precaution, polluter pays, and participatory rights. However, the current approach where enforcement of rights to enhance sustainability is thorny, this will serve to undermine the EU if it is not transparent. The EU must be frank and pragmatic to ensure that, at this crucial time for its credibility, it can effectively demonstrate its added value as a strong and sincere advocate of sustainable development worldwide.

# Index

Aarhus Convention 17, 39, 88–106, 148–149; access to information 17–18, 91, 94–95, 103–106; access to justice 17, 38, 91, 95–106; *locus standi* 96–98, 101–104, 106; public participation 17–18, 37–39, 88–89, 91, 95, 103–106
access to information *see* Aarhus Convention
access to justice *see* Aarhus Convention
Agenda 21 *see* Rio Declaration on Environment and Development 1992

Brazil: sustainable development, and 139–142
Brexit *see* United Kingdom
Brundtland Report 2, 7, 11, 22, 25–26

Charter of Fundamental Rights and Freedoms: access to information, and 94; sustainable development, and 15, 44–47, 58, 146
China: sustainable development, and 130–133
climate change 4, 23, 107–144; Brazil 139–142; EU external relations 107–114; India 137–139; polluter pays principle 78; Russia, and 133; United States, and 126–130
Copenhagen Conference 2009 112–113, 116, 140–141
common agricultural policy: sustainable development, and 43; polluter pays principle, and 81–83
common but differentiated responsibility, principle of 4, 25, 35, 40, 138
competition and state aid policy 17, 148; *see also* polluter pays principle; Guidelines on State Aid for Environmental Protection and Energy 2014
corporate social responsibility 9–10
Court of Justice of the European Union 14–16, 37, 46, 50–52, 146; access to justice 96–106; general principles, and 53–59; polluter pays principle, and 75, 83–88; precautionary principle, and 63–72; proportionality, general principle of 50–52; public participation, and 93–95, 98–99, 104; subsidiarity, general principle of 48–50; sustainable development, and 52–58

Emissions Trading Scheme: EU external relations 111–112; polluter pays principle, and 77–80, 87; Russia, and 133–134; United States, and 126–127
energy policy 43, 49, 74, 77, 79, 85, 108–109; Brazil, and 140; Russia, and 137–138; United States, and 130–133
enlargement policy *see* European Union
environmental decision-making *see* Aarhus Convention; public participation
environmental impact assessments *see* Aarhus Convention; public participation
environmental protection: Aarhus Convention, and 88, 92, 97, 100–101, 103, 104–106; Brazil, and 139–142; China, and 130–133; economic development, and 3, 13–14, 21, 145, 147; European Union external relations, and 18–19, 107–121; India, and 135–138; mandatory requirement of 56;

polluter pays principle, and 16–17, 72–87; precautionary principle, and 15–16, 33–34, 59–71, 146–147; principle of 48, 50, 52, 147; Russia, and 133–135; subsidiary principle, as a 4, 15, 33, 55, 152; sustainable development, and 3, 8, 21, 23, 25–26, 30, 40–41, 56–58; United States, and 126–130; World Trade Organisation, and 121–126

European Convention on Human Rights and Fundamental Freedoms 15, 17, 46, 58, 88, 146

European Court of Human Rights 15, 17, 58, 88, 146

European Union: climate change 110–113; Environmental Action Programmes 8, 73, 92, 115; energy policy 108–109; enlargement policy 116–118; external relations 107–121; European Neighbourhood Policy 116–117; general principles 47–58; Generalised System of Preferences 120–121; normative power, as a 116–120, 143; security of 107–111, 125; soft power, as a 116, 143; Sustainable Development Strategy 7, 114–115; trade agreements 117–121; transport policy 17, 79–81, 87, 148; *see also* sustainable development; Court of Justice of the European Union

general principles of EU law *see* European Union; proportionality, general principle of; subsidiarity, general principle of

greenhouse gas emissions *see* climate change; Emissions Trading Scheme

good governance, principle of 8, 25, 38, 48, 85, 89, 109, 120

Guidelines on State Aid for Environmental Protection and Energy 2014 81, 84

India: sustainable development, and 135–139

integration, principle of 11, 23–25; polluter pays principle, and 73, 79–87

intergenerational equity: as a subsidiary principle of sustainable development 44–47

internalisation of external costs *see* polluter pays principle

International Labour Organisation 119–120

International Law Association 3, 7–8, 24–27, 30, 34, 89

International Union for the Conservation of Natural Resources *see* World Conservation Strategy

Kyoto Protocol to the United Nations Framework Climate Change Convention 1997 23, 77, 111, 113; Clean Development Mechanism 23

multilateral environmental agreements 115–116, 119, 129

Organisation for Economic and Social Development: criteria for sustainable development 11, 35, 37, 72, 74–76

Paris Accord on the Framework Convention on Climate Change 2015 23, 113–114

polluter-pays principle 72–87; Carbon Capture Storage 78; common agricultural policy, and 81–83; competition and state aid, and 83–85, 87; costs burden 35–36, 52, 73; distortion of trade and investment, and 35–36; economic regulation, and 73–79; energy policy, and 77–81; environmental protection, and 16–17, 72–87; extended polluter responsibility 75; internalisation of external costs 16–17, 24, 35–36, 72–73, 77, 79–80, 82–83, 87, 108, 148; subsidiary principle of sustainable development, as a 34–37, 72; transport policy, and 79–81

pollution 16, 34–37, 49–50, 60, 72–87, 108, 125, 131, 133, 136–137, 140; *see also* polluter pays principle

precautionary principle 59–71; environmental protection, and 15–16, 33–34, 59–71, 146–147; free movement of goods and harmonisation of the internal market, and 65–71; subsidiary principle of sustainable development, as a 33–34

proportionality, general principle of 50–52; Court of Justice of the European Union, interpretation of 50–52; sustainable development, and 52–57 public participation *see* Aarhus Convention

right to development *see* intergenerational equity
right to information *see* Aarhus Convention
Rio+5 3, 22
Rio+20 115, 130
Rio Declaration on Environment and Development 1992 2, 7–8, 17, 22–27, 32–35, 37–40, 60, 73, 88–89, 105, 134, 141, 148
rule of law 4–5, 8, 13, 47, 51, 106, 119, 135, 149
Russia: sustainable development, and 133–135

Stockholm Conference *see* United Nations Conference on the Human Environment
subsidiarity, general principle of 48–50; Court of Justice of the European Union, interpretation of 48–50; sufficient attainment and better attainment tests 48; sustainable development, and 52–58
sustainable development: concept of 25–40; Court of Justice of European Union, and 52–58; environmental protection, and 3, 8, 21, 23, 25–26, 30, 40–41, 56–58; EU external relations, and 114–121; general principle of 52–57; proportionality, and 52–58; security policy, and 107–111, 125; social development, and 2–3, 22, 114–115, 130–133; subsidiarity, and 52–58; subsidiary principles of 2–3, 7–8, 11–15, 19, 21, 25, 27–28, 32–39, 41, 44, 47, 55–59, 70–71, 86–89, 106–107, 116, 134–140, 142–143, 145–152
sustainable utilisation, principle of 23–24

third-generational rights *see* intergenerational equity
transport policy *see* European Union
Treaty on European Union 8, 47–48, 51, 115
Treaty on the Functioning of the European Union 8, 12, 15, 44, 46–47, 56, 58, 62–63, 66, 69–70, 83–84, 92, 94, 96, 101–102, 104, 146
triple bottom line *see* corporate social responsibility

United Kingdom, the: sustainable development, and 10–11, 13, 19–20, 110
United Nations Conference on Climate Change 2009 *see* Copenhagen Conference 2009
United Nations Conference on the Human Environment 1972 21, 111, 136
United States, the 23, 111–113, 115; sustainable development, and 126–130

World Charter for Nature 2, 22
World Conservation Strategy 2, 22
World Trade Organisation: General Agreement on Tariffs and Trade 36, 121–124; *Shrimp-Turtle* case 29, 31, 124; sustainable development, and 29, 36, 121–126